For Mom
from him who
wasn't an "and others" —
love
Ella
June 1961

BITS OF SILVER

Vignettes of the Old West

BITS
OF SILVER

Vignettes of
the Old West

EDITED BY DON WARD

HASTINGS HOUSE · *Publishers* · NEW YORK 22

Contents

v

Introduction

THE CAMPFIRES of the mountain men have died. The cowboys' branding fires have dimmed. The old trails are faded, and the old songs echo back from lonely hills.

But the West That Was lives on, cherished, in our minds and hearts. It always will. The long adventure of the American frontier was our great shaping national experience. It developed our muscles, whetted our skills, gave birth to customs and inspired legends, provided heroes and villains, molded our national psyche.

Small wonder we tend to dote on its history. By and large, it is America, in the round and in the raw, at its finest and at its most brutal; people conquering a wilderness, often carelessly and sometimes ruthlessly. But here and there, too, adding something, creating, showing the true courage that is grace under pressure.

As the following pages will show, the frontier presented many faces to those who lived it. For the red men, it changed within a few decades from a burgeoning preserve to a mocking prison. For some white men, it was an open invitation to plunder and exploitation. For others, it was promise, a chance to grow in living. For some, shining beauty and new beginning. For some, dark sorrow and an unsought end.

The pieces in this collection present various expressions of that ever-changing face. A series of plunges—some surface splashings, some depth-plumbing dives—in the turbulent stream of Western history. Certain selections may come as old friends to some readers. To others, they may be exciting revelations. Altogether, they are hopefully offered as an entertaining and inspiring whole.

Hastings House, Publishers, came into being in 1936—twenty-five years ago—so the present work, made up entirely of selections from titles in its Western Americana list, may be considered as a silver-anniversary event: "Bits of Silver" in token of that way-marker met. Hastings House hopes that during the next quarter of a century it will be able to publish many more volumes that will add significantly to the story of the great American West.

Don Ward

Red Men
and White

Many Soldiers Falling into Camp

BY MARI SANDOZ

¶ *The Indian tribes of the northern Plains were strong, simple people with many virtues—courage, steadfastness, self-discipline, a quiet dignity. Notable fighters, when mounted on their tough little horses they were reckoned by United States Army officers who campaigned against them as the world's finest irregular cavalry. They offered organized opposition to the whites' advance only spasmodically but when they did so they were often effective, if only temporarily and locally. The most dramatic of such times came during the 1876 campaign against the Sioux and Cheyennes. The Battle of the Rosebud, on June 17, and that of the Little Big Horn, on the 25th, in which Custer and five troops of the Seventh Cavalry were wiped out, have been recounted many times, but seldom as forcefully as Mari Sandoz has done, telling it as it appeared to the red men themselves, in her biography of Crazy Horse, the great Oglala war chief. Crazy Horse was mainly responsible for Crook's defeat on the Rosebud and, with Sitting Bull, Gall, Dull Knife and other famous chiefs, led the combined Sioux and Cheyenne forces to their greatest victory on the Little Big Horn.*

THE NIGHT was thinning in the east when Crazy Horse stopped his Oglalas for a little resting. They were not far from the Rosebud now, and once a little wind brought a smell of water that stirred the tired horses and once the sweetness of the roses blooming so thick in that valley. But soon there was the soft owl hoot of another war party coming, so they rode in closer, for the soldiers must not escape them now.

From *Crazy Horse*. Copyright 1942 by Mari Sandoz.

Daylight came upon the warriors behind the ridge north and west of the bend of the Rosebud. Stopping there, they ate of their *wasna* and made ready for the fight. Crazy Horse loosened his long hair, tied on the calfskin cape, and threw dust over his spotted war horse while not far away the eighteen-year-old son of Red Cloud shook out a long-tailed war bonnet and put it on as though he were really a bonnet man of the *akicita*, the other young men standing away from him, even the older ones silent, for this son of the agency could be told nothing at all.

While the horses rested, the scouts were sent out to locate the soldiers, bring back word of them; but as they crossed the ridge they rode into the Crows coming up from the other side. There was shooting, a Lakota fell, two Crows were wounded, and all the warriors, forgetting about the resting horses, whipped them to the ridge and stopped there in dark rows against the sky.

Below him Crazy Horse saw the Crow scouts fleeing down the slope into the valley of the Rosebud, full of soldiers and Indians,[1] so many they looked like a resting, cud-chewing herd of buffalo, the horses grazing, the men in dark little bunches. Beyond them was the willow-lined creek, with more soldiers on the other side, and then the bluffs and the far ridge, so far that a horseman would look like one of the scattering of little trees. And between him and that place, as in the palm of a browning hand, were the soldiers, and once more Crazy Horse wished for guns, plenty of good rifles and warriors who would strike together in waves like flying hail.

As the Crows fled howling back to the soldiers, they stirred into moving, running to catch their horses or lining up and then going off every way in little bunches, many horse and walking soldiers hurrying up towards the hostiles, coming in rows, a flag waving, a bugle sounding clear in the warm air. Behind them the Indian scouts were riding hard up and down, raising a great dust, making ready to fight too, now that the soldiers had gone ahead, shooting into the hostiles.

Crazy Horse held his warriors together for a long time but there were so many soldiers and their rifle-fire was so close among them that finally they fell back to the rocks of the sec-

[1] Battle of the Rosebud, June 17, 1876.

ond ridge, hoping to draw the whites along. And they came, off their horses now, crawling from rock to rock, and when they were well scattered, Crazy Horse led a charge. It was a hot little fight, many men going down, some even from arrows. Then more soldiers, followed by the Snakes, came galloping up from the side. In the smoke and dust the Lakotas couldn't tell their friends from the scouts, so they withdrew awhile to rest their horses and to see how the fighting was going in other places.

The Crows had been getting bolder too, and when young Red Cloud lost his horse and ran away without stopping to take off the war bridle to show that he was unafraid, they rode upon him and whipped him hard, grabbing his father's rifle from him and jerking off the war bonnet, saying he was a boy, with no right to wear it. Crazy Horse and two others charged the Crows and got the young Bad Face back, not looking at him, shamed that they had seen one of their young men crying to his enemies for pity.

By now the sun was high and the fighting had spread off to the opposite ridge, the charges going back and forth over miles of rough ground, with many brave things done, many afoot and wounded ones being carried off the field by warriors whose horses were so tired they could barely be whipped out of a walk. The Hunkpapas were helping strong now. They came late, their horses were fresher and their guns still loaded. Crazy Horse was with them awhile, shooting from the ground as always. When his spotted horse was played out, he got his bay and went to the bluffs where the Cheyennes seemed to be making a very good fight. Once, when the smoke and dust lifted, Crazy Horse saw the sister of Chief Comes in Sight charge forward to where he was afoot and surrounded. With him on behind her she zigzagged back through the soldiers, bullets flying, the warriors making a great chanting for this brave thing done.

Ahh-h, the Cheyennes were indeed a strong people, Crazy Horse thought, but not the strongest heart and the longest arm, Lakota or Cheyenne, with only a bow was enough against these rifles. The warriors fought hard but always they were driven back. It was happening right now to his own Lakotas, his bravest men breaking into retreat before the bullets whistling hot around them, whipping hard to get away.

Then suddenly they found Crazy Horse before them, his horse turned into their faces, crying out to them: "Hold on, my friends! Be strong! Remember the helpless ones at home!" And with his Winchester held high as a lance he charged through them towards the coming soldiers. "This is a good day to die!" he called back over his shoulder, the calfskin flying out like bat wings behind him. "Hoka hey!"

"Hoka hey!" the strong voice of Good Weasel answered him as he turned to follow, and then Bad Heart Bull, Black Bear, and Kicking Bear. "Hoka hey!" the warriors roared out together, thundering close behind them, charging back into the soldiers among the rocks, lifting their arrows to fall among the horses. When the frightened animals began to break from the holders the soldiers jumped back on and now even the youngest Loafer could see that the whites were afraid and so pressed them harder, charging through them, shooting under the necks of the puffing horses, or from flat on their backs, until the Crows and Snakes fled from this wild charging, whipping, crying, towards the little bunch of soldier chiefs and traders' sons down around Three Stars.

Soon the whites were breaking as their scouts had, the Lakotas right among them, knocking the men from the saddles with their empty guns and the swinging war clubs, riding them down, never stopping except to pick up the dropped carbines, Crazy Horse ramming the stuck shells from them. So they drove the whole party like scattering antelope back into the valley, the warriors chasing after them. Here Crazy Horse saw many hurt ones, and many brave ones, too, particularly a little soldier chief sitting against a tree, his face all blood, still shooting with his revolver.

Now there was a loud bawling of bugles and the soldiers fell back together and made a thick new line that would be hard to break. Besides, the sun was moving away and so Crazy Horse decided it was time to try something else. Turning, he led his warriors around over the creek and down the other side, letting their tired horses walk, making it seem they were giving up. As he hoped, a bunch of soldiers and some Crow scouts saw them go and followed down the other side, and once more Crazy Horse became the old thing he was so often—a decoy, making little stands behind the others, little charges towards the soldiers across the creek, as if to hold them back. So they came faster.

As the Oglalas neared the bend of the Rosebud, signals were sent back, calling the others to come down to the narrow place in the valley, where it would be easier to fight with bows and tired horses. More and more hostiles began to string out down the creek behind the whites, who did not seem to notice these Lakota warriors coming.

But before the soldiers got to the place for fighting, the Crows with them stopped, making the wild Crow howling, pointing ahead, refusing to go to where the ridge came towards the creek, with rocks and brush for the enemy to hide. And when a messenger from Three Stars came galloping after them, the soldiers swung far out around the Indians following them and hurried back in time to strike the rear of the warriors still fighting.

So the Indians scattered. The shells were gone, even those they had got with the new guns, and the horses worn out. It had been a hard fight.

The daybreak star was in the sky when the warriors got back to the camp on the creek that flowed into the Little Big Horn. The news had been sent ahead from where they stopped to make travois for the wounded and so they were brought home in the good way, two of the older chiefs from each circle leading them in. The great encampment was fine to see, with cooking fires burning everywhere, the women moving dark about them, ready to feed the hungry warriors. There were some bad things to tell—eight men who would never charge the soldiers again, two from the Oglalas, and more wounded. It was bad, too, about young Red Cloud sneaking away to the agency like a shamed little boy, without the borrowed war bonnet or his father's fine gun. It must be hard to have a son come home like that. But that was only the act of one foolish young man, and the Indians killed were very few for so many in the fight, and the soldiers had been hurt too.

By the time the warriors had rested, scouts came riding with good news. Three Stars had fifty-seven men to haul away, dead and bad-wounded to need hauling, and it seemed that his ammunition was almost gone too. Anyway, he was turning his

dust around and going back to Goose Creek, not so hungry to
chase more Indians now. When the heralds rode through the
camps with this word, even the mourning people stopped to
make a little sound of joy.

After the news was talked over, Crazy Horse went out to sit
on a ridge above the great camp, to think about the fight.
There had indeed been something new among the warriors, as
he had asked. The old Lakota way of fighting for coups and
scalps and horses, of a man riding out alone and doing foolish
things to show how strong he was, seemed gone. Yesterday
most of them had charged in bunches, straight into the soldiers, breaking their lines, almost nobody stopping for coups
or scalps until the fighting in that place was done. And they
had driven Three Stars back. It was the biggest thing the Lakotas had ever done against soldiers who really came fighting, not
just sneaking like coyotes through the canyons, trying to keep
from being seen. Perhaps it was really bigger than the fight on
the Piney, for the soldier chief there was no warrior like Three
Stars.

And there was still the vision of Sitting Bull: Many Soldiers
Falling into Camp.

The next day the whole camp moved down to the Little Big
Horn, leaving the death lodges of the Lakotas behind, the
women keening as they looked back from the first rise. That
night the victory dances began, only the scalps of the Indian
scouts hanging from the women's staffs, those of the short-
haired soldiers thrown away as no better than so much horse
skin. They danced the things taken too, the guns, including
many of the short saddle ones, some thrown away by the soldiers when they jammed in the heat of the fighting. But one
called Good Hand, who had helped the blacksmith at the
agency, knew how to make them work very well, even those the
soldiers had broken whipping their horses.

The drumming and dancing and singing lasted all night,
the people going from one camp to the next to hear all the
great things done on the Rosebud. But the best of all was down
among the Cheyennes, where the story of Buffalo Calf Road,
the woman who carried her brother from the battle, was told
and retold. Their dancing lasted four days; the sacred buffalo

hat was brought out, a new scalp tied to it, and the ceremonial of its renewal made before all the people.

Crazy Horse never helped with the dances, but there was work and planning to be done. Scouts were sent to follow Three Stars, to shoot into his night camps and keep the soldiers watching and afraid. Runners went to the young men of the agencies, north and south, carrying the good news of the fighting in their mouths and the pay-money taken from the soldiers in their pipe cases for powder from Boucher and others who traded in the night. One morning he took a little party of Oglala boys over to the Rosebud to pick up the scattered ammunition, for it was well known that the soldiers often take handfuls from their belts, lay it down handy, and then move on with the fighting. The boys filled several unborn buffalo calf skin sacks and got very many empty shells to reload, some lead too, from bullets flattened against the rocks, and many arrow points and the shoes from the dead American horses.

"Nothing must be forgotten when iron is so scarce," he said, and told the boys some stories of the stone arrow makers, a people so long gone they seemed forgotten, the Crows claiming they were a small people like eight-year-olds that lived in the cave rocks near the Yellowstone.

"Guns are better—" a Loafer son said impatiently.

"Guns are as the eyes and the hearts behind them," the Hunkpatila said, and then spoke no more.

In the great camp were many kettles to be filled and so hunters packed in fresh meat from the buffalo herds west of the river and some went clear beyond the Big Horn to where the antelope were like a great cloud shadow running over the grass. And every day more people came from the agencies, those from the north telling of soldiers marching up the Yellowstone like the black singing cricket, so many. Ahh-h? Then the women and children must be taken to a good place, with the river between them and these new guns. There seemed no danger now from Three Stars. He was headed into the mountains to hunt the big-horn, and his Crow scouts had gone home in anger right after the Rosebud fight, and the Snakes too. So his soldiers hunted, fished, and pulled arrows from the rumps of their horses, reminders that the hostiles were watching.

On the sixth day after the Rosebud fight the great encampment moved across the Little Big Horn, the old herald on the far bank calling out where the people were to go—the Cheyennes, leading, going farthest down the stream, the Hunkpapas at the back stopping near the mouth of Ash Creek, all the others between. It was an old-time moving camp, the councilors ahead, the women fine with their bright saddle trappings, the warriors singing, the young men playing tricks and showing off before the girls, the boys racing up and down, the great horse herds a thunder on the ground as they came. By evening the five great circles and several small ones were spread along three miles of river as orderly as after weeks of living.

That night there was dancing everywhere, not of ceremonies but for the young people. Groups moved from camp to camp, singing, joining around the drums in the light of the great fires, and then going on, the prettiest girls choosing their partners from among the young warriors who had done big things on the Rosebud. It was a night of fun lasting until the stars faded into dawn.

The next morning the camps slept late, many going straight to the river for bathing when they awoke, men and women and children splashing and laughing in little parties all up and down the swift, cool water of the Little Big Horn. The sun, climbing, burned hotter, and they scattered, some to move the grazing camp horses, many to the shade of the trees along the stream, most of the women going to the lodges to some easy, visiting work like rubbing the buckskin or waving the fly brush over the sleeping children, some of the younger ones taking the turnip-diggers to the hills north of the river. Many of the warriors loafed in the shade of the rolled-up lodges, talking lazily about the fighting the other day. Even the few boys around the camps were quiet, the whole great encampment like a dog lying in the sun.

It was true that the Cheyenne prophet, Box Elder, had sent out a crier a few days ago to warn the people to keep enough horses up, that he saw soldiers coming in a dream, and yesterday a No Bow went around saying the soldiers would be here the next day. Then there was Sitting Bull's vision of soldiers falling into camp. But the people were not uneasy. The scouts said Three Stars was going farther away and that the soldiers from the north were still far down the Rosebud. Even Crazy Horse had left his lodge, to visit in the Cheyenne camp.

But an Oglala crossing the ridge on his way to Red Cloud happened to see a dust hanging like smoke on the breaks up beyond Ash Creek, with many men moving under it. He whipped his horse back across the river and to his lodge, crying out: "Soldiers coming here! Soldiers coming here!"

It was like the shot of a wagon gun over the quiet valley of the Little Big Horn, setting the Indians into a swarming. Runners started to the other camps, warriors hurried out for the herds, or got their fighting things together, and the turnip-diggers were signaled in, for already the women were crying of danger close. There was dust to be seen from here, a great pile of it just up the river, on this side, with many fast-riding horse soldiers in it.

That was true, for already they were near the upper, the Hunkpapa circle, stretching themselves into a line of blue riders from the river to the hills, their Ree Indian scouts on the higher end. A row of smoke puffs came from the soldier guns, bullets tore through the lodges, the echoes roaring all over the great camp as they moved slowly ahead, shooting. And before the soldiers' coming the women grabbed up their little ones and fled down the river, the old men and the camp dogs following. The Big Bellies hurried out too, some going along to quiet the afraid ones, others staying to help make a wall between the people and the soldier guns until the warriors could come up with their arms and horses to stand off the whites. And as the herds came flying in from the hills, the young men caught up the first good horses they reached, jumped on, and with a whooping charged off into the fight.

With many Hunkpapas facing them and more Lakotas and Cheyennes coming hard, the soldiers got off to fight on foot, and when the warriors saw this done they felt very strong. First they struck the Rees, driving them from the fight, making them drop some Hunkpapa horses they had cut off, and leaving the whole end of the soldier line open. Only one, a half-Lakota that the northern people knew as Bloody Knife, stayed with the whites, and him they cut down like a sneaking Crow found in the woman's lodge.

By the time Crazy Horse and Big Road with some Oglala warriors reached the Hunkpapa camp there was already much damage done, the lodges torn by the bullets, many knocked down, some burning. And just beyond where the fighting was several hundred warriors stood against the soldiers, with Sitting Bull, Black Moon, and Gall leading them. Crazy Horse was on his yellow pinto, stripped to breechcloth, a splattering of hailstone marks on his body, the lightning streak down his face, and the red-backed hawk on his head. And when the warriors saw him coming they made a roaring and lined up for a charge. But he remembered their need to save ammunition, and all the jammed guns they got from the horse soldiers on the Rosebud.

"Be strong, my friends!" he called out. "Make them shoot three times fast, so their guns will stick and you can knock them down with your clubs!"

He said this over and over, as another would sing a song, holding the warriors back while he rode up and down before the soldiers, drawing their fire to him as the man in his vision had, bullets like hail around him, and not touching. And when the shooting slowed down, the men beginning to jerk at their guns, making loud words, the Indians charged and the scared soldiers broke and ran like crazy men for a patch of brush and trees near the river, the warriors getting many on the way. But now they had a little hiding-place and the Indians had to crawl up over flat ground, so the fighting slowed.

But it seemed the soldiers couldn't stay still. They kept coming out and looking back up the trail and finally they jumped on their horses and retreated through the warriors between them and the river. There was no crossing, but they spurred their horses to jump the high bank into the water, with the Indians after them as after buffalo caught in shifting quicksand, knocking them from their horses with war clubs as they tried to get out on the other side, their horses slipping and falling back, the Indians making the "Yi-hoo!" the game-killing cry, each time they struck. But many got away, and with the little soldier chief in the lead they headed towards a hill, some of the warriors after them, others going back to finish the scattered soldiers and to pick up the guns and shells and round up the horses.

While they were stripping the whites one of the Cheyennes from the south country stopped to look carefully at the markings on a soldier coat. It was the same as on the one he had got in the Washita fight, where Long Hair had killed his mother and his wife. So these must be the same soldiers, these who were lying on the ground here, and who died like buffalo in the river. With the blue coat held out in his hands he ran from one to another, showing it, crying for all the valley of the Little Big Horn to hear: "My heart is good! This day my heart is good!" the water running as with a raining down his dusty face.

But now a messenger came riding, his arm pointing off across the river. More soldiers! Many more soldiers going down along the ridge on the other side, just across the river from the lower camps, where the helpless ones were. There was a fork-tailed flag ahead, and behind it a long double row of soldiers and dust, so much dust that one could hardly see the bunch of gray horses that were among them.

Hoh! It was indeed as in Sitting Bull's vision—soldiers come falling into camp. Crazy Horse saw that the big fight would be made down there. Good, let it come. He felt very strong today because the warriors were as they had been on the Rosebud, not after coups and showing off, but striking hard, striking to kill. That was what had scared the many soldiers of Three Stars away, and broke those who came here. So Crazy Horse and Gall and Knife Chief called their warriors together with their bone whistles and spoke a few words for a charge on those soldiers going against the lower camps, already so close to the fleeing people.

"A few stay here to watch those on the hill, the rest go against the new ones," Gall told his Hunkpapas, and started off down the soldier side of the river.

"Remember the helpless ones down there! This is a good day to die!" Crazy Horse said to his Oglalas. But they needed no heating words now. "Hoka hey!" they cried, lifting the new soldier guns high as they swept off down the river behind the Hunkpapas while Crazy Horse hurried to gather up the warriors still scattered over the fighting ground and to bring up as many as he could from below. By the time they got to the half-struck lodges of the lower camps he saw four men ride out

of the river and up towards the soldiers. They were half a mile
away but they looked like Cheyennes, four Cheyennes, going
out alone to hold hundreds of soldiers back from the river
crossing until the Lakotas coming hard along the bottoms got
there. They rode in a brave little row, their horses moving together as in a dance, their guns blooming into smoke together
and making a stir among the soldiers as if some were hit. Then
there was a long row of smoke puffs from their guns, but the
Cheyennes kept riding, shooting together again, four guns
against almost three hundred. It was a great thing and Crazy
Horse whipped his tiring pinto faster to where Black Shawl,
indeed a warrior's wife, had another horse waiting.

He stopped for a word of counselling with Sitting Bull and
the other Big Bellies holding the people together, making
plans for a stand or flight and a scattering if more soldiers
came, too many more soldiers. He saw Worm and Little Hawk
and limping Black Elk among the women and children, speaking calm and quieting to them, showing them all the guns and
bows and war clubs ready among them if the soldiers came
near.

"Hoka hey!" a small boy tied to his anxious mother's back
cried when he saw Crazy Horse. The women heard and made
the trilling to see that even a little one on the back knew this
man.

"Hoka hey!" answered Crazy Horse as he threw a handful of
fooling gopher dust over his fresh war horse and put some
little grass spears through his braids because they were like the
driving snow of the winter storm. Then he led his warriors off
across the river. By now many Indians too late for the fight at
the Hunkpapa camp were over the crossing and charging up
the ridge towards the front of the soldiers as Gall and the
others came sweeping along the slope, driving some of the back
ones before them. Soon the two streams of warriors would have
come together among the enemy as they did in the battle on
the Piney. But the soldiers were stopping along the ridge in
little bunches, many off their horses, the warriors already
charging the horse-holders and getting a hard-shooting defense, the guns of the whites making a roar like a hailstorm
before a wind, a great cloud of smoke and dust rising to hang
along the ridge.

With his heart singing the war song of the drums back among the helpless ones, his Winchester ready in his hand, the Oglala led his warriors through the river, around the edge of the soldier ridge, and up a ravine behind it to cut off their retreat. And as he rode, more and more Indians fell in behind him, until the fresh war horse was the point of a great arrow, growing wider and longer, the dust of its moving standing in the air.

They reached the head of the ravine just as the Indians from the river side pushed the soldiers to the crest of the ridge, and with a great whooping the fresh warriors charged the back of the retreating blue line, using mostly arrows, spears, and clubs. They were hot for this fight today, and the soldier guns seemed little more than grease popping on the winter fire, their horses jumping a Lakota that fell among them like so much sagebrush or stone. The first charge by the Crazy Horse warriors broke the line, cut down horses and men on that hill before the soldiers could make a circle. At the next charge a few Indian horses were hit, another man or two—nothing at all in the fight of this summer day on the Little Big Horn. As the hundreds of warriors circled and charged and circled again, many brave deeds were probably being done everywhere, but nobody had time to see them in this great roar of fighting that deafened the ear, the dust and powder smoke that made a darkness as of evening.

There were some good men on that hill, some still trying to shoot carefully from the knee even as the Indians closed in, but the circle was getting smaller, the dead horses and men piling up around the soldiers as their guns stuck, the breath of their revolvers died in their hands. One bold warrior rode through them, followed by a whole charge, and so the whites went down under the hoofs and spears until it seemed nobody could be alive in that bloody pile. But there were a few, and jumping up together, they headed towards the brush of the river, so very far away, the whooping warriors running them down like new-born buffalo calves, striking them to the ground, looking for more, until suddenly there were no more.

While the warriors were still sitting around on their horses, almost not believing this easy thing, two young Lakotas came back from the breaks disappointed to miss the finish. They had

been chasing a soldier who got away on horseback and were
feeling cheated because he put the revolver against his head
and fired. Now all the others were rubbed out and they only
got the killed-himself one between them, and so no plunder
at all.

Yes, it was truly a strange thing that only a little while ago
there had been several hundred soldiers and now suddenly
there were no more to kill. Even the horses were gone, rounded
up down along the river by boys from the camps. They had
been so worn out that they were not afraid of Indians as American horses usually are, just stood to be caught.

When every brush patch had been whipped through for any
hiding ones, Crazy Horse went back to the ridge of the dead.
By now they were all stripped, lying naked and white as buffalo fat where the clothes had kept off the sun, looking so pitiful, so helpless. It made him feel bad for them, so many and
dying so foolishly. Why did they have to come shooting the
people?

Slowly he went among them to see if there were any more he
knew besides the one who had died fighting so hard down at
the river, the small white man called Reynolds, who used to be
a boy living with his family in the upper Platte country. Crazy
Horse had been told that the Cheyennes liked his little-girl
sister and stole her. California Joe, the old mountain man with
the red hair on his face, had helped get her back, it was said.

There was a trader's son among the dead too, Mitch Bouyer,
the one they had seen in the fight with the Crows. Crazy Horse
was sorry about killing him, but if the Cheyennes were right,
these soldiers were the ones who had struck their people in the
winter camp on the Washita, who came to the Yellowstone
three years ago, and later made the Thieves' Road into the
Black Hills. He found nothing of their long-haired chief called
Custer, the man with the yellow hair falling loose over his
shoulder, yet they were bad people and the trader's son should
not have been with them.

Stopping his horse at the end of the ridge, Crazy Horse
looked down upon the scattered camp circles of his people, the
women back among them, hurrying like dark ants to gather up
their possessions, a few of them crossing the river and stringing
up towards the battleground to seek their own dead, to strike

the soldiers who had made it so. Crazy Horse felt almost dead too, so tired. Finally he started towards the crossing and home, the warriors who had been held away by his standing coming up beside him from this side and that, all talking of the great things done this day, especially of the four Cheyennes who rode out alone against the hundreds of soldiers, holding them until the others got there, four against so many—a truly great thing.

Yes, Crazy Horse had seen it.

Then there was Moving Robe, the Cheyenne woman who carried the staff of her brother killed on the Rosebud into the fight today, and Yellow Nose, the Ute captive among them who had been brave, and the strong Lakotas, too many to count. But the greatest deed of all was cutting off the retreat of the soldiers.

That was not a thing done by one man but by many, following the plannings as they were made, Crazy Horse told them.

Hou! and the plannings of the surround were good ones, and came from one man—

But Crazy Horse had not stayed to listen. Remembering now the other bunches of soldiers he had seen along the ridge, he went back to look at them, particularly those where a very brave little soldier chief had held the warriors off a long time. Most of these whites, too, had been struck down close together. Truly it seemed that almost nothing was done for glory or personal power today, but all for the protection of the people. It was a great battle, and it should make any man feel good.

But there were Indians lost too, their people coming to haul them away with the travois now. Then there would be keening in the villages, and angry relatives riding for revenge against those other soldiers still waiting on the hill above the Hunkpapa circle. Crazy Horse was surprised to remember them now; they had been so forgotten.

At the river crossing he saw an American horse standing alone with many bloody wounds. He thought of shooting it but he had no bow along and a bullet might be worth very much after today. So he rode away to his camp. Black Shawl was back, if she had ever fled very far, and came running out to meet her man, to see that the blood mixed with the dust and sweat and paint was not his own; that he was not scratched.

She brought him hot water and a piece of soapweed root for washing, fed him, and had another fresh horse ready so he could go to the hill where the live soldiers were. On the way Crazy Horse saw some young warriors dressed in soldier clothes, with flags and bugles, riding around in twos like the soldiers. It seemed some whites left hidden in the brush from the morning had come out when they saw the blue coats and then ran back into the bushes when the warriors began shooting with the captured guns that were good after they knocked the stuck shells loose. They had shot at some of the soldiers from the hill who tried to come down for water, too. Maybe they had hurt them but they hadn't tried very hard. After the big fight they felt too good for much more killing.

When Crazy Horse got up on the hill, he saw it was true that more whites had come there, bringing pack mules, as the watching warriors said, and that they had really been digging themselves down into the stony hill as a turtle digs into sand. But it seemed they were not satisfied with that place either, and while Crazy Horse signaled for more warriors, some of the soldiers came out and started off along the ridge towards the ground of the big fight, several miles away. They stopped on a high point where they could see very many Indians sitting on their horses down there, the smoke and dust like a wind cloud high above them. There were warriors coming across the river too, and the ones the soldiers had been fighting on the hill were trying to cut them off, so the little soldier chief led his men in a gallop back to their hole. The Indians attacked there, trying to scare them as they had done in the morning, to get at the horses. They made a few good hits but the whites seemed different now, much stronger, and they had a good place to defend. After going against them several times, afoot too, the tired Indians gave it up for that day. When the sun stood red on the hills west of the Little Big Horn, a night guard was set around the soldiers, and most of the warriors went back to the mourning camps across the river, where the death lodges had been put up for the twenty warriors killed, the medicine men working over the many wounded.

As soon as he could, Crazy Horse went to cover his head in his sleeping robe so he need not hear the keening; he tried to sleep so he need not think about the fight today and why it did not seem as good as the one on the Piney ten years ago. Many, many more were killed here, and he had lost no one like Lone Bear, and yet it seemed almost that he wished this hadn't happened. Could it be that his warrior days were over?

The next morning some of the headmen went up to look at the soldiers dug in on the hill. There was talk of making a great charge to finish the fight right away, but some were against it, saying good men would be lost, and their little ammunition used up.

"Wait," these advised. "The whites will soon come out for water."

Crazy Horse was there too, planning a few charges to try the hearts of the soldiers today, but the scouts signaled that another great army was coming up the river, many more than they had been fighting, with wagon guns. Short Bull and some of the others had stayed behind to shoot into their camps, to charge the horse herds, to make them move slower so the people would have time to get away, for they were already very close.

Once more the great encampment set out upon the trail, going up the river this time, and fast, with no beaded saddle hanging on the women's horses, no gay singing, no jokes and showing off. When the last travois pulled away past the Hunkpapa camp ground the grass of the valley began to burn, the pale smoke rolling up like midsummer thunder clouds behind them. So the long line of people hurried away towards the shelter of the White Mountains, leaving the places of the soldier fights behind—the ridge with the dead ones bloated fat in the hot sun, and the hole with the live ones, too, the last of the watching warriors from there falling in with those who guarded the rear of the people as the camp disappeared into the breaks along the river.

The battle of the Little Big Horn was done.

Sixty Lodges Standing

BY MARI SANDOZ

¶ *The Little Big Horn fight was the high point of the Indian resistance on the northern Plains. Bowing to the inevitable, the great Crazy Horse surrendered and led his band into the reservation. Not long afterward he was killed when he resisted being thrust unfairly into jail. The Northern Cheyennes were sent to a reservation in Indian Territory (now Oklahoma), a region they detested, fifteen hundred miles away from their homeland. There, dysentery and tuberculosis took their toll and, half-starved, the others faced extinction. Defying Indian agent and army alike, the pitiful remnant of this great people—two hundred and seventy-eight men, women, and children, armed with a handful of guns and a scanty supply of ammunition, with too few horses —took leave of the reservation and struck out for their remembered, beloved Montana, led by Little Wolf and Dull Knife, both Old Man chiefs and wise, respected leaders. "Sixty Lodges Standing" tells of the inception of the historic, incredible march they made, pursued and harried by thousands of troops, pausing occasionally to fight, then turning to flee again. Their achievement is chronicled fully and movingly in Mari Sandoz's* Cheyenne Autumn.

NOW IT WAS THE NIGHT, but there were no friendly clouds to run before the face of the climbing moon. Little Wolf sat alone at the deserted council fire, the big silver peace medal given him by the President in Washington shining softly on his breast. But under his shirt hung the Cheyenne Chief's Bundle and across his knee was his rifle, ready.

With his finger on the trigger the Wolf listened, looking out beyond the spread of smoky, cone-shaped lodges that stood about him, so quiet and remote in the moonlight. Here and there the diffused glow of a little fire showed through the old skins, or a few coals lay red inside a lifted lodge flap—fires that had been kept alive all through the hot summer against the chills of the shaking sickness and starvation.

Somewhere a ground owl hooted, and Little Wolf wondered how it had escaped the empty soup kettle so long, here where hunger sharpened the oldest teeth. But the owl called only once. Otherwise everything seemed to sleep except Young Eagle, blowing his love flute up on a hillside, softly, mournfully. Once more his people needed every warrior, no matter how old or how young. So he must go with them, leaving his beloved one here in the south, go even if his blood was to be spilled in a red blanket on the ground somewhere between the Fork of the Canadian, flowing so quietly back below him, and that other river, the Yellowstone, that cut its valley deep along their home country.

The Cheyenne village lay in a small pocket surrounded on all but the south by the sandy hills rising in a wall against the moon-paled sky. The new cavalry encampment was vague whitish rows of tents out of sight beyond the ridge from the Indians, but soldiers were posted along the crest of the encircling ridges, the guns ready, the cannon waiting to boom out, to burst its shells down among the smoky lodges.

No matter what happened now, this was the last night of the Cheyennes here, Little Wolf knew. All the delaying that the Indians could make was done, and tomorrow the soldiers would attack if the camp was not moving early, to be settled back at the agency. It was hard to understand these things, for the earth here was the same as that under the black coattails of the soft-speaking agent, all the same reservation set aside for their southern relatives by the treaties to which the white man had also touched the pen. Everybody except the Northern Cheyennes, who never agreed to live anywhere here at all.

A dog barked several times in a distant Indian village, where such friendly, noisy animals could still be tolerated because there was no secret movement to betray. Up along the hillside the flute still rose and fell like a sad-winged bird, but it no longer spoke of rejected love. Now it signaled to Little Wolf that the strong men selected to watch the soldier sentinels were finally all in place, ready with war ax and knife, and with arrow poised for the silent song of death if any departure was detected. They were young men but strong-hearted enough to stay their weapons if nothing was seen by the watching soldiers, no alarm given, and then to slip away behind their fleeing people, leaving the sentinels to watch the husks of the village, the sixty empty lodges standing.

For this, too, the Cheyennes must have good luck, and Little Wolf looked out to the moonlit knoll where Bridge, the medicine man, had lain for three days fasting, although he was already thin as a shin bone from all the hungry time. Bridge worked hard with his cloud ceremony, but surely the Great Powers had turned their ears from the Cheyennes, for this night laid naked every living thing. Yet the people must go, and as the flute lifted its thin cry, one figure after another crept from the quiet lodge fires, Dull Knife and the way finders going first, then Little Wolf's wife, Feather on Head, and the women after her, moving like smoke from shadow to shadow toward the little pass in the hills. They moved carefully, keeping from the moon's rounding face so no white-man eyes could see the going, nor the Indian policemen the agent had made.

Humped as buffaloes with their burdens, the Cheyennes passed, the men with their poor arms—bows or perhaps a rifle or a pistol—and the regalia that they could carry, the war-bonnets, the shields, and a few other medicine things. All who had saddles or saddle pads of antelope hair took them along. The women were bent too, with the weight of the babies on their backs and with the few goods they managed to gather for the long road north. With a hand out to keep the older children close, they tried to hurry, some stumbling a little in weakness or from the contagion of anxiety.

Behind these women came the young Singing Cloud helping her father who had lifted himself from his bed of dying so his daughter need not remain behind. In her lay the last seed of a great warrior family. If this was to be lost, it must not be to ignominious hunger and shaking in a cannon-dark-ened lodge of a prisoner people but in a fight for life. Some-

where on the long run northward the old man would slip
down and return to the grass. Then, in his vanishing the
daughter would be free, free to go to the bold young Dog
soldier Little Finger Nail, the sweet singer of the Cheyennes,
the one who drew the finest pictures of the feats of his people.

Ahead of the Cheyennes and all along the chosen path
through the watching soldiers was a thin scattering of warriors, men who would fight to the end, if they must, as so
many of their brothers had died in other places from other
soldiers while protecting the women and children. Leading
this departure was old Dull Knife, carrying the pipe, with
three good men close in the old Cheyenne way. He was sick
with malaria and dysentery too, his warrior days as a leading
Dog soldier only heroic tales around the evening fires now,
but on his breast was the beaded lizard of his medicine dream-
ing that he wore whenever the people had to be saved. Not
the grasping hawk or even fire can kill the big-eyed lizard so
long as it is watchful. Nothing except the call of the years can
bring its bones to molder in the earth. So, with this protection
and because the frightened women and children would surely
follow him, Dull Knife went ahead, although there would be
soldiers coming from that direction too, from behind and
the sides. If not in this loud throb of the drumming heart or
the next, then certainly when the sun bared the lodges standing empty.

Far back, to see that the families all got away, Little Wolf
watched; then he began to move too, slipping from one
shadowed spot to another up along the edge of the hills, looking down—the Wolf, the one the Cheyennes called their
Brave Man. Soft-spoken and gentle, he could whip any unruly
Elk warrior to his duty and still, at fifty-seven, lead him in any
battle. The Wolf had fought so hard when the soldiers struck
the Cheyennes up on the Powder Fork two years ago that it
stopped the heart. He had been like a great wounded bear in
his fury and fearlessness that time, even the soldiers said, and
when it was over, he lived to carry away all the lead the whites
and their Indian scouts could send into his flesh, as he carried
the pockmarks of the stinking, alien disease on his face. Perhaps this was because under his arm he bore the bundle
brought to the Cheyennes by Sweet Medicine very long ago,

and so was selected as the dedicated one of all the tribe, the
man who must always forget himself, as their culture hero
had done, and remember only the people.

Behind Little Wolf came Tangle Hair with some of his
older Dog soldiers, the warrior society whose duty it was never
to start until all the village was moving—a perpetual Cheyenne rear guard but greatly diminished in their stands against
the army attacks on the villages during the last fourteen years.
Now once more this was not just a war party going out, where
the warriors needed only to whip the enemy or, if whipped
themselves, to run and plan revenge another day. Now all the
people here and all those to be born so long as the sky stood
over the earth were given into the palms of their warrior
hands, to be saved or to lie scattered and lost forever on the
wind.

The two leading chiefs had good warrior sons along to help
them, two each. Dull Knife's older one, Bull Hump, was
hidden behind the troopers watching the cannon that pointed
into the camp. His knife was naked, ready to check the first
cry in the throat or the finger tightening on the signal trigger.
Little Wolf's son Woodenthigh was out there too, and the
Wolf's favorite nephew who had been given his own name.

The chiefs had two wives each, the smallest number required by the lodges of such men, with no Cheyenne ever to
be hired as his brother's pay help. There were many guests to
visit a chief's lodge, guests from the village, from other bands
and far tribes. They must be feasted and given lodge guest
presents of moccasins and robes, as well as good young stock
from the pony herds. With Dull Knife was Pawnee Woman,
the one he captured as a pretty girl from a Pawnee camp and
took to his lodge many years ago. It had grieved his first wife
so she hanged herself, and for a short time brought a silent
looking down from the women of the village as he passed. But
soon he took another wife, a young woman of strong heart,
short and sturdy, with soft, smiling eyes. Gradually she
brought smoothness to the life of the lodge and to the village
about her with the good deed, the gentle word, and the firm
hand even with her man when it was a matter of the family,
for this was always the first duty of a Cheyenne woman within
her lodge. Tonight, while the old chief went ahead of the peo-

ple, this Short One made a little song as she hurried with Pawnee Woman from shadow to shadow:

> Proudly we follow the path of Morning Star,
> The one they call Dull Knife.
> Many, many snows he has spoken for peace,
> Carrying the pipe of it in his hand
> Like others carry the bow and the shooting gun.
> Ei-eya!

She sang softly, so no listening soldier might hear as she passed with the chief's warbonnet and shield and sacred lance head on her back.

So the Indians vanished from the lodges under the veiling moon, going like the fox sneaking up a gully, not like the Cheyennes of the old days, bold as the gray wolf who stalks the ridges with his tail straight up in the air. The Cheyennes were not strong in warriors now. A year ago they brought two hundred fighting men along. But now barely a hundred remained, counting all over twelve, the age not for war but to take up weapons for defense. All the others were lost—many sick and dead from the hunger and fevers and the old, old disease of homesickness that no doctor, not even Bridge the medicine healer, had the power to cure. Besides some had deserted, and that too had to be endured.

With the warriors went the people, the weak and old and infirm too, and a few lone ones, like the woman whose husband threw her away down here in the south country. It seemed better to follow those who lived in the old Indian way, where everyone would have meat for the coals if anyone did. She felt she belonged here with the strong ones, even the women here strong enough to bring courage, and envy, to any camp—those like young Buffalo Calf Road, the warrior woman who had killed in battle and had ridden against the soldiers of both Generals Crook and Custer. In this fleeing night it was good to think of this and remember that once, long ago, another warrior woman saved all the tribe when the enemy seemed hopelessly many.

But there were other courageous young women along. The

Leaf, the wife of Bull Hump, was well fitted to the Beautiful People, as the Dull Knife family was called by the whites. The chief's older daughters had both dared say no to the covetous officers, even after their cannon stood on the hill looking down upon the lodges, the Sorrowing One's hair still cut short to her shoulder in the sign of mourning for her young warrior husband killed by the troops on the Powder. Then there was Wild Hog's pretty daughter, who, with her friend Singing Cloud, had saved three small children when the cannon balls were bursting right among them.

Pretty Walker, too, had saved a life in a fight, but it was never recounted at the evening fires for the man she saved was a soldier. She had dragged him away from the bullets because, in the thickest fighting, he had given his horse to an old woman who could not run. The daughter of Little Wolf was an independent, tall-walking girl, as was proper in that family of good leggers, the father still a foot racer, her brother called Woodenthigh because he never wore out. The girl had been called Pretty Walker so long that her real name seemed forgotten, but none forgot that she could go as calmly into the path of bullets as her father, the dedicated man.

The young women were going north to escape this country before the sickness shook away the roundness of their flesh. And following them were the hopeful young warriors, some from the southern people too, and some older men like Thin Elk, who had come slipping down from the Yellowstone country scarcely a moon ago—to visit his brother Bald Eagle, he announced when he came. Yet it was to Little Wolf's lodge he walked most often, and this time he could not be driven away as he was twenty years ago, when the Wolf was still only a war leader. An Old Man Chief could not warn anyone away from his wife. "Only danger that threatens the people can anger me now," Little Wolf had sworn in the tribal chief's oath. "If a dog lifts his leg to my lodge, I will not see it."

But tonight as the Wolf watched Thin Elk pass, helping the women in their flight, he thought of something else: the old Cheyenne saying that a coal once kindled is easiest set to glowing. The chief did not know that, while he walked his preoccupied way these later days, some of the women had begun to whisper behind the hand. Perhaps it was not toward one of the wives of Little Wolf that the Elk was turning his eyes in the card games and along the village path. Perhaps it was the daughter, the Pretty Walker, that he was watching.

But Thin Elk had brought important news of their relatives who surrendered to the fort on the Yellowstone last year. They were healthy, well-treated, well-fed. The council circle made their *"Hous!"* of approval; that was the way things were done in the north country.

Ahh-h, but all those people would be brought south too. A band of nearly three hundred were already on the way. When Bear Rope, the violent man among them, protested this angrily, his eyes red as the eagle's in the firelight, Thin Elk replied that those Cheyennes could not help themselves either. The soldiers held them in the palm, riding ahead and behind them as Little Wolf himself had been driven south. All the Cheyennes were to live in the south forever.

"It said forever too in the treaty that protected our north country—so long as grass shall grow and water flow," the Wolf recalled quietly.

As he had hoped, the bad news Thin Elk brought turned no one from the northern trail of tonight, not even after the Keeper of the Sacred Buffalo Hat became very cautious and uncertain, perhaps because he foresaw fighting, bad fighting with the soldiers. Yet the sacred tribal objects, the Hat and the Medicine Arrows, had not always brought the people luck. They were both carried along last summer, and still not a lodge was spared the sickness and the death keening, although the Keeper and his wife had performed a good curing ceremony with the Hat that was made of the head skin of a mothering buffalo cow. Even strong ones died, or turned strange, like Bear Rope, who walked so dangerously among the fleeing ones this night of silence. He had been a good man to follow in war and in the council. Now he might break into fighting at the flutter of a wind, striking out at anyone with his war ax and not even the long pipe of mediation and peace brought the light of seeing into his eyes. Afterward he would sit shaking, so cold his wives must pile the fire high all night.

But now there must be no sound, and the Rope's son-in-law moved close beside the sick man, sorrowful, yet with his strong fingers ready to stop the first sound in the bony throat. There was still death among them too this night. Just as the people started, a small girl, warm as alive, had to be left alone in one of the dark lodges, with the buckskin fringes of childhood on her dress, the first moccasins she was beading, and the doeskin doll with the braids of her dead mother's hair held in her arms. Not even her grandmother dared make a sound of sorrow now, with the soldiers all around, and the wagon gun that threw balls great as the sun, to burst with the sun's fire among the people.

So they went, their faces turned northward under the luck of a falling star, but their hearts looking back to all those who must be left behind. Silent as field mice, the moccasins ran over the bare, horse-cropped earth, keeping to the uneven ground and hollows.

Hidden, but felt by them, Little Wolf recognized each darkening of the shadows below him, knowing each one as intimately as though of his own lodge. Without questioning or hesitation the helpless ones were following Dull Knife into the pass with the soldier guns very close on each side, for his wisdom was of the old days—of the wool-blinded buffalo feeding with his nose always into the wind, snuffling out danger, of the young grass waiting under the winter snow, and the Powers of the earth and sky and the four great directions— the old wisdom of the time when a man spoke what he believed and his word was his life. But long ago something new had come into this, the *veho*, the white man, and to Little Wolf it seemed that the whites had to be met on their own terms, for now the power of numbers and of guns and the twisted tongue was with them. Now, as for over twenty years past, it seemed that the only Indian surely never killed was the Indian never caught.

As the chief counted the passing ones, their going less than the sound of a breath, he pressed his arm against the sacred bundle, but his hand gripped the Winchester. Back behind him young men rode into the deserted camp as though returning from a hunt or a visit, shouting among the empty lodges, doing it open and natural, as on any night, for the listening soldiers to hear. They threw wet grass upon the low coals, making smudges against the mosquitoes and to send the smell of smoke over the ridge to the camp of the red-faced

soldier chief, Captain Rendlebrock, who carried a smell of his
own, the whisky that made men crazy. On the hillside the love
flute still cried, the young man yearning for the delicate-
boned Blue Fringe who must be left behind. He had asked
her to come, and her relations too, for it was only right that
a young man join the woman's people, as in the old, old way.

But Blue Fringe had laughed, making a little song:

> My friend, if I go north,
> I may not be able to swim across a river,
> I mean the big Platte river.

She sang it as to a small boy. It was done at a dancing, the
Fringe repeating it to all the others who knew that the Platte
was often sand bars in late summer, where the buffalo herds
once milled around a long time before water welled up under
their hoofs.

Even though the girl made small of Young Eagle, he still
grieved that she would stay here among the Southern Cheyennes—the laughing, taunting girl who had stood within the
folds of his blanket for a few words now and then. Perhaps
he might have stayed behind, but when the agency chief
struck old Dull Knife down with his quirt in the council a
little while ago, it was settled. So the young man blew his
plaintive eagle-wing flute, while on both sides of him lay the
dark rifle pits that the warriors had dug to meet any soldier
attack with down-hill cross fire. It was known that the whites
could destroy the village with their cannon and ride over it in
one cavalry charge, but many soldiers would be killed from
the pits so long as the ammunition lasted, and perhaps some
of the Indians might escape to the horses hidden in a steep
canyon where even stripling boys could hold them against
stampede.

And there were stripling boys, lone ones, along, some
orphaned here to be taken back to their relatives, and then
that other one—the light-haired Custer son born to Monahsetah. Her father was one of the southern chiefs killed in the
Washita fight ten years ago, and Monahsetah had been taken
with the long string of captive women and children led in
triumph over a hundred miles of snow to Camp Supply.

When the young girls were selected for the officer tents on
that cold march, she was sent to Custer.

Later Monahsetah went along on his winter expedition that
pursued her fleeing people deep into Texas. When Custer's
wife was coming to him, the Cheyenne girl was sent back to
the Indians, where this son was born toward the autumn
moon. Years afterward the traders told her that he wrote
about her in a book, praising her charm, her beauty and
grace. Not until she knew that Long Hair, General Custer,
was dead did she take another man.

Now this Yellow Swallow was nine years old, but spindly,
thin as a winter weed stalk although he was fed well by the
whites. Here he was a constant reminder to the southerners
of their relatives killed on the Washita, where General Hazen,
the military agent, had told them was a good peaceful place to
camp, not knowing that Custer could strike them at dawn.
The boy had an aunt with the fleeing ones tonight, and another up near where Custer died. In that good country the
sickly Swallow might live, become strong and brave as a
young Cheyenne should be, as the son of Long Hair should
be.

Now there were only the last soldier guns, those watching
the pass, against the escape of the Cheyennes from the cannon.
Then Little Wolf's people would be out on the open prairie
where they could scatter for a few hours as though only walking out alone if seen. But first they had to slip by the sentinels
very close together here, on both slopes, with no shadows on
the narrow pass between, the ground worn smooth and bare,
and the sharp eyes of Arapaho policemen looking. The people were strung far out now, each lost to those ahead and behind in the hazing moonlight as they crept along, barely seeming to move to the watching Little Wolf, his eyes straining so
it seemed they were afire.

Then suddenly the haze and even the far shadows were
gone in a great white light that fell over everything. It
stopped the feet, the heart, but not a sound came, no earth-
shaking roar of bursting cannon ball. Instead, a summer star
broken loose from the sky was falling slowly, its light raining
down over the people flattened to the earth—the men with
their saddles for the horses, the women with the children and

goods on their backs, all small unshadowed hummocks on the floor of a great hole of light.

But no shout disturbed the silence, no signal shot, and as the meteor slowly faded from the eyes, the moccasins began to move again, hurrying even more now to reach the scattering prairie because the light reminded them of other cannons whose bursting fire sought out their camps. Even the heavy-moving woman who had to drop back into a gully for her time remembered and whispered to the one who wished to wait behind with her.

"No, no!"

"You are weak, my sister. . . ."

"No—run! Let there be no more than myself and the child for the soldiers to ride down."

When the newborn son stretched for a cry, the mother grasped the wet little nose between her thumb and forefinger, the palm over the mouth, shutting off the breath until the child seemed to strangle in the darkness. Then she loosened her fingers for a little until there would be another crying, and tightened her hold again. So the small one was taught the first lesson of Cheyenne life: no child's cry must betray the people to an enemy.

Then, with the baby that was no bigger than two good fists against her starved, empty breasts, the Cheyenne woman started again, stumbling, weak, but moving faster as her strength returned, striking straight for the trail they would take up farther out, hoping to reach there before all had passed. She stopped only to pull the bull-tongue cactus from her moccasins now and then, and once when a rider came galloping through the fading light—a white man by the sound of the saddle leather but not a soldier, for the hoofs were naked on the hard, dry ground. Still he might be a scout or a messenger with word of the fleeing Cheyennes seen somewhere. He passed almost within finger reach of the woman, but he passed. When he was gone down toward the soldier camp, she ran, her skirts slapping against her hurrying legs.

Far from the hungry lodges and the soldiers, the people were met by small herds of horses. As many as possible of the women with their children and bundles were put upon them.

Just a few pony drags had been made, only for the very old and the very sick. But first, as always, came the needs of the young men. They must get enough more horses for the rest if they were to outrun the soldiers. They would get these without trouble if possible, but horses they must take, any way they could—the way the white thieves had taken theirs. Then too, the young men must remain well mounted and ready to charge back to fight off the pursuers.

Finally Little Wolf and his son, the last riders of all, faded into the haze of the flat horizon, cutting across to where the scouts who went out last night should be waiting—if they had escaped capture by the soldiers. If not—ahh-h, it was known that many soldiers would be standing across their path, but they hoped it would not come until the people had been fed a little, with meat and with hope.

Drummed by the moccasin heels, the horses went too fast for those afoot, and for all those who had to stay behind entirely because there was nothing to ride, and the trail to the Yellowstone seemed very long for the worn moccasin and the sickened heart.

But many toiled along afoot, bent under the burdens of their children and their bundles. These were determined to go to their home country even though they must walk over fifteen hundred of the white-man miles. Two women called Brave One and The Enemy, both with babies on their backs, led the larger party, with a few old men and growing boys along. They hurried, but no matter how fast the line of dark figures moved over the dusky prairie, in a little while even the ear to the ground could no longer detect the hoofs of the horses gone ahead.

Hide Hunter

BY MARI SANDOZ

¶ *The ability of the Plains Indian to resist the encroach-ments of the white man depended basically on the condition of his commissary-on-the-hoof, the buffalo herds. After the Little Big Horn fight, the Sioux and their allies were handi-capped not only by a serious shortage of ammunition but also by the rapidly dwindling number of buffalo. The tragic slaughter of the great herds—primed by the economic de-pression of the 'seventies that lured many men into the hide-hunting business and encouraged by government and army leaders who realized its strategic implications—set the stage for the red man's final defeat. One of the white hunters who contributed to that destruction-wrought downfall while making a stake for himself was James Butler Hickok, who as "Wild Bill" was to attain lurid fame later on as quick-shot peace officer and dandified gambler in trail-end towns and mining camps.*

ALL THE HORIZON lay bleak and gray with late November, the Indians gone, the scattering of antelope quiet on the empty prairie, the white of their rumps barely showing. An eagle flew high over the breaks, soaring, circling, while on the table-land the snowbirds fluffed themselves out round and fed busily in their little circles. But suddenly they lifted, tossing like dead leaves on the light southeasterly wind. Then they were gone, perhaps to sleep in some sheltered spot, perhaps hurried by the delicate perception of a sound that seemed to germinate in the earth, a faint vibration that grew in the air.

The antelope were gone too, now, and the deer from the buckbrush along the bottoms as the sound became a far rumble that rose and spread. A wolf, whitened by approaching winter, stood on a ridge a while, looking back, his tail an erect plume against the clouded sky.

Then the buffaloes appeared on the northwest tableland, singly at first, then in twos and threes coming down the breaks, and in little strings along the narrow trails. More and more of them came, their running a deep rumble in the earth, their dew claws rattling, the ponderous humped shoulders thrusting forward, great shaggy heads down, grunting, their noses turned into the wind.

Those in the lead stopped to sniff at the frozen creeks and the fall ponds along the river bottoms, shying from the thin ice and then crowded out upon it, pushed by the dark herd behind until the ice sagged and cracked. In the deeper holes they went clear down, others driven upon them, striving for footing on the struggling mass, perhaps to go under too. And still they kept coming, thicker and thicker, crowding hard upon the leaders. This was the way two thousand buffaloes had been left in the quicksands of the Platte River when the great herd moved north in the spring migration, and why they could be driven over any bank or cliff if the scattered van could be turned, as the Indians sometimes turned them with waving blanket or with fire, to plunge over the Chugwater bluffs up in Wyoming, and in many other less likely places.

But now the main body of the herd was coming, one dark cover over all the upper forkings of the Republican River. They came by the thousands, tens of thousands, perhaps by hundreds of thousands too, for no eye could encompass them all—one great dark moving robe that reached from horizon to horizon; a fine thick robe soft as Indian-tanned that spread over all the breaks, the canyons and the broad sweep of the valleys, fitting close as fur to the chilling earth.

And as they slowed and settled to feed a little, to rest, the wind freshened. A few gray flakes of snow began to fall; then more, and by night the storm had closed down, the storm whose coming had urged the buffaloes to move very fast until they struck long grass bottoms and the protection of bluffs and canyons against the cold wind veering into the northwest. It was a swift November snow, the third of the season, and the temperature dropped far below zero. But the second night the sky cleared and the next morning the sun crept over the sparkling plains, the vast snow-swept prairies unbroken by tree or bush away from the stream lines or the steeper breaks.

The snow was light, not over eight, ten inches on the level, and the buffaloes got up, one after another, until the whole white plain seemed rising under some curious, darkening yeast. Grunting they shook themselves and went to feeding, their wool still caked with white as they searched out the tall joint grasses sticking through the shallow drifts. Their small hoofs cut up the snow on the barer stretches. Their breath wreathed the great heads and shoulders in the cold, and lifted in a pale cloud of frost that hung over all the vast herd, the sign that the eyes of every Indian, Sioux, Cheyenne, Arapaho and even Kiowa, and every white hide hunter sought.

As the sun moved over the breaks of Medicine Creek, a man pushed his way through the flap of a canvas tipi hidden in a canyon. His long black hair was tangled into his beard, his clothing stiff and dirty. He took one long habitual glance towards the picketed horses and then all around the canyon wall for Indian sign.

"Clear day, Jim!" he called back into the smoky tent. "Not a cloud no place—"

Almost at once Jim Hickok came out too, tucking his beaver-tan hair inside his short buffalo coat as he stepped into the early sun. He was cleaner than his skinner, and lighter complexioned, with flowing mustaches and a pale stubbling of beard. He looked around carefully too, and then climbed up the canyon wall to see farther, shading his eyes with a long slender hand.

"There they are!" he said, motioning towards the pale smudging along the horizon to the southwest. "A powerful big herd!"

When the smell of coffee hung in the canyon the hunter was ready, leaving his helper to fetch up the camp with the hide wagon. Rifle in scabbard and his eyes protected from snowblindness with a heavy streak of soot across his bare cheekbones, he started. He wore gun-barrel chaps, the leather saturated with buffalo tallow to keep the snow water out, with a heavy cartridge belt over his buffalo saddle coat. Even in the bulky coat Jim Hickok was plainly a slight man, with well-cut, fur-lined gloves to protect his delicate hands. Instead of the fine faunching black mare he usually rode he was on a light gray today, a little slower if it came to a run from the Indians or a buffalo stampede, but much less conspicuous against the snow.

The hunter proceeded cautiously towards the vanishing frost cloud, keeping to the broken country, to the barer, rougher ground already thawing off enough to help hide the tracks of his horse, and where he could get out of sight very fast, perhaps even stand off a dozen angry bucks, Sioux or Cheyenne. Many Indians, peaceful even a couple of years ago and content to hang around the forts and trading posts between their big hunts, were making trouble all summer and into this fall of 1867. They didn't like the settlers pushing into the buffalo country or the Union Pacific railroad that roared its way up the Platte. Now another string of tracks had come hurrying up the Smoky Hill River of Kansas like a snake chasing a mouse along a wagon rut. With the long overland haul to river shipping, only the well-tanned Indian robes had been worth the freight but now that the railroads had tapped the buffalo ranges, even flint hides, the untanned, wind-dried skins, paid out. Hunters were swarming in to kill buffaloes by the thousands, the ten thousands, generally taking nothing but the hide, leaving all the meat to stink on the prairie wind. Now the hides were priming towards winter, heavy and well-furred, but they were priming for the Indians as well, and the meat fat for their hungry roasting fires. As surely as they wanted robes and fancied juicy hump ribs they would be out after the big Republican herd too, and any man who carried as fine a scalp as Jim Hickok better keep his eyes peeled.

By the time the hunter got sight of the herd it had broken up to feed, the small bunches scattered dark over the snow as far as he could see with his fieldglasses. He swung around to approach against the wind, topping every snowy little rise on his belly. But there was no boom of hunting rifles and the buffaloes remained quiet, undisturbed, certainly not disturbed by Indians, who were contemptuous of the hideman's still or silent hunt. They took their meat and robes with whoop and galloping horses in the thundering chase and the great surrounds.

When the snuffling, grunting buffaloes were just over the ridge, Jim Hickok hobbled his horse in a draw and crept close upon a small bunch of about fifty. He pushed a wall of snow together before him, laid his rifle across the top and, selecting the leader, aimed for the lights, the lungs. The report was loud on the cold wet air, the puff of smoke very blue, but through it he saw the fat young cow give a little jump and run a few steps, bright blood streaming from her nostrils to the snow. Several shaggy heads lifted to look. Two cows up close started a low bellowing in their throats at the smell of the blood and then suddenly they began to move away, one picking up speed, the others looking, deciding to fall in. Soon the whole bunch would be in flight. But the hunter brought down the running cow and then the other one, going in the opposite direction. She was up again and headed straight for Jim, as though her little eyes had located him, or she caught his enemy scent. So he fired another, a faster shot that brought her down in a lurch, forward upon her great head, her body rocking a little as she kicked, and was still.

By now the whole little bunch was excited, rolling their anger in their deep throats, the two old bulls pawing the earth at the stink of death, hooking their horns threateningly this way and that, their long beards waggling. But they too, waited for a leader, and each time one tried to start there was the boom of the gun until the heated barrel had burned away all the snow support. Besides, the hunter would soon have to move to keep the shifting buffaloes from catching his scent and stampeding. He aimed for one of the big bulls, but let him get too far away. He missed, and then the other one too, both fine, dark-robed animals; missed them clean like a greenhorn tenderfoot popping away with a derringer. Maybe Jim had buck fever too, even after all his years with guns, or perhaps the barrel was too hot, and the stinging smoke blinded his eyes.

The hunter examined the sights, adjusted them a little and

gave himself time to cool too as he rubbed the barrel with
snow. This still hunting with a heavy rifle was very different
from the swift jump of pistols in some smoky little frontier
saloon, or shooting from a buffalo horse charging along beside
a great bull, almost within touching distance. That was sport;
this was hides and a stake that Jim Hickok needed, a new
stake from hides that were as good as gold up at the hide
yards of the new station the Union Pacific railroad had located
at Sidney Barracks on its way through western Nebraska a
few months ago.

When fourteen buffaloes were down and one crawling
away, dragging his hindquarters, the rest apparently had
enough of the thundering noise, the infuriating smell of
blood and the curious actions of the bleeding. They were
quitting the hunter, bunching their ponderous shoulders
close together as for protection but walking in their swinging
pace, ready to break into a trot, a gallop. Stiff from inaction
and cold, Jim got up and ran around the side, barely taking
the time to glance over the white prairie for Indians, who
could be coming up on him in line with the buffaloes from
any side, almost. He kept to the cross wind and dropped
down to shoot from a bank as the buffaloes passed. His buck
fever had passed and he got eight more, scattered out in a
ragged, fleeing line, the two big bulls among them, great and
black on the snow as the others all drew away, leaving them
bleak and alone. He ran after the rest a ways and the little
bunches they were tolling along, hoping to head them with
his scent. Then he noticed a tight little herd in a box canyon
quietly sunning and chewing their cuds out of the cold northwest wind. Only one, a young spike bull, was standing, his
wet nostrils out, testing the air uneasily.

This bunch Jim managed better, dropping the first two
that started to break for lower ground with a bullet apiece.
They went down in the narrow neck of the canyon, almost
closing it as they kicked and died. The others tried to climb
the steep sides or stopped to snort and bellow at the fresh
blood, their little eyes rolling. The hunter picked them off
one by one until suddenly he realized he was out of ammunition—his belt and his pockets empty, and only the two cartridges in his hand left. Not only was he out of ammunition

but he was at least three miles from his horse. It was a chilling
realization that a man so long on the plains would be foolish
enough to shoot himself out of trigger feed, that the man who
was bragged up in *Harper's Magazine* last February as the
fastest man with the draw would let himself be caught afoot
and alone in the Indian country with an empty gun.

Coke, the skinner, was nowhere in sight and there were no
shells to waste signaling him now. Surely Jim Hickok, the one
called Wild Bill, should have his famous white-handled pistols along, but they were too valuable to lose crawling on his
belly through the snow. Besides, they were better for show
than for defense and entirely too light, too short-ranged
against a wounded buffalo, or to hold off attacking Indians.

Yet the hunting this first day had gone very well. Forty-two
buffaloes were down in the little canyon here, sixty-five altogether, and the sun still high as a man's shoulder. But Jim
was stiff and wet and cold. He crawled into a clump of brushy
weeds up at the canyon's rim and looked all around with his
fieldglasses. There was what looked like a dissolving thread
of smoke far off north, perhaps from the rising column of an
Indian signal, but nothing more came, and otherwise there
seemed only earth and sky and grazing buffaloes all around.
By the time he got back to his horse, Coke was busy skinning
at the first kill and had a sirup bucket of hot coffee waiting
in a heated firepit beside the wagon. Although the hunter
was ravenous, he refilled his cartridge belt before he did anything else. He did it silently, without speaking a word to his
helper, as often happened for days between them.

The two men were not finished skinning when darkness
came but they could not risk working by the coal oil lantern
that would surely toll any murdering redskins within miles.
A good, experienced man, Coke had worked fast. He skinned
out the heads of the two big bulls with the hides, to sell for
rugs or wall robes, but the others he ringed at the neck close
up behind the curled horns. He slit the skin down the grass-
fat belly from throat to the root of the tail and down the
inside of each leg to the knee. Then he staked the head
securely by driving a wagon rod through the nose into the
freezing earth, took a hitch of rope around a thick wad of the
hide from the back of the neck and fastened it to the double-

trees. With a sharp whipcrack Jim started the horses up and ripped the skin off, leaving the tallowed carcass bare. Most of the kill was still warm and only one hide was torn, but those left over night would have to be taken off with the curved skinning knife, painfully, inch by inch. It would be tedious but that, too, was part of the business and Coke whistled a little through his teeth as they took a heavy wagon load of the hides to camp, the rest left for tomorrow.

So the two men worked come-day and Sunday, Coke shooting some too, when the buffaloes were moving out very fast, until there were only patches of snow left along the slopes, like the spotted flanks of a pinto pony. Some days Jim shot as high as fifty or sixty but seldom more than they could skin out, and as the buffaloes grew rested and more alert, particularly on windy, moving days, it sometimes dropped down to twenty. The weather remained cold and the hides pegged down on the prairie dried so slowly they had to be left behind as the herd began to drift southward. Another month free from molestation and Jim Hickok would have his stake, be ready to return to Ft. Hays and the famous customers gathered in the back room of Drum's saloon, men like General Phil Sheridan, General Custer and his brother Tom, and always at least a dozen prominent easterners come to look at the long hairs, the gunmen and Indian fighters.

But Jim Hickok waited a little too long. He had found several nervous, scattered little bunches of buffaloes, nervous from Indian chases, he knew, and so he moved the camp east, nearer to the settlements, where the herd was thinning fast but the hunting seemed safer. They still had not actually seen an Indian.

Then one afternoon as the two men pegged down a new haul of hides, hammering hard to drive the wooden pickets into the bare, frozen ground, they were suddenly surrounded by at least twenty-five mounted Sioux Indians, so suddenly not even Hickok could jump for his gun. Another party whooped down between the hunters and the rougher breaks to cut off escape that way, although there were already a dozen warriors between them and their horses, and the tent with the buffalo guns too. It was two men against at least fifty angry-faced warriors, a few with their guns up, many with arrows set to the string. In the open the longer range of the buffalo rifles would have given the two hunters the advantage until the cartridges ran out. Now they had only their Colts in the holsters laid out of the way while they pegged down the dirty hides, and the Indian weapons were drawn upon them to stop any motion toward the guns.

Coke knew a little sign talk and at Jim's low urging, he tried to bargain with the Sioux, but he got only a snarling "All!" from the man who seemed to be the leader, and the flat-fingered circling motion of the hand that indicated they were going to take everything. "Kill our buffaloes!" the man roared out, with a final accusation: "You!"

While the Indians looked steadily down their weapons the others picked up the pistol belts and went through the tent, bringing out the buffalo guns, throwing out the small kegs of powder and the bar lead and the cases of cartridges dug from the cache hole under the bed robes, sweeping everything into their yawning hide sacks to sling across their horses. Coke was shaking inside his bloody skinner's pants and Jim Hickok had to stand with his hands empty of all except the useless pegging hatchet and watch this happen, his face pale and furious under the dirt and powder smudges of the day's hunt. The Indians pushed the wagon up close to the tent. One of them stooped to it with flint and steel to burn what they could not carry away. All Jim's property was going to the bloody redskins, and his guns too, and probably both of their lives. Wild Bill Hickok, the Prince of Pistoleers, had let a bunch of dirty, skulking Indians come up on him easy as a still hunter up on the stupid buffaloes.

As the Indian fanned the sparks to a smolder in his tinder of grass, the impatient young warriors pushed up closer with their guns, arguing among themselves, others crowding in with arrows and war clubs ready. But there was a far whooping, and another Indian came down over a little rise, whipping his yellow pinto at every jump, roaring out in his harsh Sioux, "Stop! Do not harm the white men; we are not the ones to make war first!"

Slowly the warriors nudged their horses apart to make way for the newcomer with the one feather of a chief in his hair. They did it reluctantly, sullenly, some curling their lips in snarling threats. But they did move back, and the chief slipped from his horse, kicked the rising smoke of the fire to pieces, and held his hand out to Jim in the white man way. "Me Whistler," he said, making the thumbing sign towards himself as he spoke the traders' word for his name.

Angrily, arrogantly, although the chief had surely saved his life for the moment, Jim Hickok shook his long hair loose from his collar, tossing it to curl over his shoulders. "Me, I'm Wild Bill Hickok," he said. "I remember seeing you around Morrow's ranch up near the Platte—"

Hou! it was so, the chief agreed, nodding his understanding, his teeth white in the dark face. Firmly he motioned the rifles and all the rest of the goods brought back, the powder and the horses too. Then he and the two white men went inside the tent to squat beside the little emigrant stove while Coke stuffed it full of dry buffalo chips. Over a smoke they visited a little, with Coke's smattering of sign talk to help. When a big bucket of coffee boiled up it was passed around outside for the warriors, with plenty of sugar for the tin cup. There were big handfuls of raisins too, the men cracked the seeds with satisfaction, but their eyes still turned to the pile of powder, lead, cartridges and other goods that Whistler had made them give up.

In the tent the old chief reminded the hunters that he had always been known as a peace man, but all this last summer troops had chased the Indians back and forth through their buffalo country. Nobody had been caught but it was hard to make meat and robes while running. Then too, the hide men were killing the Indian's buffaloes, his cattle, taking the skins while the Indians were not allowed to sell the robes they made at all. It was an angering injustice. In addition all the soldiers marching around and the hunters shooting stirred up the buffaloes too much for the arrow, the only way the Indians could hunt now that they were not permitted to trade robes for guns and powder or to buy ammunition. Besides, it kept their men busy protecting the women and children from the whites, who had plenty of guns.

Jim Hickok said he had shot at no one here, but that he would not stop hunting. "The buffaloes belong to the man what gets 'em," he insisted, and Whistler had to admit that the Sioux had never denied any one the right to make meat. It was the waste of the herds for only the hides that grieved him and angered the warriors to fighting.

When old Whistler left, his blanket was heavy with tobacco and powder and lead. His warriors rode in single file behind him, their blankets held close about them in the golden evening light of winter, the younger men lagging a little, as though still minded to sweep back upon the guns and all the ammunition there beside the old tent.

Finally the Sioux seemed gone and then Jim Hickok let loose the fury that almost always found a swift and natural outlet in the lightning draw. By the time he quieted, Coke had gathered up much of their scattered belongings out of the dusk. He piled everything into the side-boarded wagon, spread the tent over the top and hooked up the team in the darkness. Quietly, without striking even a match, they moved out over the prairie, the wheels creaking on the frozen ground. Jim rode ahead on his black mare. She stopped cautiously every now and then, turning this way or that from some gully or washout, or to listen, snorting, clearing her keen nose. But there seemed no scent of danger and no sound except the howl of the wolves and the high thin voices of the coyotes answering them. They were made restless by the coming change of weather but otherwise too lazy for much howling, with all the meat left by the hunters, several thousand fat carcasses, the entrails easy to drag out with no hide to gnaw away.

Several times Jim had to turn his horse from the grunt and snore of sleeping buffaloes. Once he was so close in the darkness that the man-smell penetrated their stolid resting and they sprang up awkwardly, joints cracking in the darkness, and were gone in a thunder of hoofs on the frozen ground, fortunately missing Coke and his wagon, although their noses led them straight in his direction. They passed very close in the dark shaking of the solid earth, the man so stiff from fright he could scarcely climb off the wagon when they were gone.

After awhile the two men stopped to gnaw on some frozen jerky, not daring to build more than an Indian fire, a handful of broken buffalo chips glowing red for a few minutes under

a dry hide, to boil up a tin can of coffee. Then they crawled
into their sleeping robes, the pickets of the horses within
hand reach. But although Coke was soon snoring, Jim could
not forget the danger, particularly the indignities, of the day.
He was the man who, it was said, got the nickname of Wild
Bill from the wild account he gave of the McCanles killing at
his murder trial six years ago, the man who had probably
killed at least a half dozen others besides the Virginian, Dave
McCanles and those with him at the Rock Creek station of
the Overland Stage in Nebraska back in 'Sixty-one. To such
stories Jim Hickok said nothing, one way or the other. He
had done many kinds of hired-handing, from living in a company dugout as horseherder for the Rock Creek station to
house gambler in some of the best saloons in Kansas, including Hays and the other boom towns as the Kansas Pacific
moved westward up through the Smoky Hill Trail country
on its way to Denver and the gold mines. Last winter he
chased horse thieves and then drove illegal timber cutters
from the public lands for the government. It was claimed by
some that he spent most of that time up in Nebraska trapping
beaver, and there was a story that he got into a two-gun saloon
fight up there and dropped four cowboys before he got a
bullet in the arm. Although three of the men were supposed
to be dead, later accounts said the only casualty was the truth,
that Bill wasn't carrying two guns, that he wasn't even in the
saloon. But now, after many months of sporadic scouting for
the army, interspersed with short hide hunts and standing off
the hostile summer Indians, this man who stirred such story-
telling had let himself be surrounded by a little bunch of
wintertime, agency Sioux, to be rescued by one of the most
despised characters of the frontier—a peace chief.

The truth was that the fastidious Wild Bill hated the hide
business, this crawling over the prairie, perhaps through snow
or mud and fresh buffalo droppings. A man was always bloody
and soiled, always full of vermin and buffalo mange, conspicuous anywhere with his continual scratching. Yet Bill
liked the test of holding a small bunch of buffaloes together
in the still hunt as he picked them off, the clumsy animals
confused, frightened, stupidly waiting to be shot. But he
hated most of all the blood and stink of the great awkward

hides, heavy as lead and limpsy as rags while green, and then board-stiff when dry enough for the hauling wagons. What he needed was a big outfit with a cook, a lot of skinners and haulers, a big comfortable wall tent with his monogrammed bay rum bottles and a good stove for hot water to shave and to soothe the cold from his hands. Then, with enough armed help around so no devilish redskins could creep up on a man, he would only need to shoot down the buffaloes.

Perhaps he hated the isolation, the lack of admiration most of all, that and the cold which crept into his bones and kept his long thin fingers stiff as frozen tallow. He was made **for** finer things, as his mother assured him long ago, before he got into trouble back home in Illinois. But now he was thirty and had tried out several kinds of work, followed several wild geese since the fight with another canal driver in which both fell into the water. The other man didn't seem to be coming up and Jim Hickok struck out for the west, thinking he had killed a man. Since then he had moved on repeatedly over gun fights, and had actually stood trial for the killing of McCanles and the two men with him at Rock Creek. But those times were behind Wild Bill Hickok now. He usually had the law on his side these days, was the law, but it didn't pay enough, and although he had filed on two homesteads, one in Kansas and then one in Nebraska, somehow he never had much to his name except debts. He hadn't been running in luck the last year with the pasteboards, particularly not while scouting for the new regiment, the Seventh Cavalry. There were a lot of Hard Cases and cardsharpers among them and just enough Bible packers to lend a little respectability and a sense of recklessness.

Scouting wages didn't go far either, and there was the new weskit Wild Bill was having made. It would be of fine corded silk the color of a pale sand dune in the sun, embroidered in sprays of prairie roses like the one, great as a man's palm, that was pressed between the pages of the *Harper's Magazine* he always carried in his gripsack, pressed full blown beside the picture of Wild Bill Hickok, the Prince of Pistoleers. With the new weskit there would be a black broadcloth cape lined in plaid silk and boots with embroidered patent leather tops, the heels two inches high, with a little more build-up inside,

for Wild Bill liked to fancy himself much nearer six feet than
he was, particularly now that eastern visitors expected him to
be tall as they believed everyone was in the west, even men
like Sheridan, Custer and Kit Carson, no bigger than the
family runt.

But the tailor would be waiting for his money at Kansas
City, the garments to be shipped out to Bill at Hays only if
he could raise the cash ahead of time, in addition to what he
already had on tick there.

"Coke," the hunter whispered, nudging his partner. "We'll
make one more try—"

The skinner moved sleepily under his robe. "You forgettin'
all them Sioux bucks? Next time they mightn't be no old
coffee-cooler like Whistler come tearin' up to stop 'em," he
muttered.

Wild Bill and Coke stayed another month, although both
Sioux and Cheyenne parties kept coming through now, so the
camp could never be left alone, but had to be moved along
from kill to kill. Yet they were never attacked. Perhaps old
Whistler's rescue gave them general protection; perhaps it
was because they were always on the alert now and camped
in places where many Indians would die in an attack. Indians
were always spooky about getting their men killed.

In this extra month Bill got twelve hundred more hides,
good, prime, thick-furred robes that brought twice the price
of their early take. Bill hired a trader's freight outfit to haul
in his accumulated caches. Then the first clear day after he
sold the lot, the receipts augmented by a few hands of poker
with the troopers of Sidney Barracks, Bill rode southward
over the two hundred fifty miles of winter prairie to Hays,
Hays City now, the end of the track with the first train in just
ahead of the snows, and already three big dance halls opened
and twenty-one saloons.

Jim had his tailor bill paid and more than three thousand
dollars in gold and yellowbacks in his money belt. With the
swagger of its weight and importance, he headed straight for
the bath house at Hays. Later he came out in the new rose-
embroidered weskit, with frock coat and checked trousers,
the flowing cape, and the handsome boots so well fitted to the
slender feet with insteps high as a lady's. Now he was the

Wild Bill of the card tables. With his hand carelessly at his holster he went down the middle of the dusty street. He kept away from the shielding alleys and was cautious as he passed the late wagons and the hitchracks with shivering horses hunched together in the squares of windowlight. There was a wild shot or two as some galloping troopers hit town, but otherwise everything seemed quiet. Drum's saloon, too, would be duller now that little Phil Sheridan was stationed at Ft. Leavenworth, leaving his regular place in the back room empty, and that General Custer, suspended for a year, was shorn of the swank that went with the command of the Seventh Cavalry. But the brawling Tom Custer would be around, and the troopers flush from the paymaster's arrival at the post today. They and the hundreds of buffalo hunters driven in by a general blizzard off west last week ought to make good pickings.

Before Wild Bill reached the light that spilled from the windows of Tom Drum's, he stooped to flick away the dust on his boots with his handkerchief. Then he threw back the two sides of the cape to show the red silk tartan lining, settled his shining curls about his shoulders and walked easily through the saloon door, into the noise and light.

Cow Country

Cattle Roundup

¶ *For many, the story of the Old West will always be only that of the great era indicated in the phrase, "the cattle kingdom." The open-range days that contributed most to the romance of that era came to an end with the widespread use of barbed-wire fences, but the techniques of working cattle changed little, and the hard labor it involved. How some of it was done early in the present century is told in this passage from the* Arizona State Guide.

DOWN IN THE CORRALS a cloud of dust heavy with alkali and profanity filled the air. Suddenly over the top bars shot the head and forelegs of a bronc. As he landed and kicked his way to freedom his rider somersaulted in the air, then landed face-down in the dirt.

I ran to help the fallen rider, but he arose and looked at me blankly. "What's the matter? I'm not hurt." Then he roared to his pardner in the corral. "Ketch that hammer-head, I want my saddle back." This seemed an ordinary incident in a bronc-fighter's daily life.

I was the newly hired cook for the outfit and it was my first day at the ranch. Only yesterday I had been touring America in a box-car. Ditched by the freight crew in Willcox, I was hired by the foreman as a roundup cook, although I assured him I had never cooked outdoors over an open fire in my life. "You'll make out all right," he said. Roundup cooks were hard to find in 1906.

That afternoon I drove the big wagon loaded with supplies

to the ranch on the San Pedro about twenty-five miles away. The boss started me on the right road, but never having seen so much open country before I thought seriously at times of turning back. There were many faint wagon tracks called roads. I was afraid of getting lost. However the mules picked their own route. They paid no attention to me and late that evening we arrived at the ranch.

It was typical of others in the valley. The main building was of adobe with tremendously thick walls. The roof had been made by laying heavy round poles close together and covering them with dirt. Above the roof rose parapets with spaces to shoot through. It had been built in the early Indian days; and as it was directly in the path of hostiles favored between the San Carlos Indian reservation and Old Mexico, it had been the scene of many stirring happenings. Its few windows were mere slits through which a rifle could be fired. One small room served as the office and quarters of the boss, another small room was the kitchen, and a still smaller one was for the cook. The rest of the building was one immense room with ten built-in bunks, each large enough to accommodate two men if required, and a long table that made it a dining room at meal times.

One feature that interested me was the rack of twenty old-time single-shot Springfield army rifles of 45–70 caliber. They had been furnished by the government in the days of Geronimo and Cochise, and remained a mute reminder of the past. Numerous small gouges on the outside walls showed where hostiles had taken shots at the house; while inside, bullet holes in the woodwork and a pock-marked ceiling indicated a desire on the part of its occupants to shoot up something.

Outside was a barn used as a storage place for grain and ranch supplies, with a lean-to at one end that served as a saddle room. Two small sheds helped keep the sun off the wagons. An immense corral with thick adobe walls, now crumbling away, told eloquently how cattle were protected from Apaches in the old days. It had been replaced by pole corrals, all of which were grouped around a windmill and a well.

Most of the punchers were Texans. I soon learned that personal questions were taboo. If a man wanted anything known concerning his past he volunteered the information. The punchers ranged in age from sixteen-year-old Bud, a wrangler, to Old Buck with snow-white hair, who rode with Forrest's cavalry in the Civil War. Later Buck had fought Comanches in Texas and hunted buffalo, and had been up the trail to Abilene and Dodge City when there wasn't a wire fence from the Gulf of Mexico as far north as a man could ride.

The punchers were gathering horses and shoeing-up the night I got in, and over two hundred saddle horses were penned at the ranch corrals. Between roundups the ponies ran unshod, but when the work was on every horse and mule was plated. Each puncher shod his own string, although they helped one another. If a horse was inclined to kick too much, they tied up one hind foot. The shoes were put on cold; they simply rasped the hoof down, and after fitting the shoe they tacked it in place. Each puncher had ten head of horses in his string to use as he saw fit. Some in each string were gentle but any horse that was bridle-wise was classed as a gentle pony. Two bronc-fighters, or peelers as they were often called, were breaking horses at the ranch. On the roundup they rode the rough string made up of broncs (young half-broken horses) and old outlaws that were too tough for the average waddie.

Feeding this outfit would have been easy for an old hand, but it was far from simple to me. We had meat at every meal. A fat heifer was killed at sundown and hung outside to cool. Before sunup I cut off enough for the day's needs, then wrapped the rest in a meat tarp and put it in the shade. After sundown I removed the tarp and hung the meat out again. It is surprising how well a beef will keep when handled in this manner. Frijole beans, potatoes, and hot biscuits were served at every meal. Lick (syrup) took the place of butter. Dried fruit cooked with plenty of sugar was the usual dessert. Canned milk was bought in town. The outfit was running around 20,000 head of cattle on its range, but there wasn't a single milk cow in the lot. Most of the punchers were good cooks, and since they had to eat my cooking they helped me in every way. But it was some time before my biscuits were fit for a dog to eat. The coffeepot was always busy when the punchers were at the ranch. In those days coffee was called "jamoka." Tea was never used.

I had been at the ranch about a week when the roundup really started. A big wagon was brought to the kitchen door and the chuck box put in place. It was fitted with shelves to hold all the small supplies, while other compartments were fitted to hold the bulky articles. One end, which also served as a lid for the box, was hinged, and when it was let down it was my working table. Everything in this box was so compact that no matter how often we plunged down into arroyo beds or rumbled over rocky ledges the contents were always safe. A beef was killed and placed in the wagon box, together with several sacks of beans, potatoes, and onions. Then came the huge dutch ovens used for outside cooking. Next the bedding was rolled and corded. Each man carried a huge waterproof tarp inside which he spread his blankets; and between his blankets he placed his extra clothes—if he happened to have any. The war bag in which a puncher carried his tobacco, cartridges, and other odds and ends usually served as a pillow.

It was my job to drive the chuck wagon from one camping spot to another, as well as to feed the crew. Since I wasn't familiar with the range a puncher acted as pilot. Two wranglers drove the *remuda,* as the bunch of horses was called, and herded it during the day. At sundown the wranglers were relieved by two nighthawks, who herded the ponies at night.

Our first camp was on the river about twenty miles from the ranch. Here we met a neighbor from the south with an outfit just like ours, along with several stray men (small owners from along the mountains). The stray men worked as regular hands and ate with us at the wagon. In addition to looking after their own animals it gave them a chance to keep an eye on the other outfits in their neighborhood. For at this time the big outfits, and the small ones too, had an unholy reputation for branding everything they could, regardless of ownership. While the men spoke politely and softly to each other most of them wore hardware.

Every morning at daybreak the *remuda* was driven in. By holding a lass-rope in each hand the men made a rope corral while their ponies were roped out. As soon as each horse was saddled his rider topped him off. To me it was like watching a wild west show as even a gentle cowhorse is apt to pitch on a frosty morning.

The men were divided into two groups which rode in oppo-site directions of the circle to be worked. As soon as the ponies were uncocked they left camp on a trot, dropping men at regular intervals until the last two men had met. Every gully and every clump of brush was worked, as the cattle were driven in toward a designated spot at the center of the circle. It was usually around two o'clock before the drive was fin-ished.

Now the *remuda* was driven in again and fresh horses were caught and saddled, as the ponies used in the morning had been going at top speed over the roughest kind of country. A quick lunch at the wagon and the evening work began. Punchers were stationed around the herd to keep the cattle bunched properly and to hold the various cuts. By the time the ropers rode into the herd the branding irons were hot. Unbranded calves were cut out with their mothers. It was necessary to have the mother as her brand proved ownership of the calf.

With a flick of his rope a calf was heeled by a roper and dragged out to the fire, where the bulldoggers slipped the rope after flanking him, and held him down until he was ear-marked and branded. The bulldoggers usually worked in pairs, although there were always men who preferred to work alone. When a grown animal was found unbranded one puncher roped him around the horns while another heeled or roped the critter by both hind feet and stretched him out between them. A few good calves were usually kept for bulls and the other bull calves were castrated.

After all the calves were branded, the steers, fat cows, and strays were boosted out of the drag into one of the three small herds, and the work was through for the day. Every night a few stray men cut out their animals and started for home, while new men came in as the roundup neared their range.

The last thing done each day was to drive the *remuda* in again and rope out the punchers' night horses. Each puncher took his turn at standing guard. The men usually worked in pairs. Two hours on guard was the usual time but occasion-ally when trouble arose a man would be out all night. At night around the fire the men relaxed. Horses, men, and cattle made up most of their talk. By nine o'clock they were all asleep or blinking up at the stars.

In this manner the range was worked. Although the work was mostly routine it never dragged and no two days were alike. It was not unusual for a bronc to buck through camp, knocking the pots and pans four ways at once, to the amusement of the punchers and my discomfiture. Horses running at top speed often fell and men were hurt. There was always some excitement. The work climaxed at shipping time with the usual bust in town. When the last steer had been prodded into the car, the extra hands were paid off.

Back at the ranch the old hands were scattered in line camps over the range, living much like coyotes. Except for occasional trips to headquarters for chuck, they seldom saw one another. They were keeping an eye on the water, tending the hospital bunch, branding the slicks (calves that had slipped through the roundup) on their part of the range, and above all watching the neighbors and knowing where they rode. Riding alone from daybreak till dark, there was always plenty to do.

At headquarters only three punchers rode from the ranch. Two extra men were sweating (working without pay). The chuck wagon had been put away until spring. I cooked on the stove in the house. Down at the big corrals clouds of alkali dust and profanity hung heavy again, where two peelers were breaking horses.

Trailing Out from Bloody Basin

BY FRAZIER HUNT

¶ *Burt Mossman was one of the West's great cattlemen—indeed, he was one of its all-time outstanding figures. From the day in 1884 when he went to work as a kid cowboy for a little ranch to the one in 1944 when he retired from his own giant spread, he lived a life of adventure and danger, strenuous physical exertion, imaginative enterprise, community service, and hearty enjoyment. He became a range foreman, a ranch manager, superintendent of the gigantic Hashknife outfit, organizer and captain of the Arizona Rangers, and cattleman in his own right.*

When he was twenty-six years old, Burt was offered the job of rounding up several thousand head of cattle and trailing them out from the rough Bloody Basin country, along the Verde River in Arizona—murderously difficult range, lacking roads or even good trails. It was only a short drive south to Phoenix but giant cholla cactus were so thick along the way that for years not enough beef had been trailed out from the Basin even to meet interest charges on the outfit's debt. The Mogollon Rim thrust a thousand-foot-high barrier between the Basin and Flagstaff. Between the outfit and the railhead at Del Rio there was a forty-mile dry drive. Any man who tackled this job would need plenty of guts and patience, plus a big dose of luck. Characteristically, Burt Mossman said without any hesitation that he'd be glad to try it.

BURT REALIZED what he was up against before he was half-way through his inspection trip over the Bloody Basin.

He had never seen such violent, difficult country, and the prospect of gathering, holding and then trailing out the thousands of head of wild cattle ranging back in these canyons, wooded slopes and distant valleys, appalled him.

He found the three owners, Granville Graybeal, D. L. Murray and Walter Hudson, all friendly men and agreeable to matching their ranch holdings against their indebtedness to the Thatchers and Bloom. They had had more than enough of trouble during the past nine years. And now in the late fall of 1893 cattle prices were as low as they had been since the late '60's when the great Texas breeding grounds started their living streams of cattle flowing to the fattening ranges of the north.

Granville Graybeal, who had once run a dairy in Pueblo, was the active manager of the outfit. He was a bachelor, about forty, and spent most of his time at the headquarters cabin far up the Verde River. Burt liked his frankness and honesty.

"The trick is to get the big stuff out," he explained, with a shake of his head. "That's what busted us."

The two men rode north from Phoenix at sun-up on a bright Monday morning. Eight miles out of the city they watered their animals and filled their canteens in the Arizona Canal. It was forty-five miles before they'd hit water again on Camp Creek.

On north, straight in front of them, stretched the sandy wastes of Paradise Valley. Giant cholla cactus raised their heads high above the lowly cat's-claw, mesquite and ironwood.

"Those cholla are the villains," Granville pronounced with considerable bitterness. "Every time we've tried to bring a trail herd down through here, they've defeated us. Their fishhook barbs just seem to jump at a steer's tail. One swish and the brute has needled himself from hell to breakfast—and away he goes! All the cowboys in Arizona couldn't hold them after that."

Time and again, he explained, he'd tried this short southern desert route, but always the big stuff would stampede on him. Half of them would break back to the distant hills and deep canyons of the Bloody Basin. The best he'd been able to do in recent years was to bring out little batches of three or

four hundred yearlings or mixed stock cattle at a time. Oddly
enough, cows and calves seemed to quiet down a herd.

"Can't you trail out on west to Prescott, or go straight up
north to Flagstaff?" Burt asked.

"Wait'll you see the country," Granville answered, with a
shake of his head. "You can hardly get a packmule in or out
of the Basin except through this desert."

It was getting dark when the two men struck water. They
spent that night at Camp Creek and at daybreak climbed up
a steep six-mile incline and then dropped down to the Verde.
As they moved on north the country grew wilder, and Burt
began to wonder how a man could drive the company's four-
mule team and heavy wagon over the deep ruts and heavy
rocks, and up and down the steep grades.

Some twenty miles on upstream they reached a long, one-
story building that was called Camp Supply. It was the end
of the wagon road, and the four-mule outfit was kept busy a
good part of the year bringing up rolled barley and general
ranch supplies and storing them here. Horses working the
round-ups had to be grained or they wouldn't have a chance
against the aged, fleet cattle in the rough country.

Eight or ten big mules and a batch of tough burros, in
charge of a packer and his helper, packed the stuff from Camp
Supply on up the twenty-mile trail to headquarters.

Burt and Granville reached the log cabin with its pole lean-
to late that afternoon. The four cowboys who were the year-
round hands rode in shortly after they arrived. The head
rider was a level-headed, soft-spoken Texan named Hayden
Justice. Burt was sure satisfied with his looks. The boys were
busy rebuilding pole catch-corrals and packing salt, for the
fall round-up was scheduled to start in a couple of weeks.

Granville offered to show Burt over the whole Bar O O
range. Burt said he wouldn't bother him but that he'd be
grateful if he'd send him out a round-up cook and three or
four more riders when he got back to Phoenix.

"I'll pick 'em up for you at Tempe," Granville promised.

The next morning Burt and Hayden Justice rode east
across the Verde, and on up the rough East Fork, and then
over high, timber-covered slopes and ridges until they

reached the divide of the Mazatzals. On to the east stretched the great Tonto Basin, where the Grahams and Tewkesburys had feuded to the last man.

Burt was glad of this chance to look over the range and the cattle, and he kept his eye peeled for a new trail out of the Basin. He was about convinced that he'd have to turn to the western side when the great barrier of the Mogollon Rim suddenly loomed up in front of him. He threw up his hands. The Rim was a veritable stone wall, a thousand feet high, apparently blocking all hopes of reaching Flagstaff and the railroad.

Two days later he and Hayden rode west of the Verde as far as the Big Bug. The head rider described the nature of the country on northwest to the Santa Fé railhead at Del Rio, half-way between Ash Fork and Prescott. Among other difficulties there'd be a forty- or fifty-mile dry drive, Hayden explained.

"Let's try it," Burt solemnly pronounced. He liked and trusted this narrow-hipped cowboy, who reminded him so much of Charlie Wall and Warren Carpenter. But he couldn't understand why the old management hadn't broken the trail.

"Them farmers couldn't drive a bunch of milk cows down a fenced lane," Hayden answered. "I'll bet we can make it, boss."

Back at headquarters Burt looked over the riding stock he had inherited. There were some forty excellent mountain horses, chunky, short-coupled animals with good feet and strong hearts. Hayden pointed out a brown riding mule named Daisy, and pronounced her the best mountain animal in the remuda. She had a black mate named Bessie, who he claimed was almost as good as Daisy.

The horses and the riding jennies had to be shod all the way around. Burt teamed up with Hayden, and in one day the two fitted and nailed on forty-four Burden shoes. Great care had to be used that the iron calks of the front shoes did not stick out behind the hoofs, where they might be tramped on by the front tip of a hind shoe. A man's life often depended on his horse being properly shod.

The night chill of the high places was still in the dawn air on the late fall day when the pack outfit and the men and remuda started out from the cabin and, single-file, headed north up the Verde. Each man had a string of three grain-fed horses, and two of the boys had either Daisy or Bessie as one of their mounts.

Three big pack mules carried the bedrolls, and the cook had his pots and pans and grub tied down on a trio of burros. The packer closed up the rear of the column with his eight mules loaded down with heavy burlap sacks of rolled barley.

They made camp in a flat valley that had a small creek cutting down its middle. At daybreak Burt led his eight men off to the right and up a series of steep rocky hills. They dropped off one at a time and when the quarter-circle net was completed each man was on his own.

They were after beef, but that took in everything that was two years old or better, including dry cows. The calves had been branded back in June.

It was wild, dangerous work. A man would catch sight of a big-horned critter, and take after it on the dead run. If the beast chose to high-tail it down a rocky, gullied mountainside the man and horse had no choice but to follow at the dead run. When the rider could keep the critter headed for the round-up grounds he was playing in luck. Two or three men stayed below to hold up the wild stuff as they'd come piling down the steep slopes.

That first night the gather was eased into a corral, and the men got a good sleep. For two days the same round-up grounds was used, then the little herd was moved on down the canyon and a new camp and holding ground laid out. Men had to day-circle and night-herd the catch from here on.

Once a small herd had been brought together and broken to trail, it was easier to hold the wild additions. But there was constant trouble. The old mossy horns would wait their chance, and quick as a flash they would break out of the herd and race for the rocks and gorges they had just left.

Often the men would tie a wild critter to the horns of a fairly tame animal, until the fight and the urge to escape had left him. There was little use trying to be humane with the big, aged brutes. Many of the old steers and bulls were as dangerous as grizzly bears, and they would fight until they played out from sheer exhaustion.

Burt did his full share and more. He had never seen such reckless cowboying, but it pleased him. A man had to pull up the cinch of his saddle and tighten the strings of his own nerves each time he took after one of the big fellows. Death lurked on every stony hillside and canyon wall. Many of the older critters had been defying capture for years, and hundreds had neither been branded nor castrated and their horns were long and sharp.

But the danger and excitement suited Burt. There was something primal and deeply satisfying about roaring down a rocky slope after a thousand-pound steer. It took a man with *cahones grandes* to drop his rope over a big brute's horns and then bust him wide open. It was a hundred times more dangerous than ordinary roping, and the thrill it gave a rider lifted him into the realm of pure exaltation.

Burt reveled in his own accomplishments. He had two big Mexican vaqueros who didn't even know the word fear, and he determined to keep up with them. They had a cruelty he lacked, but he asked no odds when it came to dangerous riding, roping and tying down.

Each man carried a small saw-blade tied under the leather skirts of his saddle, so that he could saw off the tips of the thorns of the wilder critters. When they'd finished this operation, the two Mexicans would cut the cord just over the steer's knee-cap, so that the animal would never be able to run again.

Burt's own favorite method of taming an old battler was to cut two holes in an empty barley sack and then pull it down over his horns. The steer could only see the ground at his feet. Then he would haze the animal to the gathered herd, and usually the aged reprobate would seek the center of the circle and stay there. Several times Burt ordered his men to stop sewing up the eyelids of the worst of the critters. It was too cruel to suit him.

For long, hard days the men worked the rough country, up and down the canyons of the Verde. Men were badly bruised and cut, muscles strained and joints sprained, and clothes torn to rags, despite the heavy leather chaps. But the little herd grew, and in less than a month it numbered around a thousand head.

It seemed a wise thing to stop the round-up and make the try of trailing out the big stuff that was now gathered. Burt wanted to make this first trail herd at least fifteen hundred head of beef, but he knew that every day he delayed he ran the chances of a stampede and a breaking back into the hills of all the wild stuff they had worked so hard to get down. Men and horses were almost exhausted by the additional work of standing day and night guard over the gather.

Many of the hoofs of the tougher, older animals were worn down to the bone. It was pitiful to see the limping, suffering veterans plodding down the rocky trail toward the big flat that Burt had picked out for a final holding ground.

There was nothing to do but cut back the critters with the worst hoofs. They would never be able to keep up with the herd on the terrible drive that lay ahead. What was needed was a rest of two or three weeks to let the cattle recuperate, but that couldn't be done in this open mesa.

At the western end the flat narrowed and Burt posted Hayden opposite him, with a man on each side. Then he had the herd trailed out and slowly moved between him and Hayden. As each hundredth critter would go by Burt would shout "Count!" and tie a knot in the string he held. Each made it exactly one thousand and eight head.

The trail drive, accustomed now to day and night herding, moved out quietly. The second afternoon they hit Bug Creek and followed it until dark, when the cattle were bedded down on a rough flat back from the stream. The whole country looked as if it were cut into strips of steep arroyas and dangerous washes, and Burt was worried. There was a spooky feeling in the air.

He had every man tie up a night horse, and he assigned half the men to ride circle, with the relief coming out at midnight. The change in the night shift had barely been made when the first bolt of lightning ripped through the black night. The big steers already on their feet were off before the second flash cut across the sky.

Burt and Hayden had been with the first shift, and when they stretched out on their tarp for a little sleep each held the reins of his night horse in his hands. At the first crash of lightning they jumped for their ponies.

It was pitch dark and the footing was dangerous, but the two men raced toward the sound of the running cattle. In some strange manner the herd, on its own accord, broke into several bunches, and the two top riders separated.

It was difficult to turn the leaders of the several batches and for what seemed miles each man raced alongside his hold. Burt gave his horse his head, and several times he was conscious of his pony leaping over dry washes that he could not see and that might have meant death to them both.

When dawn broke he found that he was holding some five hundred exhausted cattle. Slowly he trailed them back toward camp. At one steep-banked gully he counted ten head floundering about with broken legs. He would come back with his rifle and end their misery.

The riders began to dribble in, each man driving the few head he had rounded up. An hour later Hayden showed up with two or three hundred. When all the men were accounted for and they had breakfast, Burt had the cattle strung out for a fresh count. They were out exactly thirty head. Burt figured that maybe the only real loss was the ten that had piled up in the arroyo. The other twenty probably had headed back for the hills of home.

Late that afternoon Burt had the cattle thrown into a tight circle and a double guard posted. At dawn they would leave the Bug and start the forty-mile waterless drive across Lonesome Valley.

The men fed themselves and their horses in the dark, and only a suspicion of light was breaking out in the east when they began the long, dry drive. If the cattle had been in good shape the forty-odd miles could have been covered nicely in two days, but there were too many sore-footed brutes to figure on pushing through that fast.

At noon the following day, when the herd was checked and the men ate their cold biscuit and chunks of meat, Burt suddenly changed his mind and decided to try to reach water that night.

A rough, twelve-mile downgrade lay ahead. At the bottom and cutting across the trail flowed a living stream, as broad and almost as deep as a "mother" irrigation ditch. Before the cattle had covered half the distance Burt posted riders ahead of the leaders.

Suddenly an old mossy horn lifted his head and sniffed the air. He bellowed and struck out at a lumbering trot. Others followed. They could smell the water that awaited them six miles farther on.

The men swung their ropes and ponchos in the faces of the crazed cattle, and yelled until they were hoarse. For a time they managed to slow down the leaders, but when there was a mile or two still to go Burt waved the men aside. When the stronger animals reached the creek, the herd was spread out for more than a mile.

That night the cattle were quiet, and for two days they were held on grass along the stream while Burt rode ahead the few miles to the railhead at Del Rio and ordered two trains. He would go with the first train with one of the boys, and send Hayden and another man with the second. He had orders to ship to a siding called Thatcher near Pueblo and put the cattle on company grass.

Burt was completely tired out. He'd made it, but it had been an exhausting experience. The cattle were gaunt and many of them had lost as much as a hundred pounds. He was positive now of two things. First, he must locate and fence a big pasture, where he could hold the foot-sore steers that were gathered until they were in shape to start for the railroad.

And then he must find another way out of the Basin.

Burt had his eye on a valley that was roughly six miles square. On two sides were sharp hills and cut-banks, ribboned with deep ravines and dry gullies.

He figured that by stopping up the rocky draws with cedar poles, and then stringing barbed wire across the two ends, he could have a tight holding pasture that would be almost as big as a township. The western end narrowed down to less than two miles, and a stream cut through the center.

He rode south to Phoenix, and shortly he had his wagon packing up the wire and staples to run a four-wire fence. His pack-train was assigned to bringing the stuff on from Camp Supply, while his men cut cedar posts from the timbered slopes that half surrounded the pocket.

While he was fencing the Big Pasture, he made several exploring trips in the hope of finding a better way out for the cattle. Riding off to the northeast with Hayden one morning, they made their way up and down canyons and steep rimrocks to the cabin of an eccentric ex-Confederate soldier, called Old Hutch. The odd character ran some thirty mares, and raised and broke mountain horses. At this time the Territory was paying a bounty of twenty dollars for the scalps of mountain lions, and Old Hutch did considerable hunting.

The cabin was perched on a high mesa, and there was no one at home when Burt and Hayden drew up. It was well after two, and they had had no dinner.

They entered the cabin and found a pan of stew simmering on a bed of live coals in the corner fireplace. On a littered table was a plate of hard soda biscuit. The whole place was dirty and unswept, but the visitors helped themselves to the food and enjoyed their lunch. The stew tasted like tender meat from a yearling, and Burt grinned when he wondered if he was not eating his own beef.

On their way down the opposite side of the ridge, they ran into Old Hutch at work in a small irrigated plot of ground. His beard was long and matted, and his clothes were as crudely patched as Joseph's coat. Hayden knew him and introduced him to his boss.

"Wal, you fellers ride on back to the cabin and I'll git you somethin' to eat," he drawled, scratching his gray beard with his dirty fingers.

"Thanks," Burt said, "but we helped ourselves to that stew of yours."

"Good God!" Old Hutch exclaimed.

"It was good, too," Burt added.

"Say! That was a panther I killed yestiddy. I was cookin' it up fer my dogs."

Hayden slid down from his horse and stepped over behind a cat's-claw bush. He was a hard man, but his stomach apparently was easily upset.

Burt and Hayden next turned to the east side of the Verde in their search for another way out of the Basin. Over to the north it was even rougher and wilder. Like explorers touched with some half-mad zeal they rode on and on.

On this second venture they took along a packmule and Burt swore he would not turn back until they had found and marked out a new trail. He led Hayden into country his head rider never knew existed. Often they'd have to backtrack to get out of a deep box-canyon, or off a high mesa that had sheer cliffs a hundred feet high.

Finally they could see the great Mogollon Rim looming ahead and trailing far off to the eastward toward Apache land. It was a challenge, an affront, a dare to the stubborn Burt. Like the crack of a pistol he sprung the proposition of leading a herd straight up over the Rim.

Hayden drew in a deep breath and the crow's-feet around his gray eyes fairly cracked. "You're the boss," he slowly said. "We can shore try her."

Burt had made his play and he meant to stick to it. He was relieved and happy. He had a goal now that would be well worth the fight it would take to gain it.

His brother Thad, eleven years his junior, had written that he'd like to join Burt at the Basin. He'd tell him to come on and see the fun.

With the letter went the ticket money. For almost ten years now he'd been sending money home. When he left the Monticello outfit he bought the best team and wagon the ranch had and got a man to drive it to his father's place. He'd sent Dana to college for two terms and he was now arranging for his sister to go to school in Iowa. And never a month went by that he didn't write his mother an affectionate letter. Usually there was a yellow-back enclosed.

When Thad arrived Burt was surprised to see how big and strong he was for seventeen. Before long he grew a full blonde beard, and the boys got to calling him "Mormon Bishop."

Thad seemed to enjoy fighting and Burt suddenly realized that he himself had been the same sort of a kid. He'd learned to control his temper and accept responsibility the hard way. That was a part of growing up.

Thad had worked on one or two New Mexico ranches and

he was a good roper. Burt assigned him the brown mule
Daisy, and he took considerable pride in the way the boy and
the little jenny tied into the big stuff.

But he had Hayden keep an eye on the kid so he wouldn't
bite off more than he could chew. It was mighty easy to get
killed in this wild country.

The second round-up was well along when Burt spied an
old mossy horn in a rough patch of scrub cedar that clung
with a grip of death to the rocky slope of a hillside. He had
his coiled rope in his left hand, alongside his reins, while the
loop hung ready in his right hand. Here in this dangerous
country even the Texans did not tie hard-and-fast, but dallied
around their saddle horns so they could turn a critter loose
if they got in a jackpot.

Burt was riding a fine roping horse named Snort, and he
jabbed in the spurs and went after the steer, hell-bent for
election. The big fellow broke for the open, then dodged back
into a patch of pines. In and out, up and down, he led the
chase. Just about the time horse and man and steer were all
three pooped out, the critter half-slid down the slope to where
it debouched into a rough flat, with a spring over to one side.
Burt managed to make his catch and flip the rope over the
steer's side, then taking a quick dally he turned Snort to the
left and busted the old mossy horn with a bang. In a matter of
seconds he had him cross-hobbled, his piggin' string tied fast
from a front foot to the opposite foot behind. Then for good
measure he tied together the front feet.

Burt stumbled over to a big rock, and cursed slowly and
fervently. He was mad clean through. Snort stood with head
down, breathing deeply while the sweat rolled from his heaving sides. This ornery critter had pretty near caused the death
of both of them.

After a good rest, Burt stepped up and rode off. Mister
Steer could lie there for the night and think things over.

The next morning he rode in and slipped off the rope that
tied the front legs together, but he left on the cross-hobble.
Then he prodded the critter to his feet. The animal glared at
him, hate smoldering in his eyes.

Burt hit him across the rump with the hondo of his rope, but he would not budge.

He hit him again. The mossy horn bawled, and swung his vicious horns as if he would take to him. But he did not budge. Yet Burt knew he was half-dead from thirst, and there was water less than a hundred yards away.

Burt rode off. The next morning when he returned, the steer was lying down. Again he got him to his feet, but again he failed to drive him to the spring.

The third morning Burt came back with a little batch of tame cattle. He cut the hobbles, but the steer wouldn't even get up. He would look up at Burt with hate showing in his blood-shot eyes. He was weak and dying of thirst, but he would not budge.

Burt got down and twisted his tail. He tried every means he knew of to get him to his feet. But the animal willed to die.

Three mornings later when Burt rode in, the old warrior was dead. He had not given in to man. He had been captured but he had not been vanquished.

Burt couldn't help but be touched by the dumb brute's stubborn hate and his inner courage. This time it was man who had been defeated.

Things were a lot easier this year, with the Big Pasture to fall back on. As soon as he'd get a batch of a hundred or so gathered, Burt would drive them to the permanent holding grounds. There was plenty of grass and water there, and it was working like a charm when it came to healing the sore hoofs.

By the end of June he figured he had gathered as big a herd as it was safe to handle in one trail herd. There was silent disapproval among most of the men when Burt announced that he would point the drive straight up the East Fork of the Verde, and cross the deep canyons of Strawberry and Fossil Creeks. Then he'd lead them up over the Mogollon Rim, and on across the high mesa to Clear Creek and on to Flagstaff. The cowboys whispered among themselves that the new boss must be touched by the altitude.

In 1875 General George Crook had built a Military Road from the little-used army post of Camp Verde on southwest to Payson. By far the most difficult stretch was a narrow wagon trail that he had hacked, foot by foot, up the rocky slope of the Rim. It had been used very little, and for a number of years now it had been abandoned. The flash rains had cut deep gullies across it and dug out chunks of the rock bed, until the Rim Road was all but impassable, even for a man on horseback. Burt knew the risks he was running, but he was going to tackle that Rim come hell or high water.

His count was 1770 head on the morning he started out from the Big Pasture. Soon he was breaking trail through a fearsome land. At times he pointed the herd along the side of canyons so steep that the midday sun could barely reach the dancing stream two thousand feet below. Often he was forced to lead the cattle down rocky slopes to water, and then fight his way up the opposite banks.

His men grew quarrelsome and short-tempered, and there were constant bickerings and fights. His kid brother Thad actually seemed to enjoy the daily brawls as much as he did his meals. Burt played no favorites.

Day and night he was in the saddle, keeping his men awake and working, wearing out his mounts, doing double turn at night guard—tireless, indestructible, omnipresent. His will never weakened, and he drove his body with a stern, quiet fury.

The third night out he tried to hold the herd on a bed ground half-way up the slope of a canyon wall. Shortly after darkness the cattle broke and went thundering down the dangerous incline.

But Burt had outthought them. Just before twilight he had sent two men with axes to a spot down the creek bottom where the canyon narrowed. His roving eyes had noted the narrows, and also the fact that cottonwoods had, by some miracle, gained a foothold here in the rocks.

"Cut down enough trees to bottle up the trail," he had ordered. "Then if these damn dogies want to stampede, let 'em!"

The barricade stopped the wild, frightened cattle, but it was a hideous night. All that next day he held them there, while they quieted down. At dawn on the second morning he led the way out of the river bed to a high mesa, and then cut on northeast along Strawberry Creek, in the direction of the little Mormon settlement of Pine.

Turning due north, they followed the deep canyon of Fossil Creek to a point where they could look up at the Mogollon Rim, cutting directly across their path. They were now at the foot of the abandoned Military Road that led up the side of the Rim.

Like a giant snake the trail twisted and wound its way up the long, tortuous slope. At times it would disappear from the view of those standing at its base. To the eye, the Rim looked as impregnable and forbidding as the high walls of an ancient citadel.

Burt sliced off thirty head of big steers, and with a man ahead and the trusted Hayden behind started the little batch on the great adventure. They trailed out single file, and Burt eagerly watched the line wind up the uncertain path hacked out of the side of the Rim, until it passed out of sight. It was a terrific gamble he was taking. He was betting seventeen hundred head of cattle against a hunch. Five minutes after the first bunch had left, he started up a second group, with no rider in front but with a seasoned man behind. There must be no crowding and the steers must set their own pace. He knew that Hayden and his helper would locate a good holding ground—if and when they reached the top of the Rim.

When he had started up the sixth batch, and had only a single man remaining behind with him, he called a halt until the riders could return. He had told Hayden to keep one boy to help him hold the herd at the top of the Rim, and not to let the other riders start down until the sixth bunch of cattle arrived.

The minutes dragged by for Burt and the boy waiting below. Finally they caught sight of a rider coming slowly around a curve high up on the trail. Five men were following him. Burt knew his hunch had paid off.

The boys had strange tales to tell of the terrible Rim Road. At times the cattle, traveling single file, had to hug the inside of the rocky trail while they picked their way around great boulders and across dangerous washouts.

All day long Burt sent out his little batches of cattle, moving a total of two hundred head on each journey. It was twilight when the last critter took to the Rim Road, and he motioned to the horse wrangler to lead off with his remuda.

Early in the afternoon he had sent up the cook and his pack outfit.

Hayden was holding the big herd a mile or two back from the lip of the Rim, in a wide draw with a creek in its bottom. The worst was over. They had conquered the Rim.

But ahead lay a fifty-mile dry drive through rough country splotched with patches of cedar and hemlock. It was a high land and while it had no deep canyons or tough mountains, it was difficult to take cattle through.

Burt and Hayden criss-crossed the country ahead, one on each side of the trail herd, searching for water-holes and springs. The second day they located enough water off to the east to take care of the horses and mules. Burt ordered that the drags be held back, and when the main herd, already half-crazed from thirst, was well ahead he trailed the forty head or so of weakened, sore-footed animals to water.

The nights were unbelievably cool and sharp, and as long as there was sufficient light Burt kept the herd moving. It was around four the afternoon of the third day when the tough old steers in the vanguard caught their first whiff of water. A tiny breeze was blowing from the north, and it carried with it the promise that set the hearts of these weary, thirst-mad cattle beating high.

Burt knew that five miles on ahead lay the great Mormon Lake, and he made little effort to hold back the herd. When he finally reached the lake with the drags, he pushed back his hat and grinned happily at the sight of the big critters standing bellydeep in the cool waters.

There was a little grass on the slopes stretching away from the lake, and he decided to let the cattle loiter here for a day. Half the time they would quietly graze and then they would walk slowly into the water and stand there contentedly chewing their cuds.

Burt instructed Hayden to move the herd on the second day the dozen miles or so on north to the center of Clark's Valley, and hold them there while he jogged it to Flagstaff and ordered the stock trains. There was plenty of water and grass in the valley, and it would be good for the beef after this hard, grueling drive.

Burt came back with bad news. A railroad strike was on and

there was no freight moving either way out of Flagstaff. They'd have to hold the cattle and take things easy. A little later when the beef herd had fully settled down the men could take turns twisting the monkey's tail in Flagstaff, ten miles on north.

When the strike started there was a carload of oranges in the freight train that had pulled in at a siding. The oranges were spoiling and an enterprising merchant had bought them for a song by telegraph, and was selling them at 50 cents a crate. Burt hired a pack mule and brought out four crates, and each boy could eat more oranges than he'd had in all his life.

The second day they staged a ball game with the precious fruit, but it quickly degenerated into a battle royal. When it was over, most of two full crates had been used up. Burt was plenty disgusted. He bluntly told the boys he'd see 'em all frying in hell before he ever bought them another orange.

On that first visit to Flagstaff Burt arranged with a local bank to honor his checks. He knew the boys would want the money coming to them when they rode into town. The result was plenty of big heads, but the only man who gave him any trouble was old Jim, the cook.

At best he was an evil-tempered, cantankerous cuss, but when he came back roaring drunk he was nothing short of a public menace. When he failed to pick a fight with the boys, he grabbed the iron rod that was part of his cooking equipment and went to work on his pots and pans. Then he bellowed his challenges and started for the men.

Burt slipped his six-shooter in the waistband of his trousers and got to his feet. Apparently he'd have to pistol-whip this crazy cook to keep him from killing somebody.

Burt was still thirty feet or more away when one of his pet hands, a weazened, bow-legged little Texan named Mat Lee, rode up. A few months before this Mat had been bitten on the wrist by a hydrophobia skunk, and Hayden had hustled him down to Pete Latourette, the Frenchman down on Deadman Wash, who'd cured him by applying a magic "mad stone" that was supposed to be found only in the stomach of certain rare deer. Anyway, Mat didn't die.

Quite unconscious of what was going on here at the camp,

Mat stepped down, unsaddled and slipped the bridle off his pony. He was dragging his saddle by its pommel with his left hand, and dangling his heavy, silver-mounted bridle in his right, when Jim spied him.

The drunken cook made a bee line for the unsuspecting and undersized Mat. He swore he'd tear him limb from limb. Finally Mat spotted him, staggering straight toward him and waving the murderous iron rod.

The little cowpoke waited until Jim was just the right distance away. Then he swung his bridle over his head and the heavy California bit caught the cook squarely alongside the temple. It knocked him as cold as a mackerel. Mat had not even dropped his saddle, and he walked on to his bedroll as if nothing had happened.

Burt pretty near broke a hamstring laughing.

The herd was held for a full month at Clark's Valley. By the time Burt rode in with the news that the strike was over and the stock cars were arriving, most of the stuff had put back the tallow they had lost.

Two days later the men cut out 550 head and started them for the shipping pens. That would make up a full trainload. Every two or three days after that they'd slice off around half a thousand head and ship out.

Things had worked out all right, despite all the hard luck they'd had. But Burt was cured of the Mogollon Rim business.

The Big Creek trail and the dry drive to Del Rio on the west side was plenty bad enough, but it was a boulevard compared to this East Fork, Fossil Creek, Rim route.

That was too much like driving a herd through hell with a million red devils making it extra tough for the trail boss.

Cow Camp Chuck

BY FAY E. WARD

¶ One of the most impressive and most useful books published in 1958 was The Cowboy at Work *("All About His Job and How He Does It"), an encyclopedic treatise on roundup equipment, brands and earmarks, packs and packing, mustanging, ropes and roping, "building" a quirt, etc. In most of these cases the text depends for its full effectiveness on the hundreds of detailed drawings—like the text itself, the work of veteran cowboy and rodeo man, Fay Ward. There is one little chapter—"Cow Camp Chuck"—however, that needs no visual aids; these recipes present an interesting contrast to the ubiquitous American cookbook.*

THE FOLLOWING RECIPES are cow-camp favorites and if properly prepared will prove to be a treat to those who have never sampled them before. They are dishes which only the experienced roundup-wagon cook knows how to build and prepare properly.

S. B. STEW, OR SON-OF-A-GUN

In polite society this concoction is often referred to as Son-of-a-Gun, but that is a very mild version of its real name. Naturally, the polite name makes cowhands and cow-country folk grin when they hear it used by tourists and such. The ingredients, procured from the carcass of a freshly slaughtered beef, are as follows: brains, liver, heart, sweetbreads, kidneys and marrow-gut. Wash them all thoroughly and cut them up into small pieces about an inch square. Put them in a Dutch oven with a piece of suet tallow about the size of a prairie oyster (see below) from a four-months-old calf and enough water to cover. Season with salt and chili powder. Boil until the meat is tender. Mix a small handful of flour with some of the juice or some warm water, add to the stew, stir thoroughly, and let cook about thirty minutes longer. (*N.B.* Marrow-gut is a particularly choice bit of cattle anatomy, the tube connecting the two stomachs of ruminating animals and containing a substance resembling bone marrow. Recipes often specify the quantity to be used by the foot! The best suet tallow is the fat found around beef kidneys.)

CRISPED MARROW-GUT

Procure the marrow-gut, free from foreign matter, from a freshly slaughtered beef, wash thoroughly, and cut into pieces about two and one-half inches long. Fry in hot, deep fat in a skillet or Dutch oven until nearly crisp. Remove the marrow-gut, salt it, pour off the fat and return the marrow-gut to the skillet to keep warm.

PRAIRIE OR MOUNTAIN OYSTERS

These dry-land oysters are the testicles removed from male calves when they are castrated, or cut. When the calves are branded and marked, the male calves are cut and the oysters are saved and taken to the cook who prepares them in the following manner:

Surplus tissue is removed and the oysters are split open, carefully washed, and then fried in hot, deep fat in a skillet until they are thoroughly cooked; then they are removed from the fat, which is poured off. The oysters are salted and returned to the skillet to keep warm, as in preparing marrow-gut.

CORNED TOMATOES

To a large-size can of tomatoes add a can of corn. Season with salt and pepper, add a chunk of fat and stew until done.

TOMATO RICE

In a skillet brown a cup of rice with just enough fat to cover it when it is well spread out in the pan. When the rice is cooked to a golden-brown color, slice a medium-size onion, add it to the rice. Let this simmer until the onion is about half-cooked, then add a can of tomatoes, season with salt and a little chili, and let cook, covered, until the rice absorbs most all the moisture in the tomatoes. Stir to prevent burning when nearly done.

BLANKET STEAK

There's different ways of fixing steak, but this way is one that "will make a hand let out a couple of holes in his belt when he gets started to wrapping himself around a span of them." The best cooking utensil to use for blanket steak is a Dutch oven. Put the oven on the coals and then cut some fat off the steaks to melt. Prepare the steaks by dropping them in water, salt them, then roll them in flour and put them in the hot oven with the melted fat. Have the lid of the oven hot before it is put on. When the lid is on, pile on some good live coals and let the steak cook until done. Remove the steak when done and add a couple of tablespoons of flour to the juice and stir until smooth. Then add water, salt and pepper. Let stew until thick enough to make a good gravy.

SOURDOUGH BISCUITS

To make the starter, soak half a cake of yeast in half a cup of lukewarm water for about half an hour, or until it is soft. A teaspoonful of sugar added to this increases the action of the yeast. Then build a batter with the yeast and the water it was soaked in, another half cup of lukewarm water, and enough flour to make a thick consistency, or about one and a quarter cups. Stir thoroughly. Place in a stone jar or an enamel pot and put lid on same. Set where the dough will keep warm. If the nights are cold, it is best to wrap the jar in a heavy cloth to keep the dough warm. During the mixing the yeast plant should have developed and the batter should be full of bubbles. Usually the result is better if the mixture has longer than twenty-four hours to stand. If you can let it stand that long, increase the batter the second evening by beating in another half cup of lukewarm water, a teaspoonful of sugar and just enough flour to make a good thick mixture. Let this set overnight and it will be ready for use.

In making biscuits, pour out nearly all of the starter into the mixing pan, add about half a teaspoonful of soda, a pinch of salt and flour enough to make a good thick dough. Knead and work it thoroughly, for the more it is worked the better. Pinch off the dough in pieces about the size of a billiard ball, dip the tops of them in fat and place in a Dutch oven or baking pan.

Always keep a little starter in the jar; add to it some lukewarm water and enough flour to make a thick batter. Stir thoroughly and set aside until wanted. If one does not have yeast to start the dough, a few spuds boiled in water until they fall to pieces can be used. Add flour and a little sugar to the potato water and stir until a thick batter is formed. Then set away in a warm place so it will raise. After that handle as previously explained for good results.

Sourdough flapjacks are made by mixing the starter with a little sugar and lukewarm water, as well as a little soda and a small amount of flour to make a good batter.

A COWHAND'S COFFEE RECIPE

To two gallons of boiling water add two pounds of coffee. Boil two hours, then throw a horseshoe into the pot and if it sinks, the coffee is not yet done. "Trouble with most coffee-makers, they're too generous with the water," says Frank King.

S. B. IN A SACK

To two-thirds of a quart of flour add two cups of suet which has been chopped fine and one teaspoonful of salt. Add a large handful of raisins and sufficient water to make a heavy dough. Mix and roll in another third of a quart of flour. Place in a small sugar sack and boil in a pot of hot water for one hour.

S. B. SAUCE

Beat 1 egg, add one cup of sugar, a hunk of butter about the size of an egg, three tablespoonsful of hot water and the juice of a lemon, or some lemon extract, or a wine glass of brandy. Cook in a double boiler until thick. Pour on S.B. pudding (S.B. in a Sack) and watch 'em take to it.

SUCAMAGROWL

This is not so hard to take as its name might imply and it is a good substitute for pudding or pie. The ingredients are:

3 cups of water   1 cup of vinegar
2 cups of sugar   2 tablespoons of flour
2 pinches of cinnamon
   or nutmeg

First, put the water and vinegar together and bring to a boil. Mix the sugar and flour together and stir this mixture into the boiling liquid until it is thoroughly dissolved. Let cook for fifteen minutes and then add the spice. Have a dough ready, like a biscuit dough prepared with baking powder. Break it off by the tablespoonful and drop the pieces in the simmering liquid. When the dumplings are done serve them right off on tin plates while they're still hot.

High Color

Hail the Glorious Overland!

BY ELLIS LUCIA

¶ *The West has enjoyed a surfeit of at least one thing—color. From the time of the explorers and the free-ranging mountain men to today's dude ranches and neoned gambling casinos, including gold stampedes and silver stampedes, prairie-schooner pioneering, cattle-driving and trailtown didoes, railroad-building and Indian-fighting, the accent has always been on color, in scene and in action.*

One of the great and revealing experiences for any greenhorn tenderfoot was to spend several days bouncing around on the seat of one of Big Ben Holladay's Overland Express coaches . . . another was to put in some time really living, in one of Colorado's booming, hurly-burly silver camps. . . .

YOU GOT DOWN to the station early to weigh and check your baggage and to be assured of a seat. Travel was heavy and there might not be an extra stage today. Your luggage was a pound overweight, so you paid another $1.10. You crawled into the Concord's cramped quarters, scrambling for a forward-facing position. You were jammed between a plump rancher and a burly gambler. If you were last aboard, you perched on a hard jump seat in the center, with your knees pressed against the others'.

When the weather was good, and you'd smarted up to stagecoach travel, you preferred the open-air seat behind the driver, or riding on the roof. You got a sweeping view of the unceasing landscape from there, the air was fresh and invigorating, and you wouldn't have to risk holding a squalling baby on your lap.

From *The Saga of Ben Holladay.* Copyright © 1959 by Ellis Lucia.

The snappy six-horse string of chestnuts trembled eagerly in their splendid harness. The air still held its nighttime chill, for it was shortly before eight o'clock. A thousand pounds of mail and express were loaded aboard. The driver stashed the heavy express box, perhaps carrying one hundred thousand dollars, away in the forward boot. He scrambled up beside the messenger, who was armed with a sawed-off shotgun. The coach shuddered under his weight. The driver pulled on the brim of his hat, spat tobacco juice into the dust, and blew "last chance" on his horn. Then he released the brake. The leather ribbons slapped the broad backs of the beautiful team.

"Hi-ya . . . Hi-ya . . ."

The coach gave a sudden lurch as the horses surged into motion. The jehu lashed out with his long whip, more for show than need. The loyal mustangs were happy for action, anxious to hit their full stride. Heads were high, manes and tails blooming on the air. Traces jingling, the bright-red and yellow coach wheeled down the main street past the stores, saloons, dance halls and honkytonks, heading for the open country. Merchants, housewives and small boys paused in utter fascination to watch the Concord go by. The spectacle was a never-tiring one, to be matched only in later decades by the steam-spouting locomotive and the interurban trolley.

The flying hoofs hit a steady pace, while the dust rolled up around the coach. The broken prairie stretched yonder, in jagged buttes, calm valleys and small streams lined with cool elms and cottonwoods. The coach bounced onward through sun and shadow. Here and there you caught glimpses of ranches with their mud shanties and plots of new land under cultivation. Game was everywhere in the Platte valley. Deer, antelope, elk, sagehen, grouse and prairie dogs caught the passengers' eyes as they rocked along.

A swing station was reached. Passengers had little time to stretch their legs. The hard-breathing team was replaced quickly by another, this one shiny black with long, freshly-combed manes. You were on your way again through rocky crags and purple canyons.

Seas of buffalo sometimes blocked the stage, causing lengthy delays. In the deep forests were deer, bear, sheep, mountain lions, and flocks of brightly colored birds. You saw miners grubbing for gold and blue-uniformed troopers on patrol. Bands of peaceful Indians moved restlessly beside the road with wives, children, and all their worldly goods loaded on horse-drawn travois, followed by hordes of barking dogs. The stage skimmed swiftly past slow-moving freight caravans and Oregon-bound wagon trains. Folks waved to the driver, and dogs gave momentary chase, soon to be left panting in the sagebrush. . . .

Another station, this one bigger than the last one. It was a home depot, with hotel accommodations and a great spread of stables. There'd be a forty-five-minute stop here while you and the others put away a hefty meal of venison steak and fried spuds. You stretched your aching legs and watched as bulging mail sacks were unloaded. Another new team was in place. Then you were back aboard and noticing a newcomer had crowded things up.

"Pack 'em; pack 'em in like sardines!" Big Ben ordered, and his drivers acted accordingly. It was like a city rush hour on the way to the gold camps. Twelve to fifteen sometimes squeezed into a nine-passenger coach, with others hanging on topside.

The great team—Prince, Lightning, Old Ben, Belle, Lucky and Nell—was stretching its full gallop along the sandy road. Several tons of coach and contents hurtled onward, thundering over small bridges, catapulting through dry washes. After initial talk passengers grew sullen, silently enduring this discomfort to get where they wanted to go. They held little interest in each other, except when there was a pretty woman aboard. Then there were moments of gallantry and perhaps the beginnings of a new romance. The thing might end in a gun fight beside the halted stage, while driver and messenger calmly smoked their Holladay stogies in bored disinterest. The stifling heat, the choking dust, the crowded conditions, the constant rough motion brought out the worst in people. There were numerous duels for one reason and another, and the rugged mode of travel even caused cases of nervous breakdown.

You made about one hundred uncomfortable miles a day, with meal stops fifty miles apart. While food was good at the home stations, lunches taken aboard the coaches often spoiled. Dysentery, a common affliction, might prove embarrassing before the next swing station was reached.

You felt each rut and each bump of the entire run to Denver, Salt Lake or the Comstock, despite the highly-touted springs of leather and coils in the seats. If you traveled under the stars, you learned to sleep on the bounce. You wished to hell it would end. Teams dragged the coach up steep mountain grades, where you viewed with mixed doubt and fear the dark canyons below. Then you were skidding around corkscrew turns, heading downgrade on a mere shelf with a cavernous drop-off just beyond your shoulder. After a while you developed confidence in the Overland's trustworthy leaders and wheelers. But at times the stage went on its side, or became stalled crossing a river where the bridge was out. Aching and stiff, you lent your shoulder to righting the upset coach or getting it out of the mire. There were broken axles and broken wheels and brushes with Indians and holdups, and times when you swore "Never again!" Only you would, for despite its faults, it was still the best mode of travel on the frontier.

One thing was certain: riding the great Overland—or any other stage line—was an unforgettable experience. Finding that you'd survived, you reflected on those days as ones of magnificent beauty along a vivid spectrum of yellow plains, shining mountains, dense forests, deep-running rivers, and blue, blue lakes. A century later railroad, bus and state travel folders would sing the praises of these very things to lure visitors to the land of the big sky. If you took the cross-country trip in one single teeth-jarring gulp, it was not so pleasant. You had to possess a sense of humor. It took weeks to recover from the bruised muscles, stiff joints, skin sores and blisters, the crowding, the strong odors, the frightening pace, the continual fear of Indians and road agents, the constant rocking motion, the endless days of torrid heat or bitter cold . . . the delays . . . the primitive conditions . . . and always the powdery dust boiling up from the spinning wheels.

The most terrible thing about a stage was the cloud of dust that hung around you, coming from the hoofs of the horses, wrote Mrs. George A. Custer, wife of the general. *You couldn't see anything. You breathed and you ate dust. You were always trying to wash the dust out of your eyes. Then there was the heat in the summer, suffocating and sickening. When the stage stopped at swing stations, you were only able to stagger out and it took some time before you began breathing normally and seeing clearly.*

Others enjoyed the ride, like good-humored Sam Clemens, on his way to Virginia City, Nevada, and General James F. Rusling, who traveled clear to California on the Overland. Clemens was charmed by the stages, the pounding horses, the pony express flying by, the scenery and wild life, the drivers and roustabouts, as well as by his encounter with the killer, Jack Slade. So was Horace Greeley, who, with daredevil driver Hank Monk, had a scalp-tingling trip over the Sierras to Placerville to keep a speaking engagement.

Not so, however, Demas Barnes, a mining inspector. Admittedly, Barnes was prejudiced, for he'd gone West for the express purpose of criticizing the Overland. He related:

It is not a pleasant but an interesting trip. The conditions of one man's running stages to make money, while another seeks to ride for pleasure, are not in harmony to produce comfort. Coaches will be overloaded, it will rain, the dust will drive, baggage will be left to the storm, passengers will get sick, a gentleman of gallantry will hold the baby, children will cry, nature demands sleep, passengers will get angry, the drivers will swear, the sensitive will shrink, rations will give out . . . the water brackish, the whiskey abominable, and the dirt almost unendurable. I have just finished six days and nights of this thing; and I am free to say, until I forget a great many things now very visible to me, I shall not undertake it again. Stop over nights? No you wouldn't. To sleep on the sand floor of a one-story sod house or adobe hut, without chance to wash, with miserable food, uncongenial companionship, loss of a seat in a coach until one comes empty, etc., won't work. A through ticket and fifteen inches of seat, with a fat man on one side, a poor widow on the other, a baby on your lap, a bandbox over your head, and three or four persons immediately in front, leaning against your knees, makes the picture, as well as your sleeping place for the trip.

There was a day when all the West rocked on thorough-braces, and the nation did likewise. The Overland under Big Ben Holladay reached a pinnacle of efficiency. It was a stupendous machine made up of thousands of well-trained, superbly moving parts of flesh and wood and leather. Its cogs were wont to fall into their proper places with admirable precision. Its gears meshed smoothly and without noise, except when some outside force ground them to a screeching halt. But teamwork, loyalty, daring—and a spark of madness —soon had them turning again.

People cursed the Overland when it ran, swore vengeance when it didn't. It was like the daily paper. Whether the Overland arrived on time or not was a sensitive barometer of how things were going. A prancing team of six and a gaudy coach of vermillion spelled progress to villages and towns. The daily or triweekly stage schedule was a citation to evoke strong civic pride. The rolling, often-embattled Concord inspired such Western artists as Frederic Remington and Charlie Russell.

So they came West, and Ben Holladay carried them all— merchants, bankers, barkeeps, cowpokes, drummers, soldiers, freighters, gamblers, saloonkeepers, dance-hall girls, prostitutes, wives, sweethearts, gunslingers, tenderfeet, Indian fighters, trappers, traders . . . a host of others who stepped from the Overland and faded into the lives of the mining camps and army posts. Edwin Booth, Lotta Crabtree, Mark Twain, Lola Montez, P. T. Barnum, Schuyler Colfax, the nabobs of the Comstock, congressmen from Washington, the desperadoes fleeing Alder Gulch, adventure-bound European princes . . . It shuttled them all from one corner of the wide-open West to any other.

Step right up to the rough-hewn counter. Buy your ticket to anywhere. The world is right before you, through the door marked *Overland.*

The Silver Camps

FOR YEARS miners in Colorado had an eye only for gold. Out-croppings of silver ore were often not recognized or were deliberately ignored. Even when appreciated, there was little knowledge of how to work them profitably. A tenderfoot at Central City worked almost a week before he learned that it was impossible to pan silver. Stamp mills of the type used to crush soft "blossom rock" were erected at great expense and total loss, for they contributed nothing toward solving the difficult problem of extracting "values" from hard and refractory silver ores.

As early as 1865 miners at Georgetown, on the South Fork of Clear Creek, uncovered large silver veins and began to work them as local gold diggings played out. For many years, up to the great Leadville strikes in 1878, Georgetown was the most productive silver camp in the state. Into this town in 1869 came Louis du Puy, one of the most fabulous characters of the Old West, *hôtelier extraordinaire,* born to wealth and position as Adolphus Francis Gerard at Alençon, France, in 1844. After a varied career as a journalist and soldier in Europe and America, he drifted west and appeared in Georgetown as Louis du Puy in 1869. Injured in a mine accident four years later, he used the funds collected for his benefit by friends to buy the Delmonico Bakery on Alpine Street, which he transformed into the renowned Hotel de Paris by excavating wine cellars, adding a second story and a wide wooden veranda with elaborate iron scroll work. He placed

86

a gilt lion at the gate, a metal stag along one wall, and a gilt statue of justice on the roof, along the peak of which ran a *cheval de frise* of gilded spikes. With its many mirrors, pieces of sculpture, paintings, tapestries, and lavish gilt furnishings, the interior had more than a touch of Parisian splendor.

Here Louis du Puy ruled like a feudal lord, refusing to pay taxes, threatening to shoot whoever came to collect them, and summarily turning out into the street all guests who incurred his displeasure. More than one Bonanza King was flatly informed that his name was not wanted on the register of the Hotel de Paris. This stimulated business, curiously, for everybody was anxious to achieve the honor, a genuine social distinction, of being accepted as a gentleman by fastidious "French Louis." But whether the woman on the arm of a guest was a "lady" did not concern him, for he was simply not interested in his friends' marital status. If they properly appreciated his food and wine, and had something to say on the subjects that Du Puy liked to discuss, which was everything from art to socialism, that was enough. "This house is my own, and if I want guests, I invite them," so this singular frontier innkeeper once explained to a distinguished academic. "If you are a college man, surely you know that no gentleman invites himself to be the guest of a stranger."

Characterized as "an innkeeper who hated his guests, a philosopher and poet who left no written record of his thought, a despiser of women who gave all he had to one, an aristocrat, a proletarian, a pagan, an arcadian, an atheist, a lover of beauty, and, inadvertently, the stepfather of domestic science in America," Du Puy was naturally the talk of the town. The people of Georgetown at once admired and breathlessly gossiped about him, particularly when he took in Sophie Galet, "Aunt Sophie," the widow of a French cabinet maker, who soon became mistress of all parts of the hotel but the kitchen, which Du Puy jealously guarded as his own province. Tongues wagged faster upon the death of "French Louis" in 1900, for his will revealed that "Aunt Sophie" had fallen heir to the Hotel de Paris, which still stands as a landmark in Georgetown, harboring many not-too-faded remnants of its former splendor.

Just above Georgetown the camp of Silver Plume, so named

because the white metal was found in feathery, plume-like veins up and down the mountain sides, had been founded in 1870. Other silver camps began to boom throughout the mountains at the same time. In Wet Mountain Valley, in the southern part of the state, a precipice encrusted with horn silver led to the founding and naming of Silver Cliff, which soon became Colorado's third largest community. Far across the Continental Divide, in the southwestern corner of the state, in what became known as the San Juan country, the camps of Ouray, Silverton, Placerville, Telluride, Ophir, and Rico sprang to life. The first of these, established in 1875 and named for Chief Ouray of the Ute, always a friend of the whites, soon had a population of 1,800 and was holding Sunday services in an unfinished saloon, with beer kegs and cases of whiskey as pews. Silverton was named when an excited miner exclaimed, "We may not have gold here, but we have silver by the ton!" The occupation of Placerville is obvious from its name, while Telluride was christened for the tellurous nature of its ores. On Nigger Baby Hill above Rico rich veins of silver were struck in 1879; shortly, a local Maecenas brought in a piano, the first in the region. The instrument arrived in sections, and half the town had a hand in assembling it in the owner's mansion, built of logs and canvas, but graced with elaborate French windows.

A feud broke out between Silverton and Ouray when the Ouray newspaper, *The Solid Muldoon*, reported that "the mines here are producing like mad." Its Silverton rival retorted that "the mines are not as mad as the men who believe that they are anything more than a flash in the pan." Ouray replied that it was only natural that Silverton should throw mud, for "they have a plentiful supply of it, all of their roads being between six and seventeen feet deep in the stuff." The newly founded camp of Ophir was dragged into the squabble when the *Solid Muldoon* expressed the wish that it would begin to live up to its name, which was that of the fabulous mining district of Biblical fame. The citizens of Ophir, having no newspaper to make a reply, drove a herd of burros into Ouray. Each burro bore the name of a prominent Ouray citizen on its posterior, and when the county judge met his namesake, he was so enraged that he could scarcely be restrained from arming himself with six-shooters and a double-barreled shotgun and making a one-man raid on Ophir.

But the silver era, the most spectacular and lurid in the mining annals of Colorado, really began with a series of almost incredibly rich strikes along California Gulch, which had been virtually deserted since the early days of the gold rush. Miners at that time had been greatly troubled by heavy red sands that clogged up their sluices and impeded washing operations. In 1874 "Uncle Billy" Stevens, an old prospector, and A. B. Wood, a trained metallurgist, assayed the sands to discover that they were carbonates of lead with a high silver content. Tracing the sands to their source on the upper slopes, Stevens and Wood staked out a number of claims, one of which, subsequently developed as the renowned Iron Silver mine, produced more than $15,000,000 in its day.

No sooner had their secret leaked out than thousands of men came swarming into California Gulch for a second time to make other rich strikes on Iron, Fryer, and Carbonate hills. Almost overnight an uninhabited pine flat just below timberline, boxed in by the towering Mosquito Range and the Continental Divide, sprouted a mushroom—and a toadstool—crop of cabins, tents, pine-bough shelters, banks, grocery stores, "fancy parlors," smelters, charcoal ovens, wine theaters, gambling saloons, boarding houses, ten-cent lunchrooms, restaurants with Parisian chefs, bicycle clubs, "Lady" barber shops, shaft houses, beer gardens, temperance societies, grand opera houses, and unsightly mine dumps—a pulsating mass famed as the city of Leadville, as wild a camp as this continent or any other ever saw. As hysteria mounted, the belief grew that the town and surrounding mountains rested upon a foundation of almost pure silver. Every piece of rock in the vicinity was carefully examined. All more curious stones were sent to local assayers, some of whom shared the current frenzy. As a joke, a broken grindstone was submitted to an assayer, who solemnly reported that it ran more than a hundred ounces of silver a ton. Another excitedly reported that the handle of a New England stone jug ran fifty ounces a ton.

Prices rose rapidly, and many great fortunes were founded upon ruthless profiteering. Squatters were driven from their

holdings as prices of lots soared swiftly from $10 to $5,000;
stores rented at $400 a month. Staple groceries sold at four or
five times their price in Denver; a barrel of whiskey often
netted a profit of $1,500. The simplest meal usually cost at
least $1. Rooming houses turned away hundreds each night,
and men were glad to pay $2 for the privilege of sharing a
frowsy bed with a stranger in a makeshift room crowded with
a dozen cots. A large tent advertised itself as the best "hotel"
in town, and the Mammoth Palace, a vast shed lined with a
double tier of bunks, was packed day and night to capacity,
five hundred guests paying fifty cents each for an eight-hour
sleeping shift. Men fought for a place to sleep on draughty
saloon floors, paying high for warmer spots near the stove.
Hundreds died of pneumonia, and scores froze to death during the bitter mountain nights. A black smallpox plague, one
of the worst in the history of the West, took a heavy toll.
Many a corpse was buried at night to hide the mounting
death rate.

   And still the host poured in. All but the Chinese and Indians were welcomed. Men of all occupations and of almost
all nationalities, with the Irish in the majority, crowded the
narrow dusty streets day and night. Bearded miners in shape-
less denim or canvas trousers, heavy boots, and red or pat-
terned flannel shirts jostled elegant dandies wearing top hats,
carrying "peering glasses" with mother-of-pearl handles, and
sporting silver-headed walking sticks. Painted girls with bare
shoulders and knee-length skirts stared enviously as splendid
equipages rattled past bearing the favorite courtesans of the
moment, breath-taking in their lace flounces, ostrich plumes,
and flashing jewels. More than one rode along smoking a
great black cigar. In quiet rooms above noisy gambling
saloons, soberly dressed gamblers and Carbonate Kings played
for stakes so high that $1,000 was often won or lost on the
turn of a single card—not infrequently, a marked card.

   The wildest extravagances were the order of the day as the
Carbonate Kings struggled to outshine one another. Companies of personal guards in gaudy uniforms followed them
as they whisked by in their enameled carriages. Their wives
and mistresses blazed with costly gems, and their houses were
filled with every luxury. Gold watches became the symbol of

success in Leadville. Mining barons bought them by the gross and often wore them in lots of three and four at a time. The élite of Central City might prefer the soft luster of pearls, but the Carbonate Kings had eyes only for the multicolored fire of diamonds. The first purchase of Jack Morrissey, who had been a day laborer before he made his strike, was a magnificent diamond-studded gold watch; unable to tell the time, he held it out to anyone asking the hour, saying, "See fer yersilf, thin ye'll know I'm not lyin' to yez." Another Irish roustabout named Gallagher did not forget his friends of less prosperous days; he completely outfitted them with new clothes and invited them to an elaborate banquet at the fashionable Tontine. One of his two brothers built a rambling castle to please his wife, who remarked, after fortune had smiled upon them, "We're gittin' out of Californy Gulch this viry day. Thim Irish trash up there ain't fit to associate with the likes of us. We're goin' to have a fine house in Leadville, and b'Jasus, it'll have an L on it, too!" An enterprising Denver business man paid $7 each for empty champagne bottles picked up in Leadville alleys; filled with a fizzy concoction of brown sugar, water, and yeast, they were resold to the Carbonate Kings at preposterous prices.

All of Colorado followed the pace set by the "Magic City," as Leadville christened itself, not too extravagantly. With all eyes now focused upon silver, strikes were made throughout the mountains. Across the Continental Divide, Aspen suddenly boomed to rival Leadville for a time. Altogether, more than $100,000,000 of silver was taken from the mountain for which the town was named. From the Smuggler mine here came the world's largest silver nugget; it weighed more than a ton—2,060 pounds—and was 93 per cent pure silver. Soon Aspen had its Hotel Jerome, with an elevator that crept up three floors and down again under hydraulic power, and a celebrated opera house in which appeared many of the great players and singers of the day.

The current frenzy was reflected in the names that lucky prospectors bestowed upon their mines—the Ton a Minute, the Long Lode, the Montezuma, the Silver Queen. The Mary Lee, the Ruby Mae, the Mrs. Kelly, and many others honored sweethearts, mistresses, and wives. More than one cast a coy

hint, such as Fanny B. Mine. Others were fancifully christened the Butterfly Terrible, the Bopeep, the Sun and Moon,
the Gin Shot, the Wobbly Legs, and the Old Lout. The City
of Paris doubtless mirrored the romantic dream long cherished by some old "sourdough" and expressed his resolve to
taste the utmost in luxury if he should strike it rich. There
was a Lucullan streak in most of the Bonanza Kings.

The archetype of the day was Horace Austin Warner
Tabor, a Vermont-born stone cutter, the best known of the
Carbonate Kings of Leadville. With his wife and baby son
he had come to Colorado in the rush of 1859. From camp to
camp they moved, following each new strike, but fortune
escaped them. Tabor took to storekeeping and served as postmaster in several towns; his frail wife, Augusta, took in
boarders and sold pastries. Settling down at Oro City in California Gulch, Tabor, still a postmaster-storekeeper, watched
the growing silver excitement with little interest, for he had
given up all hope of ever striking it rich. The boom pleased
him, however, for it meant additional customers and new
poker partners. As a matter of routine, he grubstaked two
itinerant German shoemakers, August Rische and George
Hook. The partners helped themselves to a jug of whiskey
without Tabor's knowledge, and just outside camp stopped
to sample the liquor. Having "sampled" most of it, they began to dig, for the spot seemed as good as any to their un-
trained eye. Almost immediately they struck a rich silver vein.
Tabor's grubstake entitled him to a third share in the Little
Pittsburgh mine, as it was named, from which he realized
$500,000 in dividends within a short time.

As his star rose, "Tabor luck" became proverbial. He
bought a mine "salted" with ore stolen from the Little Pittsburgh. To save face, Tabor ordered his men to continue digging, and within eight feet they uncovered a vein that netted
him $3,000,000. All Leadville jeered when he bought an un-
worked claim for $117,000 and spent $40,000 in liquidating
all claims against it. A few days later he brought in the
$10,000,000 mine famed as the Matchless. Tabor soon owned
an interest in most every better mine in the district, and extended his investments to other States, to Mexico, even to
South America. Always politically ambitious, he became

Leadville's first mayor in 1878–79 and Lieutenant Governor of Colorado in 1879.

By 1880 Leadville had an estimated population of 25,000 to 40,000; a local newspaper placed it at 60,000. The camp now had a hospital, two large and many small hotels, fourteen smelters, two banks, the Leadville *Chronicle* and other newspapers, and a telephone exchange. The operators at the exchange were all male, for the curses hurled at the inexperienced operators would have shattered more shell-like ears. Twenty-eight miles of streets wound up and down the gulch and pine flat. In summer the dust was settled by ladling water from a barrel balanced on a one-horse cart dubbed the "squirt wagon." The derelict who constituted the "street-watering department" and collected what he could from householders along his route, was old Abe Lee, the prospector who had first struck gold in California Gulch and later struck it rich in silver at the Dana mine, quickly squandering both fortunes. The water system was the pride of the camp; so little solder was available when the mains were laid that the pipes were "wiped" with silver.

Tabor presented Leadville with an opera house, still to be seen on Harrison Avenue. At its opening the old trouper Jack Langrishe presented *The Serious Family,* a comedy, and *Who's Who,* a farce written by Langrishe himself for the gala occasion. There was no lack of pleasure resorts, high and low; for Leadville could and did boast of 120 saloons, 110 beer gardens, 118 gambling halls, and 35 bagnios conducted by Sallie Purple and her scarlet sisters. The spiritual needs of the community were tended by the ministers of seven denominations, although, as the *Chronicle* remarked, "all here have one God in common; it is the Crucified Carbonate."

Into the "Magic City" swarmed gamblers, confidence men, harlots, desperadoes, and shady characters of every kind; and their depredations were so extensive and brutal that the local *Chronicle* spoke frequently of the year 1879 as "The Reign of the Footpads." Holdups were frequent on the main streets in broad daylight. "Get out of town! Stretch your legs before we stretch your neck!" came the ominous warning, but "agents" went on stealing everything they could lay their hands on— timber, charcoal, ore, champagne, oysters, picks, stagecoaches, hay, whiskey, children's clothes from school cloakrooms, bricks, jewelry, shrouds from the dead, coffins, shoes, race horses, revolvers and rifles from police stations and armories, wagons, trousers from sleeping drunks and occasionally from those on their feet and sober, outhouses, front porches, even entire cabins and houses, from the rooftree to the foundations. Claim jumping, sometimes by prospectors who honestly felt that they had been cheated, sometimes by gangs of desperadoes eager for plunder, led to pitched battles in which many were killed. All of the great mines were heavily guarded night and day, and it was highly dangerous to set foot upon the property of a Carbonate King without authorization. George Robinson, owner of the Wheel of Fortune Mine, was shot to death by his own mine guards when he neglected to warn them of his coming.

In the popular mind H. A. W. ("Haw") Tabor came to symbolize this gaudy era of the Carbonate King. Tabor removed to Denver, gave it several large office buildings and the renowned Tabor Grand Opera House, and divorced his wife Augusta because she failed to evince a taste for "high life." Diverting part of the silver flood pouring in upon him, Tabor sought a seat in the United States Senate, the goal of every Bonanza King, and managed to have himself elected for a period of thirty days, to fill the unexpired term of Henry M. Teller of Central City, who had become Secretary of the Interior in President Arthur's cabinet. While in Washington, Tabor married young and beautiful Elizabeth McCourt Doe of Oshkosh, better known as "Baby Doe," a fascinating divorcée popular in Central City, Leadville, and Denver. Scandal broke when it was discovered that their dazzling marriage, performed at the Willard Hotel in the presence of President Arthur and other notables, was the second union of the pair, for Tabor upon the basis of a fraudulent divorce had married Mrs. Doe several months before—in fact, before a second legal divorce from Augusta had been granted. This unfortunate affair made Haw many new enemies, many of them among his former friends who remained loyal to Augusta.

But Tabor ignored enmity and criticism. With an annual income estimated at $4,000,000, he was too powerful to be seriously harmed by gossip about his foibles and indiscre-

tions. Commenting upon his later ruin, a friend remarked
that "Tabor was spending money as if the United States mint
were his personal property." His lavish tastes provided the
irrepressible Eugene Field, then editor of the Denver *Tribune,* with much material for his "Odds and Ends" column.
Field reported a fictitious interview with Tabor in which the
Carbonate King was described as "shaving with a diamond-
studded razor before a French plate glass mirror, eight inches
thick, framed with pure Etruscan gold. His elegant toilet
articles included an $80 silk sponge, especially imported for
him from the East Indies, a $50 razor strop, a $125 shaving
mug, and a $25 shaving brush of ostrich down." When Tabor
had, first appeared upon the floor of the Senate, the blazing
diamonds on his fingers, in his cuffs, and on his broad shirt
front had evoked from an elder statesman an audible "My
God!" Traveling to Washington, he had created a sensation
on the train when he pleasured the passengers with a sight of
his $250 silk night gown, trimmed with point lace, rose in
color, and his gold-embroidered night cap. Upon his private
armies in Leadville—the Tabor Highlanders, the Tabor
Guards, and the Tabor Light Cavalry—he bestowed the most
magnificent uniforms. The Highlanders appeared in black
doublets trimmed with royal blue and red braid and facings,
Royal Stuart kilts, white sporrans of goat hair, and Prince
Charlie bonnets, while the Guards wore scarlet trousers with
a gold stripe, blue coats, and brass helmets. Tabor liked to
appear in uniform as commander-in-chief of these units, of
the Highlanders especially in spite of some carping criticism
about "Haw's knees in those damn kilts."

In 1890 the passage of the Sherman Silver Act sent the price
of the white metal rocketing. At the same time new rich
strikes were made to the south on the Rio Grande River,
notably by N. C. Creede, who with a partner named Smith
discovered the Holy Moses lode on Mount Campbell, now
Mount Moses. The district had few indications of silver, but
the men sank a shaft into the mountainside to open a remark-
ably fine vein. Not a profane man, Creede attempted to match
the jubilant obscenities of his partner by exclaiming, "Holy
Moses!", and so the mine and mountain were named. The
following year Creede crossed the mountain to the site of the

town that bears his name. Here two old German prospectors were working the Last Chance claim, and Creede staked the claim next to theirs, striking the rich Amethyst lode. News of this strike brought a rush to these hills with their network of silver veins, and the once quiet gulch resounded with the clamor of thousands of men. Creede was soon on every tongue. In Denver, so a traveler reported, the name "faced you everywhere from billboards, flaunted at you from canvas awnings stretched across the street, and stared at you from daily papers in type an inch high; the shop windows, according to their several uses, advertised 'Photographs of Creede,' 'The only correct map of Creede,' 'Scalp tickets to Creede,' 'Wanted, $500 to start a drugstore in Creede,' 'You will need boots at Creede, and you can get them at ——'s.' The gentlemen in the Denver Club talk Creede; the people in the hotels dropped the word so frequently that you wondered if they were not all just going there."

Not even the Leadville rush surpassed this new stampede. No racial discrimination existed in Creede; Chinese were everywhere, with "a washboard in one hand and a can of hop in the other." Ute Indians were almost as numerous as the Irish. "There is not a brick, a painted front nor an awning in the whole town," wrote Richard Harding Davis in 1892. "It is like a city of fresh cardboard, and the pine shanties seem to trust for support to the rocky sides of the gulch in which they have squeezed themselves. In the street are ox-teams, mules, men, and donkeys loaded with ore, crowding each other familiarly, and sinking knee deep in mud. Furniture and kegs of beer, bedding and canned provisions, clothing and half-open packing cases, and piles of raw lumber heaped up in front of the new stores—or those still to be built—stores of canvas only, stores with canvas tops and foundations of logs, and houses with the Leadville front, where the upper boards have been left square instead of following the sloping angle of the roof. . . . It is more like a circus tent which has sprung up over night and which may be removed on the morrow, than a town."

Within a month the narrow canyon was crowded with ramshackle structures. Rooming houses and "hotels" were filled within an hour of their completion; reservations were often

made before the foundations had been laid. Saloons prospered in flimsy tents where undressed boards laid across two
chairs served as a bar for dispensing beer at 25¢ a glass and
"raw licker" at $1 a gulp. The doctoring of liquor was a fine
art here. A man approached a saloon keeper with the suggestion that if he were given "a barr'l of strong whisky, a couple
of plugs of tobaccer, some alcohol, and some distilled water,
he'd make three, or mebbe four, barr'ls of the kind of likker
the boys cry for." The overflow of the town spilled down the
river to the neighboring camp of Jim Town, often called Gin
Town for the huge quantities of this drink consumed in the
local grog shops. The two camps were really one, but they
stubbornly and fiercely preserved their separate identities.

Here Bob Ford, slayer of Jesse James, was shot to death in
his own saloon in 1892 in much the manner that he had murdered his bandit chief. At Ford's funeral, which was conducted by the sporting gentry of the town, there were no
flowers but quantities of wine and champagne. Later Ford's
body was shipped to his home in Missouri, and that same day
his open grave was used to bury a Negro murderer. Ford's
slayer, a youth named O'Kelly, had killed Ford, it was rumored, to avenge James's death, and feeling ran high against
him. He was saved from lynching by the intervention of the
renowned "Soapy" Smith, born Jefferson Randolph Smith,
who in the camps of Colorado and later in Alaska built up a
lucrative racket by hawking soap on street corners. His "spiel"
consisted of the startling announcement that many of his
cakes of soap were wrapped in $50 and $100 bills and that a
chance to draw for them cost a mere $5. Some cakes were
wrapped in bills, to be sure, but no one but Soapy's "shills,"
or come-on men, ever had the luck to draw one. Smith had a
genius for organization and in Denver recruited a company
of gamblers and confidence men to fleece Creede. Within a
few months he was virtual boss of the camp, appointing officials and managing public affairs with an iron hand. His dic-
tatorship was a rather benevolent one; he established some
semblance of law and order, founded churches and charitable
organizations, and kept his horde of crooked henchmen from
going too far. Curiously, it was a public-spirited act that
finally broke Soapy's power. No one but him could have saved

O'Kelly from the mob intent upon lynching him, and this demonstration of power set the "respectables" in the camp to thinking, with the result that Smith and his henchmen were ousted. Smith accepted with good grace and quietly departed, subsequently establishing himself during the Klondike Rush at Skagway, Alaska, where he died at the hands of vigilantes, having fleeced one too many victims. His old gambling saloon in Creede, the Orleans Club, still stands. The bar at Soapy's Place, as the saloon is now known, is still as hospitable as it was in the days when "Dictator" Smith used to shout, "This one's on the house."

The town was early noted for its all-night illumination. Giant flares burned from twilight to sunrise, and this inspired Cy Warman, composer of "Sweet Marie," to write the jingle with the refrain, now known throughout the West, "It's day all day in the daytime, and there is no night in Creede."

The politer side of social life was cultivated by the Ladies' Social Club, the Creede Study Club, and the Ladies' Bicycle Club, whose members pedaled about the winding mountain trails in voluminous bloomers. Denouncing this costume as "disgraceful," a respectable citizen was horrified one day to catch sight of his wife pedalling down the street in Turkish pantaloons. He informed her that as she had a bicycle, she could pedal it straight back to Illinois where she came from; and she went, but by train.

The silver boom ended abruptly and disastrously. The Sherman Act obliging the U. S. Treasury to purchase 4,500,-000 ounces of silver annually at $2 an ounce was repealed in 1892. The mints of India, one of the largest markets, suddenly ceased minting silver coins. To top all, came the severe nation-wide panic of 1893. As silver prices toppled, the mining camps were overwhelmed. Frantically, the advocates of free silver sought to avert disaster. The repeal of the Sherman Act became a national issue, dividing both political parties. In defense of the act, young William Jennings Bryan was nominated for the Presidency on a free silver platform after gaining fame with his "Cross of Gold" speech, which he concluded by thundering, "We shall answer their demand for a gold standard by saying, 'You shall not press down upon the brow of labor this crown of thorns, you shall not crucify mankind upon a cross of gold!' "

But silver was doomed. Mine after mine closed down; some towns were soon wholly abandoned. Many of the Bonanza Kings lost their fortunes. Their private armies were disbanded; jewels, horses, and mansions went under the auctioneer's hammer; pretty mistresses were left to shift for themselves; more than one millionaire went back to pick and shovel or to the grocery counter. A few weathered the storm, having invested wisely in other fields, notably the Guggenheims, who laid the basis of their great family fortune in the smelters of Leadville.

Even Tabor went down in the crash of '93, losing his entire fortune in spite of frantic efforts to salvage some small part of it. Made postmaster of Denver to spare him the humiliation of utter destitution, Tabor died in 1899, breathing his last in a small room in the Windsor Hotel, Denver, a famous hostelry built by Tabor years before at the height of his career. "Hang on to the Matchless!" was his final injunction to Baby Doe. This she did with grim determination in the face of almost insuperable difficulties, living alone in a one-room shack near the mouth of the mine, rejecting all offers of assistance, stubbornly believing that the great lode was not exhausted and would some day produce another fortune. Bitter and suspicious, obsessed with the idea that "they" were conspiring to steal the Matchless, she drove visitors from the mine at the point of a shotgun. The story of the second Mrs. Tabor came to its tragic end on March 7, 1935, when her frozen body was found in an unheated shack standing on the dump of the Matchless. The single small room in the cabin was littered with mementos of early days, bundles of newspapers, outmoded garments, and unopened presents from people who had admired her courage and invincible faith and wished to help her. Boxes of shoes and warm clothing had not been touched by the proud old woman, who was found in rags, with burlap wrapped around her feet in place of shoes.

But Leadville, however shrunken from what it was in the great boom days of 1880, is not a ghost. It has always retained its high spirits. It is not paralyzed by a wistful nostalgia for days that are gone. Leadville, indeed, is growing again. It still mines silver, gold, zinc, lead, and manganese, and in the neighboring camp of Climax on Bartlett Mountain is one of the world's most valuable mines from which comes almost three-fourths of the world supply of molybdenum, a rare metal used in making radio tubes, chemicals, dyes, and high-speed machine tools. No bonanza of earlier days poured forth greater treasure in as short a time as this mine, shares of stock in which, according to *Time*, rose 116,900 per cent between 1926 and 1936. During World War II, Climax enjoyed probably the most phenomenal growth of any Colorado mining camp and Leadville shared in this boom.

Bad Actors

Billy the Kid Breaks Jail

BY FRAZIER HUNT

¶ *One view of the Old West that is superficial but under-standable—particularly as it has been nurtured lately by the dubious fare of television programming—has it populated largely by gun-toting Bad Men and Good Guys, most of them afflicted with itching trigger fingers. The view is grossly exaggerated, but the sober truth of history bears out the legend sufficiently to satisfy most of us. Bad men, whether out-and-out criminal types or those unable to adjust even to the rudimentary social controls of the frontier, existed in long supply. Foremost in legend, and impressive if some-what perplexing in truth, was a smiling, small-statured fel-low born Henry McCarty and known variously as Billy Antrim, Kid Antrim, William H. Bonney, and during the flowering of his brief and violent career as Billy the Kid, or simply The Kid. Whatever were the motives that impelled him to action—and he has had scores of apologists and sym-pathetic delineators, as well as critics and detractors—he was outside the law, a killer who died a fugitive from justice. In his biography of The Kid, Frazier Hunt has been kinder to Billy than have most recent commentators. Here he tells the story of the Kid's escape from the Lincoln County jail, where he was awaiting execution for the murder of Sheriff Brady.*

APRIL 28TH was a Thursday, and Billy had now been in close confinement at Lincoln exactly one week. Bob Ollinger's big calendar showed that he had fifteen more days on this bright, sunny earth, before May 13th rolled around.

Early on Wednesday morning Pat Garrett had checked in

From *The Tragic Days of Billy the Kid*. Copyright 1956 by Frazier Hunt.

at the prison room. He'd be riding over to Los Tablos to collect taxes and the next day he'd jog on west to White Oaks.
He told Ollinger and Bell that he supposed he might as well
order the lumber for the scaffold while he was at the Oaks.
Certainly he had no heart to go through with the hanging. It
was grim business to be a sheriff. He'd be back along about
Saturday: that was three days off.

It was the first time that Pat had left Lincoln during the six
days that Billy had been held a prisoner. He had treated the
boy with every consideration, but he made no bones about
warning the two guards that they must be constantly on the
alert. They must never let the Kid see the back of their shirts.
There was nothing intentionally mean in Pat's warnings to
his deputies: he wasn't trying to rub it in on the Kid. Actually he probably had a soft spot in his heart for the boy.

After Pat rode off Ollinger took his double-barrel breech-
loading shotgun from the armory in the closet near the head
of the stairs on the second floor and brought it into the room
where Billy was held. He thumbed the lever that opened the
breech of the valuable gun and put in two brass shells.

"There's nine buckshot in each of them shells, Billy," he
remarked. "The man that gets one of them loads will feel it."

Billy grinned over at him when he answered: "You better
take care you don't get a load of them buckshot yourself,
Bob."

Ollinger patted the shiny gun and set it in the far corner
of the room by the north wall. It was well within the pro-
hibited territory that Billy could enter only on threat of instant death.

Nothing unusual happened the rest of that Wednesday or
during the long morning or early afternoon of Thursday, the
28th. Late April is probably the loveliest time of the year in
this high country of central New Mexico. But the boy, sitting
in his chair by the open window, handcuffed and wearing leg
irons, was hardly thinking about the warm, bright day and
the friendly street noises. He was thinking about freedom.
That fatal day of May 13th was approaching pretty fast.

Just about now Garrett would be ordering the lumber for
the scaffold. Ollinger told Billy in great detail just how high
the drop was, and how it would be erected in the open space

behind the courthouse. The hanging was even going to be a public affair.

Billy had been extra quiet all day. Things had come out exactly as he had hoped. It meant a good deal that Garrett was a full day's ride away.

It was mid-afternoon when Bob Ollinger called to the three or four minor prisoners who were jailed in the room across from the wide, central hall. He motioned them to march on down the stairs to the back door and then on across the street for their dinner at Wortley's Hotel. From the open window the Kid could look down on the path that led to the street. He watched Charlie Wall limping along behind Ollinger. Charlie's wounds were almost healed.

The Kid waited for a few minutes, then he asked Bell if he'd mind taking him down to the privy. There was nothing unusual about the request. Bell told him sure he would: lead the way. The Kid shuffled from his chair on through the adjoining room to the wide hall and down to the far end, and then he turned to the right and slowly clanked down the stairs.

Bell patiently waited outside in the warm sun while the Kid went inside the outhouse. It was too nice a day for anything to happen. By rights a man should be taking a little siesta along about this time. He could sure use one on this quiet, hot afternoon, when there wasn't even the suspicion of a breeze.

Ollinger and the prisoners were across the street eating their dinner; Pat Garrett was a good forty miles away; and here at hand Bell was daydreaming. This was the moment.

There are many versions as to what happened during the next sixty seconds. Over a period of three decades Lt. Col. Maurice G. Fulton, long Professor of English at the New Mexico Military Institute at Roswell, explored every possible angle that might lead to the solution of the drama that now swiftly unfolded. A year or two before his death in 1955, the distinguished scholar arrived at what he was certain was the accurate sequence of the deadly happenings. His conclusion can be accepted either as completely factual or as near the truth as will ever be ascertained.

The day before, when Sam Corbett had shaken hands with Billy on his visit to his prison room on the southeast corner of the second floor, he had managed to slip into the Kid's manacled hands a tightly folded note. The doomed boy patiently waited his chance to read it and then probably swallowed the paper. He learned that a six-shooter wrapped in an old newspaper would that night be tucked under the wooden *vegas,* or round poles which supported the dirt roof of the adobe privy.

So on the afternoon of the following day when Ollinger and his prisoners were well along with their meal at Wortley's Hotel, the Kid asked Bell to take him downstairs to the outhouse. And the easy-going Bell remained outside. In the hot, lazy sunlight there was no need to be concerned over the boy.

The Kid located the gun wrapped in the newspaper and concealed under a *vega* near the door. It had been placed there some time during the night by Jose M. Aguayo, a high-class young New Mexican who had been friendly to the McSween faction but had been too young to take an active part in the terrible feud of three years before.

The Kid reached up his arms and pulled down the bundle. He took out the six-shooter and saw that the gun was fully loaded. He managed to stick it under the waistband of his trousers, the butt concealed by his manacled hands. He waited a plausible length of time and then pushed open the door and stepped out into the bright light.

When he reached a spot three or four feet away from Bell, he jerked out the six-shooter and pointed it at Bell's middle. Unquestionably he disarmed him at once. The Kid did not raise his voice as he spoke to the guard. Bell was to march through the rear door and then up the stairs. He'd have to kill Bell if he shouted for help or did not do exactly as he was told.

Bell led the way, the Kid walking a pace or two behind him. Bell made straight for the back door, then up the three stairs to the landing and turned up the longer series of steps that led to the upstairs hall. It is probable that the Kid's intentions were to march the guard either to the room at the right of the stairs, or to another room where Bell could be held while the Kid made his next move. Billy might have figured on forcing Bell to unlock his handcuffs and his leg irons.

In the hall not far from the top landing Bell suddenly turned and made a break for the stairs, possibly following a tussle with the Kid. Billy, holding his gun in his manacled hands, managed to shoot when Bell was halfway down. He missed, but the slug careened off the left-hand wall of the stairway and entered the guard's body just below his left armpit. It plowed its way through to his right side.

Bell managed to keep his feet and lunged around the lower platform into the downstairs room. Then, calling on some subconscious reserve force, he staggered through the rear door.

He fell into the arms of Old Man Gauss and was dead by the time he was laid on the ground.

Swift as a kangaroo the Kid leaped in short jumps down the hall and into the room of his confinement. He grabbed Ollinger's shotgun and crossed to the window that looked down on the pathway that followed the east side of the building and ran on out through the little gate to the street.

Ollinger was at that moment coming through the gate, his drawn six-shooter in his right hand. He had heard the single shot and, as he had hurried from the eating house, he had remarked that Bell must have had to kill the Kid.

"Hello, Bob," the Kid shouted down when the deputy was directly under the open window.

When Ollinger looked up the Kid, awkwardly holding the long heavy gun in his manacled hands, pulled the trigger. The buckshot felled Ollinger like a bolt of lightning.

The Kid swiftly hobbled across his prison room and through the sheriff's office to the hall. Turning to the right he crossed to the front balcony and in short jumps reached its east end. He could see Ollinger lying inside the gate and a little beyond the east corner of the building. He laid the shotgun over the railing, pointed it downward, and managed to pull the left-hand trigger. Then he tossed the gun at the dead figure of the hated Ollinger.

"Take this, too, damn you!" he shouted. "You won't follow me any more with that gun."

He could see the men under the porch of the hotel across the street, and he shouted for them to stay where they were. Swiftly he returned to the hall, sped down it to the room on the right in the rear. He crossed to the closet at the northwest corner and tried the flimsy door. It was locked, but he threw his weight against it and the lock gave way.

Two or three Winchesters rested, butts down, in the rear corners of the closet. Several Colt revolvers hung from scabbards and gunbelts on hooks screwed in the back wall. The Kid picked out a Winchester, examined it, and then chose a Colt with its belt filled with shells.

He hobbled out of the room and turned to the right and the open window at the bottom end of the hall. He saw Old Man Gauss on below and ordered him to throw up a file, that if Gauss did as he was told there'd be no trouble.

The Kid now made his way up the corridor and out to the front balcony. Charlie Wall and two or three of the prisoners were still standing under the overhanging porch of the Wortley Hotel. One man, consumed with curiosity, started across the dirt street just as the Kid stepped up to the railing.

He shouted for him to go back. No one must cross the street or come near the building. He'd kill anyone who did.

There is no certainty as to just how the boy got shed of his handcuffs. He had large wrists and it is barely possible that he managed to pull his small hands through the steel cuffs. It is far more likely that he forced Gauss to search Bell's pockets and when he found the keys to the handcuffs to come upstairs and remove them from his wrists.

According to Gauss' story, he was told to locate a file but the best he could do was to find a prospector's pick-axe, with a steel point on the long shank, and he tossed it up through the open rear window to the Kid.

The Kid finally succeeded in loosening the rivets on one of the iron shackles, thus freeing one foot. Time was fleeting and he decided to tie the loose anklet and the chain to his belt.

He was now fully mobile, although he was still somewhat handicapped when he walked. The sound of the dangling chain links clanking as he walked must have sounded like the happy music of jingling spurs to his ears. It meant that he was going somewhere.

He was free. He wouldn't have to hang on May 13th. He had outwitted them all.

It was a good hour after he had killed his guards before Billy was ready to pull out. He was in no hurry. He knew that no informer had ridden up the single street of Lincoln and on to the west in front of the courthouse, to carry word to Pat Garrett; he had seen to that himself.

Pat was still forty miles away. That meant that at the very earliest he couldn't be on his trail until the following evening, probably not until the second day.

In the opposite direction, to the east, no deputy sheriff or law officer lived within fifty miles: that would be on the Pecos near Roswell. Everything had broken in his favor. He'd have at least a twenty-four-hour start.

He filled two cartridge belts with .44 shells that would fit either a rifle or a six-shooter. There is a legend that he now strapped on a pair of revolvers—although all his life he had held two-gun men in contempt.

The pony was a little frightened when Billy, with his rifle held in one hand and with his leg chains jingling, swung on board. Before he could get his feet firmly in the stirrups Collie bucked him off.

After Billy had been thrown, Gauss caught the pony and led him up for a second try. This time Billy had the old German hold his rifle until he had mounted and quieted the horse. Then he reached down and took the rifle in his right hand.

Across the street, under the porch of Wortley's Hotel, the crowd watched the performance. A few years later Charlie Wall told a young cowboy, who eventually became the great cattleman and founder of the Arizona Rangers, "Cap" Burton C. Mossman of Roswell, that he could easily have picked off the Kid with a six-shooter—but that he was on the boy's side. So were almost all the people there. They hoped he'd have luck and make it safely out of the country.

Billy waved his rifle at the friendly crowd. Then he let out a yell and touched his pony's flank with his iron shackle. Collie threw up his tail and started off at a gallop.

The Kid took the west road on up the Canyon of the Rio Bonito. He was as wildly joyous as an eagle suddenly freed from its cage.

No one moved until he was well out of sight.

৪৹৫৹৫৹৫৹

The Worst Outlaw Since Sam Bass

BY HAROLD PREECE

¶ *Sheriff-baiting Rube Boyce was a different kind of bad man. There seems to have been little if any malevolence in him, which, while a credit to him as a human being, has kept him off most rosters of the eminent out-of-law. His brush with Texas Ranger Ira Aten is told in a chapter from Harold Preece's life of Aten,* Lone Star Man. *The Jim Epps referred to at the beginning of the chapter was a Tennessean whom Ranger Aten arrested on an old murder warrant and sent back to his home state for trial; later, concerned by the plight of Epps's wife and children, Aten wrote a letter recommending leniency that was instrumental in getting the accused man set free to return to his family.*

JIM EPPS looked up his deliverer, who had been his captor. He rode into Camp King and found Ira thumbing another sheaf of "catch-'em papers."

"Thank you, Mr. Aten," Jim Epps said feelingly. "That letter you wrote sure helped me when the prosecutor read it."

Ira felt a surge of something even more gratifying than a

Ranger citation. "I'm glad to hear that, Mr. Epps," he answered modestly.

Jim Epps's hand strayed gratefully around his throat. "Reckon they could have swung me just on my confession. I'm back home 'cause a lawman that lawyer never saw had a heart."

Ira didn't know what to say; he was struggling for words when Epps added:

"You know I ain't throwin' off on the law, Mr. Aten. But not many officers woulda put theirselves out for somebody in my fix. They'da been more interested in makin' a record than in savin' a man's neck."

The two shook hands. Jim Epps mounted a waiting horse. Then the settler rode back into happy obscurity and out of a Ranger's life.

Yet not quite out of his life. Their first encounter had left Ira tortured by a recurrent vision of Jim Epps dangling from a rope while a woman and six youngsters grieved. Now their second meeting became still another goad to a law enforcer's conscience. As poignantly as he recalled that sorrowful family in the canyon, Ira kept remembering an obvious truth voiced by its head—far too many officers would have been far more concerned with a record than a life.

Once again Ira found himself wondering what kind of record he wanted to make.

Courage was a recognized part of the reputation he had already built. Alertness and natural ability, too. All of them combined had earned him promotion from private to corporal within a very short time. The foolish part of his early romanticism had long since been outgrown. Its better part had remained to give his work the inspiration and imagination that made him an outstanding, completely trusted member of the force.

But the postscript to Jim Epps was a new element welded into ambition—the simple element of mercy.

Mercy, which Ira's good common sense would never let be diluted into sentimental drivel over "a man who ought to be hung."

As a Ranger and a frontiersman, Ira believed that ropes were often necessary and highly effective instruments of justice. Yet in a larger focus he wanted his record to be more than a footnote to a sheaf of death warrants.

His broader understandings met their first test a few months later. The test involved a man who was the complete opposite of Jim Epps—a wild man who had flirted many times with hemp but had managed to dodge its kiss.

Rube Boyce was a town rowdy who had launched himself on a lurid career of posse racing by shooting his own brother-in-law in a family fracas. Ira described him as being "one of the real bad men of western Texas in the early days."

The acquaintance was incidental rather than one dating from a sprint between lawman and outlaw. Boyce was enjoying a stretch of freedom in Llano, a hill country county seat, when Ira went there with a Ranger detail to guard a court whose sanctity was threatened by a scorching Texas feud.

Two families—the Carters and the Cogginses—had been improving already notable reputations for marksmanship by pot-shooting each other in the convenient Packsaddle Mountains of Llano County. At a former hearing, stemming from the feud, the warring clans had started aiming at each other in the district courtroom. They had finished the battle on the streets of Llano town, leaving men lying in the dust.

When the second trial opened, armed Rangers were present to help Sheriff George W. Shaw preserve order. Ira was assigned to guard duty in the courtroom. His chore was to keep an eye on the spectators and be sure that nobody testifying was "bullet knocked" out of the witness chair. He kept Carter partisans sitting on one side of the courtroom and Coggins warriors on the other. The presence of the Rangers made the truculent clans mind their decorum. What puzzled Ira, as the trial went along peacefully, was the odd behavior of Sheriff Shaw.

A tall, whiskered man with a face that was both hard and sad, Shaw kept himself posted below the judge's rostrum when he wasn't escorting witnesses to the chair. Ordinarily, a Texas sheriff maintained a hawk's watch on a trial as tense as this one. But Ira sensed that he sometimes wasn't even listening to the testimony of men living in his own jurisdiction. Often he barely heard instructions given him by the judge. Ira noticed that he was forever gazing into the middle of the crowd except when a bang of the gavel made him jump to duty.

"What's bothering the sheriff?" Ira whispered to a deputy on the third day of the trial.

The deputy jerked a thumb. "The fellow over there."

Ira looked toward a section of benches that had been set aside for Llanoites who were neutrals. He saw a robust man who kept watching the proceedings with eyes that laughed at all the embellished follies of jurisprudence. Occasionally his chest would vibrate in some suppressed belly rumble when the judge was pompous or some witness fatuous. Now and then someone would glance around to see how this spectator was taking the trial before turning a head to hide an unbidden grin.

There was a certain negative magnetism about the man. A defying, elusive something that Ira just couldn't put a finger on. And obviously nobody felt whatever it was more uncomfortably than the stiff, lonely figure who was the sheriff of Llano County.

Ira saw Shaw's eyes stray again toward the fellow. There was a subtly teasing response on the face of the man as their glances met—like the subtle challenge of a confident wolf knowing that it can conquer a hound wanting to spring but not quite daring.

All afternoon Ira was fascinated with the byplay between the upset man of law and the man who might be anybody. The sheriff was fidgeting visibly as the session drew to a close. But his tormentor still showed that provoking self-assurance.

When the day's tourney of law ended, Ira followed the man into the corridor. There he stood, watching with twinkling eyes as Rangers supervised the downstairs exit first of Carters, then of Cogginses, making sure that none carried forty-fives.

Ira turned to the fellow as the last feudist began treading steps.

"Don't believe I've met you," he said. "My name's Aten— I'm here with the Ranger detail."

The man nodded and put out a hand. "So I know. Guess we should have met before. I'm Boyce—Rube Boyce."

Ira's hand froze in the clasp. Rube Boyce, smartest of all

the tribe of stagecoach robbers. The man some Texas officers declared to be "the worst outlaw since Sam Bass."

By God! Ira thought; *George Shaw ought to have jugged him long ago for his damned impudence.*

The Ranger saw that same satirical gleam that had been disturbing to Sheriff Shaw. "Hear you Rangers are camped outside town. Maybe I'll drop over to chin with you some night."

The cheek of this damned highwayman! Ira withdrew his hand.

"You do that, Boyce," he said curtly, then walked away.

Around the campfire after supper Ira and the outfit recounted the sizable legend of Rube Boyce, who took what he wanted and twiddled his long gunman's fingers at the law. In Kimble County, a further extension of these hills, he had slain his brother-in-law. Kimble was such an undeveloped patch of rock and brush that, for several years, its "courthouse" had been two tall trees serving as twin gallows for felons condemned under their branches. A posse of cowpunchers had taken out after Rube, following the killing, but he had outrun them.

Then he had turned up as the nimble brain of a gang preying on the stagecoach lines of western Texas. Finally Rube and his followers had been bagged after robbing the Austin stage. His henchmen took their medicine of sentences served in the state penitentiary. But, as a Ranger remarked with a long sigh, "keeping their head man locked up was like trying to stuff a wolf in a tow sack."

Rube Boyce had also been condemned. Convicted, Ira guessed, while jousting in his peculiar game with the judge who had tried him. His wife had visited him often in the Austin calaboose, bringing him victuals to supplement "the jail grub which would just about keep a man alive." The jailer, feeling sorry for the pitiful girl, always admitted her for a tryst in Rube's cell after first making the customary check of her basket for hidden firearms.

Never a weapon or a getaway tool turned up in the straw container. One day Mrs. Boyce came while her husband's lawyers on the outside were engaged in some legal maneuvers for a stay of sentence. Perfunctorily, the jailer examined the basket to find nothing but fried chicken and trimmings. Graciously he then let the girl into the steel boudoir.

Two hours passed. Time to bring the baton down on the love symphony. The jailer went to Rube's cell—to find a forty-five pointing through the bars at his head. As Ira heard the story by the Llano campfire, the jailer walked into the cell; Rube Boyce and his wife walked out. They made their way to the unguarded hitching rack outside the building. There Rube boarded a good horse that was waiting and stayed ahead in a two-hundred-and-fifty-mile race to Mexico.

The jailer was released by a sheriff whose tongue blasted louder than Rube Boyce's six-guns ever had. A dropped basket on the cell floor spelled out the answer. When the angry sheriff ripped it apart, he found something never detected by his underling—a false bottom had concealed a cozy cache for a gun.

Nobody thought of prosecuting Mrs. Boyce. In fact, no Texas jury would have convicted a woman for standing by her man. Texans who detested outlawry chuckled over the break engineered by a slip of a girl. Public sympathy, as Ira remembered, began churning for the poor young wife left without the support of her husband. The romantics who kept shifting their Robin Hood projections from one knight of the swag to another now started making a popular hero out of a highwayman.

Jesse James—Sam Bass—now Rube Boyce. They had all "stolen from the rich and given to the poor," in one of the most enduring motifs of popular mythology. A climate of sympathy began generating in Texas for Rube, now enduring the less genial climate of Mexico.

He sweated out several years in the torrid southern republic, liking the country as little as had the batches of Texan filibusters rounded up and thrown in *presidios* for violating a nation's sovereignty. Pesos from Mexican gaming tables came as easily to him as dollars had from American stage lines. As Ira had heard it said, "You could always count on Rube Boyce having a pocketful of money and a headful of sense."

But Mexican heat can evaporate even the cockiness of a Texan. Rube started writing letters to friends back home swearing that "he'd rather live in hell than in Mexico." It was another way of saying that he was just plain lonesome for Texas.

His wife found him a pair of smarter lawyers who got his case transferred on some technicality to the Federal Court in Austin. Rube returned to do a second jail stint while awaiting re-trial. This sojourn behind bars passed off tranquilly, Mrs. Boyce's visiting privileges being restricted. Rube made his due appearance before the court whose authority came from the Yankee capital in Washington. To the chagrin of Austin's sheriff, he was acquitted and walked away from custody, happily holding his helpmate's hand.

And now, as Ira had seen, he was a thorn getting sharper in the flesh of Llano's sheriff.

More days Ira watched the unfolding farce in the Llano courthouse. Even the way in which Rube Boyce toyed with a button on his shirt irritated Sheriff Shaw. His flick of an eye toward some demobilized feudist made the sheriff bristle. If he bent over to adjust his boot laces, Shaw's gaze would travel downward, too. Then when Boyce would look up again, Shaw would try to counter a barely sarcastic twinkle with stern visage, his whiskers vibrating, in a slow fitfulness, like grass ruffled by some puckish slow wind.

The other Rangers also began noticing that daily tussle between two men sharing nothing but strong wills and instinctive mutual dislike. At first Ira sympathized with the sheriff as a brother lawman and remained coolly aloof toward the slyly insolent highwayman. Sympathy, though, soured into gradual disgust as Shaw kept proving such a ready victim of every obvious trap.

"Rube Boyce surely gets the sheriff's goat," Ira remarked on another night in the Ranger camp. "And George Shaw stakes the goat right out for Rube to get."

"Yeh." A comrade laughed. "But I can't feel very sorry for Shaw standing up there every day and letting himself be hurrahed by a card-shark bandit."

Ira's own feeling for the sheriff began cooling. True, the presence of such a notorious bad man in the county was a standing reproach to George Shaw's dignity as its law enforcer. His humiliation was compounded by the fact that Rube Boyce was now technically as clean as the teeth of the hounds that the sheriff used to bay horse thieves out of the Packsaddle Mountains. How would any rural sheriff feel about a stellar, if inactive, outlaw taking up residence in his county and not even being able to order him out?

Rube Boyce had been a challenge to George Shaw on the day he was born, Ira decided; some men were just natural-born enemies. But an officer was also expected to show natural self-control when dealing with an opponent whom some freak-ish process of justice had placed beyond his reach.

Then, much to his own surprise, Ira found himself getting friendlier with the outlaw. It began with a comment about the weather or, perhaps, some observation about quail hunt-ing. Then it progressed to other and longer talk during re-cesses. For a while Ira wondered if Rube Boyce was trying to make a psychological ally of him in that silent feud with Sheriff Shaw. Finally he concluded that Boyce just wanted to be friendly in that normal camaraderie of Texans, always re-laxed and sustained unless tempers flared suddenly.

One Friday night the gunman strolled casually into the Ranger camp. "Howdy, boys," he said in greeting. "Told Ira over there I'd been meaning to stop by some night."

Ira winced, feeling uncomfortable because the outlaw had for the first time referred to him by his given name. But that mention placed an obligation of sociability upon him. So he poured Rube Boyce a cup of coffee from the campfire pot and found him a box to sit on.

Boyce sipped and gossiped. Crime was a subject of mutual interest between lawmen and outlaw, if from different view-points. So there was much reminiscing about the gun slinging and banditry that gave the Lone Star State its continuing accent of notoriety. Ira noticed, however, that the guest was careful not to implicate himself in any flow of recollection, nor any other long rider about whom a fact mentioned was not general knowledge.

Rube was the smoothest bad man he had ever met, Ira thought. A man who made Sam Bass look like the crowing country boy Sam was.

After a while talk became concentrated on stage and train robberies. Rube Boyce helped himself to a second cup of coffee, then said in a voice whose matter-of-factness was edged with something else:

"Reckon the handiest bunch of stage histers was the one that robbed the coach at Pegleg Crossing nine times without being caught."

Ira almost jumped from the log where he was sitting. Memories swirled around him in an angry, churning fog. Recollections of those cold weeks and that mocking vigil when a Ranger patrol had kept searching, in stirrups caked with ice, for the Pegleg robbers. Other remembrances, too. The wheezing coughs of his comrades as they lay in their blankets on the frosty ground, sleeping in boots that didn't keep feet from freezing. The lonesomeness of the men for their girls in warm Uvalde. His own relief when he'd been given a rest from the howling "blue northers" to collect taxes on Devil's River.

And here, sitting carelessly before him, was the probable leader of the band that had given the Rangers such a futile, merry chase. Had Rube Boyce, from some safe hide-out, many times spied on his weary pursuers and had more enjoyment out of it than he was now getting from taunting Sheriff Shaw? Was this an extra little gloating game that he'd started with the Rangers?

With difficulty, Ira managed to restrain himself. "Yep, Rube," he said with forced unconcern. "Those fellows who kept sticking up that stage certainly knew their oats."

Ira had hoped to maneuver the outlaw into some slight boast, however indirect, that would lead eventually to an admission of the Pegleg robberies. Instead, Rube stood up, stretched his muscles, and yawned lazily.

"Well, good night, gents. I'm moseying on back to the little woman."

After the visitor had gone, a Ranger said laughingly, "Ira, he sprung your trap before you ever got it set."

Ira couldn't help but laugh, too. "Guess so, Charlie. And I can't figure what bait to put out next."

Next morning Ira went to court expecting that Rube Boyce would try the same sort of artful psychological mayhem on him that he was performing on Sheriff Shaw. The gunman had taken him down the night before in a rather pointed way. And foxing a Texas Ranger before a crowd of people would be a much greater coup than the wordless bulldozing of a small-town sheriff. Ira was wondering how he would thwart such a ribbing. But he was determined not to let himself be flustered as George Shaw had been.

To his astonishment, Rube saluted him with an admiring grin and a jovial wave of a hand. The baiting of the sheriff continued. That was now as much a routine of the trial as the pen scratchings of the court clerk and the wrangling of the lawyers. But whenever Rube's eyes rested on Ira or any other Ranger, his expression was one of friendliness and respect.

"Seems like old Rube's kind of cottoning to us," a Ranger commented during the noon recess. "But what a picnic he's having out of Sheriff Shaw."

"Yes," Ira answered quietly. "He hates the sheriff. And the sheriff's deathly afraid of him."

A night or two later a local citizen ran breathlessly into the Ranger camp and almost fell into the fire. Ira gave him a steadying hand. "What's the matter, friend?" he inquired.

"Rube Boyce is drunk and getting ready to shoot up a saloon!" the townsman panted. "For God's sake, stop him!"

The commander of the detail said, "That's Sheriff Shaw's job. We're here only on court duty."

The citizen gasped. "George Shaw would no more get through the door than Rube Boyce would drop him dead. And we don't want no decent folks killed by that goddamn gun slinger."

Four Rangers, including Ira, were assigned to quell Rube Boyce. The townsman led them to the saloon where Rube was making his ruckus, then bolted. Shots were echoing from inside the place. There came the sound of crashing glass as whisky bottles, used for targets, dropped in shattered pieces to the floor.

"Whoopee!" the Rangers heard Boyce yell. "This is a hell of a fine night! Hooray for hell, gentlemen!"

More shots—more bottles crashing—shouts of alarm from Rube's captive audience.

Ira addressed his fellow Rangers. "He's finally busted loose —he's hitting at this place to do in the sheriff. Two of us had better go in the back, two in front." And one of them, he said to himself, might be expected to die.

A pair of Rangers walked into the saloon from the back door. Ira and the fourth man strode through the front entrance. At that moment Rube Boyce thrust out a leg to kick over a gambling table. Poker chips and stacks of silver coins scattered across the floor. Gamesters took whatever cover they could find or sprawled quiveringly on the floor.

"Rube!" Ira called. Then again, sharply: "Rube!"

The gunman wheeled around drunkenly. His forty-five was bobbing in his right hand, but his grip firmed when he saw two Rangers standing there.

"H-mph!" he grunted. "Come for a fight? All right, by God, I'll drill both of you!"

Ira answered coolly, "You might drill one of us, Rube, but not two of us. The man left would fill you full of holes before you got in your second shot."

Rube stared at the wobbling gun in his right hand, then at the raised revolvers of the Rangers. Ira saw that he wanted to aim, but that whisky had fogged his vision. The terrified customers were taking advantage of his confusion by tearing through the doors.

Swiftly Ira reached out and grabbed the desperado's pistol. "You're under arrest, Rube. And if you'll look behind you, you'll see that you'd have had four men to kill."

Boyce jerked his head around to see the pair of Rangers who had entered from the rear. "Four men to kill," he repeated heavily, then slumped into the one chair his boot hadn't upset. "I was just having a little fun cleaning out this saloon. Take me home to my wife."

Ira leaned over the chair to search Boyce for more weapons, and found none. "We're not taking you home, Rube, but I'll let your wife know where you'll be. Come on."

Another Ranger helped the gunman to his feet. Ira placed Boyce's pistol in his own pocket. Escorted by two officers walking beside him and two behind, the bandit started toward the Llano jail.

The party had gone no more than a block when they ran into Sheriff Shaw and the sheriff's chief deputy. Boyce's hand reached quickly for the weapon that wasn't there. Then he brought his palm upward, his fingers twitching in the reflex action of a gun fighter who has been thwarted.

He looked hard at the county lawmen, then at the Rangers. "Six men to kill," he said in a hoarse whisper. "You devils framed this—"

Boyce didn't finish the sentence because Sheriff Shaw had reached out to grab him by the collar. "Damn you!" he shouted. "I'm going to tear you apart with my bare hands! I'm—"

Ira interrupted. "You're not going to do a damn thing to a man who's drunk and disarmed, Sheriff. Take your paws off of him."

He turned to the outlaw. "Rube, we four didn't bunch with these two as you think, but you're going to stand trial for what you did tonight." To the county officers he said curtly, "You fellows go on ahead to the jail. We'll bring Rube there."

At the jail, Ira sent a Ranger to inform Mrs. Boyce that her husband was being locked up. Then he laid down his own kind of law to Shaw, the lawman.

"This prisoner is under the protection of the Texas Rangers, Sheriff. Remember that after we leave him with you."

Next morning Sheriff Shaw triumphantly escorted Rube Boyce in handcuffs to the Llano justice of the peace. Suffering from hang-over and humiliation, Rube paid a large fine, then went home with his wife.

After that hectic night, Rube Boyce's game with the sheriff became a different one, with Llano's bedeviled law man gaining the upper hand. Rube stopped making his daily appearances in the district courtroom. From Sheriff Shaw's regular tormentor, he turned into the sheriff's regular guest. And by oddly contrasting circumstances, a Texas Ranger found himself being an instrument of mercy for Rube Boyce, the uproarious road agent, as he had been for Jim Epps, the penitent onetime offender.

An unwilling instrument, it was true, as Rube kept visiting Llano saloons to wreck them. When it came to the fundamental principles of law and order, Ira was unequivocally on the side of Sheriff Shaw and told the gunman so. But time after time Ira found himself intervening with Shaw for Rube's personal safety after delivering him into custody for hell raising.

"Aten," the sheriff snapped on one such occasion, "I don't like your interference. You Rangers are here today and gone tomorrow. But I have to put up with this rattler three hundred and sixty-five days a year—and he's a standing menace to the community."

Ira felt the sting of the rebuke and wondered what he would do if he were in George Shaw's place. But he had little time to grope with the question as he guarded the courtroom by day and curbed Rube's rampages by night.

Every other evening Rube Boyce blew up somewhere. The Rangers would find him standing in the middle of wreckage and liquor puddles yelling at the shaking customers:

"Help yourself, boys! Everything in this place is free!"

He gave the Rangers no resistance, except argument, whenever they came after him. But the saloonkeepers were protesting bitterly to Sheriff Shaw because evening trade was dwindling as patrons stayed safely at home. On alternate nights, when Rube was out of jail after paying his fine, he was always at the Ranger camp. There anybody whom his wife sent looking for him could always locate him.

"Rube," Ira commented one night, "I see your play now. You're trying to push Sheriff Shaw into a showdown."

Rube Boyce puffed on a corncob pipe and answered nothing.

"You've taken him down enough," Ira persisted. "If I was the sheriff here, you'd get that showdown."

Boyce knocked the ashes from his pipe. "Ira, that would be a fight between two real men," he answered gravely. "Sheriffs are hardly worth killing. They're just cowpunchers and plow pushers who've talked enough jaspers into voting for them."

After Boyce had left, Ira understood now why the desperado held George Shaw in contempt. Shaw rated as a pretty capable sheriff. But to Rube Boyce all local officers were so many glorified nincompoops. Outride them across a county line, and an outlaw could turn back to spit at them. Dependent they were on vote hustling, every two years, for their jobs. Else return to cowpunching at twenty dollars a month or plow pushing for even less.

Rangers were something else again. They represented that society of larger stature against which Rube Boyce, a desperado of stature, had declared war. They were men fit to be his opponents. Fit, too, for the occasional truces accorded between equals.

Under different circumstances, as Ira would say later, Rube Boyce "might have made a wonderful Ranger." He was "shrewd and cunning—and fearless." But other circumstances had molded him into something else—something no upholder of law could accept just because Boyce had an interesting tongue and an engaging jib.

Underneath it all the outlaw's friendliness with Rangers was only a truce. A foe he still was by definition—and in fact. But who and what was a modest Texan named Jim Epps?

A contrast between two men started Ira on comparisons of two counties. Llano County, where George Shaw tried to enforce the law, and Uvalde County, where Jim Epps tried to obey it.

Two ordinary, average counties they were, varying a little here and there because they were in opposite sections of the state. More than two hundred other such counties, with their individual peculiarities, made up Texas. County by county, since the days of the Lone Star Republic, regular or volunteer companies of Rangers had gradually brought law and order to the sprawling commonwealth.

They had done it, most often, with the help of average officers like George Shaw, who wrangled ballots. With the help, too, of average citizens such as Jim Epps, sometimes giving their votes to raise a man from plow pushing, sometimes withholding the decisive slips of paper to send him back.

Rube Boyce had no more respect for a ballot box than he had for another man's purse. By calculated taunts, he flouted George Shaw's authority in the sheriff's own courthouse. By calculated terror, he would grab Jim Epps's purse on a train or a stagecoach.

Epps had impulsively killed a love rival in Tennessee. Boyce had committed a more reprehensible crime when he killed his own brother-in-law in Kimble County. Yet that average man had finally returned and offered himself for trial. The smarter man had simply thumbed his nose at warrants to commit more planned infractions of the law.

"Jim Epps would have surrendered as peacefully to Sheriff Shaw as he did to us Rangers," Ira reflected. "But if sheriffs or Rangers go out to take Rube Boyce—*bang!*"

Appreciation of Jim Epps suddenly made Ira feel more respect for Sheriff Shaw.

"The sheriff's trouble with Rube Boyce is a lot more dangerous than the one between the Carters and Cogginses," Ira said worriedly to fellow Rangers. "They're finally submitting to law and settling their troubles in court. After we leave, Rube Boyce will stop paying those fines to the J. P. He'll kill Shaw, then lope away to take in more towns."

The Carter-Coggins trial was nearing its close. A wise district judge had done much poulticing of old sores as the proceedings had gone along peacefully under the watchful eyes of the Rangers. Both families, Ira knew, would go back to their ranches under agreements of peace that ordinary people generally kept.

But there was still the other feud. The one now involving only two men—yet that could have serious repercussions throughout Texas.

Ira feared there would be "a showdown shooting as sure as shooting" after the Rangers departed. Sheriff Shaw might be able to stand up to Rube Boyce because of the increased self-confidence gained from having had the outlaw in the lockup so many times. But the overwhelming probability was that Boyce, the professional trigger man, would rub out the country sheriff.

Only outlawry would gain if that happened. Gain everywhere in Texas. Once more Ira, as in the Epps case, gave himself a personal and private assignment. It was to stop the two-man feud before leaving Llano County.

The evening came when Ira knew that the Rangers would be making their last arrest of Rube Boyce. The usual call came from some townsman for what the rest of the detail was beginning to call "the Boyce squad." With the same three men who had gone with him the first time, Ira went to a saloon to pull out the roisterer.

Two behind, two ahead as usual, the Rangers began marching Boyce along the street. Again they met the sheriff and his deputy. The outlaw, reekingly drunk, began spitting oaths at Shaw. This time the county lawman lost all self-control.

He jerked out his pistol and struck Boyce's skull with the barrel. The full force of the blow was warded off by one of the Rangers raising his arm quickly, but blood flowed from a gash in Boyce's scalp to pour down the outlaw's face.

"Damn it!" Boyce bellowed. "You're the first man who ever buffaloed me and you'll be the last." All four Rangers tussled with him as he tried to get at Shaw. The sheriff swung the pistol again. Two Rangers pulled the cursing bandit out of his reach. The other two grabbed Shaw by the arms.

"Mr. Sheriff," one of them said, "you must not interfere with our prisoners. When we put a man in jail, he is *your* prisoner, and not until then."

The pair led Shaw down the street. Boyce was later taken to jail. Next morning he silently paid his fine, his wife there as usual to lead him home. All day long Ira felt a glum sense of futility as he conjectured what must be shaping up.

Rube Boyce was not one to take a pistol whipping from another man. Shaw's ill-advised action had canceled any chance of avoiding that showdown. The outlaw would demand an accounting.

On the night after the buffaloing Rube Boyce made another visit to the Ranger camp. His head was bandaged and smelling of strong salve.

"Hear you boys will be pulling out in a couple of days," he said. "Thought I'd drop over to have a last smoke and say good-by."

"Better not say good-by, Rube," Ira responded; "if you kill George Shaw, we'll be looking for you. And we'll find you."

Rube rolled a cigarette. His tense lips barely moistened the paper. Crumbs of tobacco flittered down on his trousers.

"Hell," he mumbled disgustedly, "I'm sure losing my grip." He jammed the sack of Bull Durham into his shirt pocket, then announced:

"I'm not drawing on George Shaw."

Ira gaped in astonishment at Boyce. What was going on in that smart, bruised head?

Rube tossed a pebble at a scavenging field mouse. "I know what you boys are thinking," he said pensively. "That somebody the Rangers ran so long was just a tinhorn and not worth all the bronc dust. That it just took one taste of George Shaw's gun butt to make me call calf rope." The bandit was having trouble explaining himself to his equals. "It wasn't old George who laid down the law to me—'cause he ain't much law. 'Twas my wife."

The Rangers were silent. A man's relationship with his wife was his own business. You didn't pick him about it.

"Yeh," Rube continued. "After she put this bandage on, she told me I was gonna be a daddy."

"A daddy!" Ira repeated in amazement. Somehow a man who had robbed stagecoaches didn't stack up as a proper father. Then, recovering himself: "That's good, Rube. Congratulations."

The outlaw had that sheepish grin of all expectant fathers. "Yep! Told me, too, that kid wasn't gonna live on the run like its folks. Said she was fed up to the craw on running. On running and on waiting, like she did those years I was in Mexico."

Rube Boyce rolled another smoke in hands now growing steady. He blew a slow, twining column of smoke from his nostrils before speaking again.

"You can't blame her. I reckon you can push a gun till you're dead. But you can push a woman just so far."

A Ranger asked tactfully, "Now that you're settling down, Rube, how do you intend to make a living for your family?"

Boyce removed the cigarette, holding it crosswise between two fingers. "Same way I've been doing lately—flipping the cards. She's not gee-hawing me on that so long as I don't play a six-shooter for trumps."

Smart gal, Ira thought. A woman, tired of running, might lure a maverick into a sort of working domesticity. But she didn't try to pen him up with a humdrum trade. Not unless she wanted to push him back into the brakes and the dry gulches.

"You know," Boyce observed, "a wife is like a bird mating. She'll fly fast with you for a long time. Then she starts picking up straws for a nest."

His eyes flickered slightly toward Ira. The Ranger caught the message emphasizing the pledge that the outlaw was giving with his lips:

"If it hadn't been for you boys, George Shaw might have done me in last night. After you go, there won't be any shoot-ing—not if George Shaw don't pick one to save his ugly face."

Ira arose from the campfire. "He won't, Rube. I'll see to that. You stay here till I get back."

Ira saddled his horse and rode into town. As he dis-mounted before the barred jailhouse, he was wondering what he would say to the local lawman.

He tied the horse to a metal stake in front of the structure. He'd just tell him that he ought to call it square with a family man named Rube Boyce, like Ira had with a family man named Jim Epps.

Epps was a good citizen. Boyce never would be much more than a hobbled maverick.

But even a maverick took care of its young, Ira reckoned.

⣿⣿⣿⣿⣿

The Killing of Jack the Ripper

¶ *"Jack the Ripper" was an Arizona gunman who was bound to get paid off in his own hot-lead coin sooner or later. Fortunately for posterity, his sanguinary end was ob-served by a literate bystander who thoughtfully recorded a straightforward account of it.*

IT WAS on the day before Thanksgiving in 1906 that I reached Benson from Boston on my way to Mazatlan, Sinaloa. As the

From *Arizona, A State Guide*. Copyright 1940 by The Arizona State Col-lege at Flagstaff; 1956 by Hastings House, Publishers.

northern terminus of the railroad to Guaymas, the only gateway into Old Mexico on the west coast, Benson's trade with Mexico was enormous. Cowboys, miners, Mexicans, and Chinamen filled the town streets. Saloons abounded, and gamblers were plentiful.

All the railroad trains to Mexico were tied up. At the time I arrived there was a strike on the line. As a result of this delay Benson hotels had filled up with bankers, drummers, mining men, and Mexicans bound southward. Since there were no theaters, automobiles, movies, or Y.M.C.A. building, these strangers, in accordance with the custom of the day, naturally gravitated to the saloons. One such place opposite the railroad station was the principal gathering point. Its bar was on the left as you entered. On the right was a roulette wheel, next a big cast-iron stove, then a couple of card tables, and at the far end an old piano. An immense coal-oil lamp suspended from the ceiling near the front of the room was the main source of illumination. A small oil lamp on the piano relieved the darkness of the rear.

The place was owned by Jesse Fisher and the principal bartender, who also acted as croupier and card dealer in emergencies, was a character well known in southern Arizona as Jack the Ripper. His real name was unknown to most people. If you wished to attain a ripe old age, you did not ask people questions concerning their names. The etiquette of those days was very strict on this point.

Each new train left additions to the stranded crowd, and Thanksgiving Eve found a hilarious bunch recklessly playing the games and drinking in Fisher's place. Several "hostesses," a common saloon feature of the times, added to the liveliness. Thanksgiving Day came, and still no Mexican train service. Jack the Ripper ran the roulette wheel that morning. The play was quite heavy but about one in the afternoon most of the patrons left to enjoy their Thanksgiving turkey, and the games closed temporarily. I remember Fisher and Jack checking up the roulette wheel then. First they put the money representing the bank—in other words, the money backing the table—into one canvas sack. The rest was the house winnings or profit for the morning. This counted up to $612. Fisher put this into another sack, except for the odd $12,

which he shoved over to Jack as a tip or extra fee for his expert handling of the crowd and table. Jack was dissatisfied.
"Hell, twelve dollars is damn little for making you six hundred dollars in only a few hours—you're stingy," he said to
Fisher. He repeated this several times, but otherwise did not
seem very sore, and a few hours later he and Fisher left together for their Thanksgiving dinner, leaving a bartender in
charge. They returned around six o'clock, both very friendly,
although it was apparent that they had taken some liquid
refreshment with their meal.

More trains had passed through in the meantime. The
crowd was larger, all the games were running, someone continually banged on the tinny piano and some of the hostesses
tried to sing. It rapidly developed into a large night. Spurred
and armed cowboys entered, just arrived from their ranches,
and in accordance with the Arizona law that required guns to
be removed within thirty minutes after reaching town, they
gave their forty-fives to the bartender and then danced with
their spurs on. Arizona-wise drummers drank just enough to
get comfortably litup in a sociable way, and then drank
enough to stay in that mellow condition. One immaculately
dressed Easterner held aloof from the rest of the crowd, drinking only a little wine occasionally. We thought him somewhat snobbish, and speculated whether or not he were a
preacher, until he suddenly slapped a couple of twenty-dollar
gold pieces on the bar, collected all the hostesses, and invited
the whole house up to have a drink. Gold and silver were the
only mediums of exchange in those days, and anything
smaller than a two-bit piece was absolutely unknown in these
parts.

I sat on a stool in back of the roulette wheel taking it all in.
It was vastly different from anything I had ever seen or heard
of in Boston. Occasionally I bought a cigar or put a few chips
on the roulette game to pay the house for the space I was
occupying. It was a bitterly cold night outside, and the hotel
rooms were bare and cheerless. Everyone was in a good-
natured mood. Several rich landowners from the interior of
Mexico were present. They seemed to turn up their noses at
our American whisky. Not being able to get their native
mescal, anything short of sulphuric acid was tasteless to them.

Fisher, the owner, drank but little. He had to keep order. I remember his telling one of the girls she had better wear longer dresses when she appeared on the streets, lest she get the whole outfit in bad with the law. I looked—the girl's dress was actually a full five inches from the floor! The only discordant element was Jack the Ripper. Every time he passed near Fisher, he would mutter "stingy."

The drinks flew around faster. Soon a rather large hostess was sitting on the knees of a little bandy-legged cowpuncher, telling him her troubles. The Mexican grandees started playing the wheel in a big way. They selected a few numbers and piled the limit on each. Had any of those numbers ever come up the Mexicans would have been the new owners of the saloon, wheel and all.

At last I decided to retire. Everyone was getting woozy and the hour was late. As I started for the door I was startled by seeing Jack the Ripper produce the house gun, a big forty-five, from behind the bar. Like a chump I stopped to see what he was going to do. A few others saw him at the same time. They were more experienced. Those that could threw themselves down in front of the bar out of his sight. "Bang" went the Colt. The bullet shot out the big coal-oil lamp, causing semi-darkness. I made one grand dive for that cast-iron stove. If there had been anything larger near, I would have selected it. As fast as I was, a New York drummer was faster. He got there first and calmly tossed me back. One glance at the doorway showed me I was too late there also. It was jammed to the top. About twenty men had tried to go out at once, and they appeared piled up there like cord wood. "Bang" went the Colt again, and the chimney of the small lamp at the rear crashed. I made a second dive for the stove, but the big-nosed drummer repelled me. Again the Colt spoke, then a man yelled and another gun joined in. It spat a fusillade, and by the sing of its slugs I knew it to be a Luger automatic, a new type of gun just appearing in Arizona at that time. Burnt powder smoke filled my nostrils. This was plainly no time to fool around without cover. Remembering my football training, I tackled low and hard and heaved the drummer into the open where he began to squeal like a stuck pig. Then I took his place behind the stove. Unless you have been in a similar situation, you will never appreciate the beauty and advantages of a big old-fashioned coal-oil burner over the little tin heater of today.

The Colt spoke again, and the Luger soon answered with a second volley. Evidently its owner had slipped in another clip. Then I noted that each "zing" of the Luger was accompanied by an ominous "zip," sounding pretty much like when you shoot into a wild bull.

By the noise from the rear I knew the door there was also jammed. There was no more shooting and the front door was soon cleared of its human dam. Not knowing exactly what might happen next and fearing the guns were simply being reloaded, I leaped outside and then stopped, standing as close to the building as I could and right beside the doorway. I correctly guessed that the near-by doorways were already filled with my late companions, who would probably welcome me much as the drummer had.

From the time the Colt was first fired, until the last Luger slug "zinged," I do not think more than twenty seconds elapsed. There must have been a full moon, for outside it was almost as light as day. There was no more shooting. Everything grew deathly quiet. I was the only person in sight on the main street. Soon a few cautious heads appeared above a stone wall across the road that separated the highway from the railroad grounds. The doorways around disgorged their occupants. Townspeople appeared and soon a great crowd collected. I turned my head before they arrived and cautiously looked inside. The interior was quite dim. The crazy little lamp on the piano was smoking badly and giving a little light, its smashed chimney strewn over the top of the piano. The moonlight helped me to see that Jack the Ripper was still at the bar, seemingly leaning over it on both elbows. As I looked, he slumped over backward to the floor.

It happened that Harry Wheeler, then a lieutenant of the Arizona Rangers, was in town. He appeared and took charge of the proceedings. An inquest was immediately held. Then we learned that the user of the Luger automatic was Jesse Fisher. With his left hand he was holding on to the place below and behind his left hip where Jack's third shot had punctured him. It was only a flesh wound, though rather inconvenient. Jack the Ripper was dead. Fisher stated that when the Ripper shot out the lights he thought it was simply friendly fun, but when the third shot stung him where it did he felt he must stop the racket lest Jack hurt some one else. Of course all the other witnesses corroborated Fisher and he was freed on the spot. All the Luger slugs hit Jack's breast and a silver dollar would have covered the place where most of them entered. They made one big hole right through his body. Pretty good shooting in the dark!

Late the next morning I went down town—to find business going on as usual. A new bartender was on duty in Fisher's saloon. Hardly a word did I hear anywhere about the shooting of the night before. The Benson of those days had seen too many saloon killings to become excited over this little affray.

❧❧❧❧❧❧❧

Pocket History of a Bad Man's Progress

BY PAT JAHNS

¶ *John H. ("Doc") Holliday built up a fearsome reputation as a coldblooded killer, always ready to pit his gun skill against that of any or all comers. Seldom was he called upon to measure up to that malign reputation, which perhaps was just as well for him, for—in the words of biographer Pat Jahns—Doc was "a rotten shot." The only man he ever killed was Tom McLowry, who caught a blast from Doc's shotgun during that famous and disputed fracas at Tomb-*

From *The Frontier World of Doc Holliday.* Copyright © 1957 by Pat Jahns.

stone's O.K. Corral (described in the "Fact and Legend" section of this book). Doc deliberately fed the popular belief in his own deadliness, sneering as he did so at the human race, venting on it the hatred he felt for himself. He was a semitragic figure, wracked by disease, punishing the bottle both to keep going and to forget the failures and frustrations that dogged him, seeking some kind of twisted fulfillment in a barren world.

The boy who was to become Doc Holliday, one of the West's most notorious bad men, was born and raised in Georgia. He attended a dental school in Baltimore and when he returned home he had, besides a dentist's degree, chronic pulmonary tuberculosis (then called "consumption"). A physician gave him six months to live . . . perhaps a couple of years if he'd move to a high, dry climate. So young John said good-by to his family and to the girl he loved, his cousin Mattie Holliday, and rode the trains and the boats to Dallas, where he began to practice his profession in partnership with an older dentist, and to develop the twin proficiencies at card-playing and whisky-drinking that were to mark his career. He lived for fifteen years, a semi-tragic figure, sometimes a sodden wreck, at others a brooding misanthrope, occasionally a charming companion. Here his biographer, Pat Jahns, picks up his trail in Dallas. . . .

JULIAN BOGEL's "swell" saloon began to see a lot of Dr. Holliday. The days were slipping past, faster than he had ever imagined that time could go, with the inevitable end moving swiftly, if silently, toward him. If one could not bear it, one could forget it. Dr. Holliday was no saint, no soul of iron. He could not bear it.

Nobody knew what to do for consumption but everybody had a suggestion. Five-mile walks twice a day, each followed by a cold bath, at least had the advantage of cutting short a painful existence. The patent medicines of the day stopped all the pain and left you feeling tip-top, but also a drug addict; this complicated matters dreadfully when it came to making out the death certificate. Many doctors prescribed whisky for relaxing the tension and gloom which are such unfavorable attitudes in consumptives, cheerfulness and a hopeful outlook being half the cure. Consequently the papers were flooded with whisky ads, recommending the purely medicinal value of their product. "Positively guaranteed to cure consumption," the distillers boasted. "We have thousands of testimonial letters in our files." Whether large quantities of whisky will cure anything but sobriety is not for persons outside the medical profession to argue, surely. Something, we are not sure what, arrested (for a while unknown to him) the progress of Dr. Holliday's chronic pulmonary tuberculosis. At any rate, he became a heavy drinker.

All of the actions of "Doc" Holliday, starting here in Dallas and continuing to his death from what had in the last days become the miliary type of tuberculosis, show the behavior pattern of alcoholism. The disappointments and insecurity which he had known in his childhood were climaxed by the shock of finding himself to be dying; all this resulted in a personality maladjustment, a neurosis, in the inability to live with the real Dr. Holliday. When drunk as a skunk he was another person, a person he could bear to be. Sober, he was as mean as all hell, hating himself and everybody else.

It didn't come all at once. He was a respected businessman in Dallas for some time and only slowly slid into the half-world of the saloons and gambling halls, maintaining a footing in both camps almost until the last. The nights were so dreadful: the pain, the imagined horrors, the fear, the tossing and coughing, staring at the blackness of despair. He had to forget, and since the nights were the worst he began to spend them quietly drinking himself into amiability. There were the friendly girls in the cribs and the jolly girls in the honky tonks; there was the burlesque-show atmosphere of the variety show and the blood-and-thunder dramas at Field's Opera House. There was in a quiet corner of every gambling house the mainstay of the business, the faro bank. . . . He was known as a gambling man and a steady drinker. His personality began to warp more and more; he became increasingly untrustworthy, untruthful, unpredictable and uncaring about his reputation—glossing over his behavior as if he thought himself invisible. His irritability when sober exploded into violent swearing outbursts when he was crossed by anyone. Daily his attitude toward responsibility faded. Sick mentally as well as physically, he was content to live his life at night in the saloons, the gambling hells, the honky-tonks and the disorderly houses in the southwestern part of town.

In such surroundings most men possessed a gun. Dr. Holliday's was probably the popular single-action Colt 1873 model, caliber .45. This was the famous "Peacemaker," and despite a hammer-fall that practically knocked the gun out of your hand, it was widely used and prized for being rugged, dependable and far-shooting. If you had a grip of iron you could even hit objects with it. Shooting, that is. In the longer barrel-lengths, of course, it did make a dandy bludgeon. But Dr. Holliday probably had his cut off short for hiding, which could help explain even better than the heavy hammer-fall some of his remarkable feats of shooting.

Sometimes he would help out his gambling friends by dealing faro for them. (The professional gambler as a rule *dealt* faro and *played* poker.) His attention was so completely taken up with watching the betting, taking in the money and paying it out that, even with the aid of the lookout and the guy on the hearse, he had not a second to think of himself. If he made a mistake in favor of the house there was a loud angry scene, which gave the bank a bad name. If he made a mistake in favor of the players, the owner of the bank might clobber him one with a spittoon, just as a hint not to do it again. Dr. Holliday, not being one to take anything off of anybody, had built his house on a volcano. The house of counted days. . . .

At last the two years were up.

He was living on borrowed time—but behold the tragicomic picture, the dying youth, the fair-haired boy pursued by a cruel fate. Only he doesn't die. The new days keep right on showing up; they are going to for years yet. But he doesn't know it. He doesn't know that he has been, as it were, reprieved. And at last his nerve breaks. It is New Year's Day, 1875.

"Dr. Holliday and Mr. Austin, a saloon-keeper, relieved the monotony of the noise of fire-crackers by taking a couple of shots at each other yesterday afternoon. The cheerful note of the peaceful six-shooter is heard once more among us. Both shooters were arrested." So the *Dallas Herald* of January 2, 1875, chronicles Dr. Holliday's sole shooting scrape in Dallas. The paper makes it out a piddling affair and doubtless its only result was that Dr. Holliday, his poor reputation now completely ruined, was requested by the law to make himself scarce. At any rate, he left town pronto, because in less than two weeks he was in jail again, this time in the little log hoosegow in Fort Griffin, Texas.

The friends he had, gamblers, saloonkeepers, bunco-steerers, prostitutes, familiarly called him Doc. He belonged to their world, particularly since his arrest. He was, in this January of 1875, twenty-three years old, of average height, very thin, very pale, with blond hair, blue eyes that some-times seemed gray, and had an expression of constrained emo-tion—sometimes sorrow, sometimes petulance, sometimes rage. He spoke with a soft southern accent, dressed with ex-treme neatness and cleanness, and was, in this age of mag-nificent beards, clean-shaven except for a blond handlebar mustache. He appeared to be a gentleman and indeed, when stoked to the gills with the demon rum, his manner was pleas-ant and refined. Then he was feeling no pain, in every mean-ing of the phrase. When he was dead sober the tense nerves stretched through him so tautly that the most ordinary of experiences sandpapered him raw in a second and he fought back with virulently expressed hatred for everything and everybody. Just to keep matters straight, he managed to stay pleasantly soaked most of the time.

Being a small railroad town of average size for a farm and ranch trading center of the times, Dallas had its gossip and its social frame into which everyone fitted. Consequently, no one was surprised when Doc finally got into a shooting scrape; it had been expected for months. Now he was not wanted in Dallas: he was a trouble-maker and a souse. He'd been in one shooting scrape and no one knew when he'd succeed in kill-ing someone. Neither did they see why it should happen in Dallas. Such things were bad for business.

Doc had seen the mile-long ox trains stacked high with buffalo hides come rolling into Dallas from Fort Griffin. He had heard that it was hell-on-the-border, that anything went.

That the hunters and skinners threw away their money like water when they hit civilization again after weeks in the wilds.

Fort Griffin was the southern metropolis of the buffalo hunters. Acres of drying hides sent up a stench that marked the town like a beacon for miles and gave the local goings-on a peculiar flavor and gustiness. Conrad's Gen'l Merchandise did a land-office business in ammunition and supplies for the hunters, and a dozen saloons, most of them with a dance hall or honky-tonk attached, supplied anything else that might be desired. One of the last of the great cattle trails, known locally as the Dodge City trail, ran from Bandera, Texas, through Fort Griffin, to Doan's Crossing on the Red River, to Camp Supply on the north fork of the Canadian River in Indian Territory, to Dodge. Only Fort Griffin could call itself a town along the way, and many of the trail bosses outfitted there entirely or in part. All summer long the herders fogged in to see a real live town and have a drink if nothing else. In keeping with the "wild" west character of the town, an army post was located within whooping distance.

When Doc came rolling in on the stage he saw a bunch of unpretentious frame and adobe buildings and piles of buffalo hides scattered among the cottonwoods beside the Clear Fork of the Brazos River. A bluff rose immediately behind this little flat and on top of it was situated the army post for which the village was named. Only the year before Shackleford County had come into being and control had passed out of the hands of the army. A gang of toughs, gamblers, skin-game operators, prostitutes and drifters had immediately set up business in town and was flourishing mightily.

Doc found a prosperous-looking spot and went to work. No more the fancy plush chair with the adjustable head and foot rest, no more the finicky drilling, no more the hard labor of extraction. There remained the professional manner. He did his day's work at a round wooden table under a hanging kerosene lamp, sitting on an uncomfortable straight wooden chair that helped keep him alert, watching the cards, the faces, the hands; concentrating; coughing.

Men standing behind the players, watching, were expected not to crowd close, not to talk, and not to give the hands away;

no interruptions to the game were permitted. Three-card draw, jacks or better, was the usual type of poker played. A houseman dealt but did not play, taking a percentage of each pot for the house. If everything was perfectly square and aboveboard, the suckers as a rule still got taken, by their own stupidity.

There would have been playing this winter other professional gamblers, hunters and skinners, soldiers from the fort, ranchers and herders from nearby, and perhaps the fabulous Lottie Deno.

Away from the quiet of the poker tables and the faro bank, making a background of gayety and liveliness, was the honky-tonk where, upon a small stage, appeared such variety acts as could be lured into the wilderness, and where pretty girl hostesses circulated among the customers, urging them to buy drinks at the bar that ran down one side of the room. The variety acts were of the not-good-but-loud type: the constant pratfall, the clumsily-contrived local joke. A chubby blonde in tights prances out to wring her hands through "Lorena," "I'll Remember You, Love, in My Prayers" and "Silver Threads among the Gold." A dapper fellow of the comic persuasion follows, distributing his humor to all fields in turn; the army joke, the one about how the buffalo skinner stinks, one about the most popular man in town and one about Grant's administration, interspersed with dirty jokes of the less subtle sort. Somebody does a clog—expertly dodging the missiles thrown by boys who want to see girls. The blonde hastily reappears minus part of her costume and her former look of pain, but no one cares. The riot at least temporarily averted, a blueshirt yells, "Harrigan and Hart!" another, "The Mulligan Guard!" The professor at the piano rips into "The Regular Army O" and all is joy on the Clear Fork of the Brazos.

After the soldiers finished celebrating the last chorus of their favorite song, a hit from one of the many New York stage successes by Harrigan and Hart, the dump had indeed livened up. Ed Harrigan's "Muldoon, The Solid Man" followed, a song which was known the world over and gave "the solid Muldoon" to the language of the times. Then the party began to get rough, "Sweet Evalina" being sung in its original off-color version, "Marriage Bells," the sporting-house anthem, being delivered, the can-can danced with whoops resembling the battle cry of the Comanches, a drunk being dissuaded from reciting "Thanatopsis," and an impromptu bottle-throwing contest coming off.

In the dance hall next door a hunter and a soldier fell to blows over one of the female entertainers and proceeded to wreck the surroundings pretty thoroughly before being chucked out. Shots resounded from the gun of a drunken herder who knew of no other way to express his emotions. A peal of giggles rang through the night, there was a scurry of running feet, a lamp crashed. . . .

At this time the legitimate merchants were still making plenty of money, with bacon, for instance, seventy-five cents a pound. But soon the herds would be killed off and the buffalo hunters would vanish, the Indians would be pacified and the forts abandoned, the easy money and the gamblers would be gone—and only the respectable ranchers and farmers would be left.

While Doc had apparently drawn to a pair of deuces and filled in the health game, his luck was lousy in other quarters. He must have arrived in Fort Griffin in time to coincide with one of their morality campaigns. And, since news of shootings travelled so fast in these dull times, the Fort Griffinites knew they had a potential killer on their hands and didn't want him any more than Dallas did, so they gave him a boot on his way. At any rate, he was indicted by the Grand Jury on January 12, 1875, for "gaming in a saloon," along with Hurricane Bill, Liz, Etta, Kate, *et al.*, charged with keeping a disorderly house, and flung into Fort Griffin's tiny log jail. This is precisely the reception a person with a reputation as a gun-punk and a hard drinker could expect in any community, west, east, up or down, for a choice in locations. It was necessary to be wicked in a certain way, to have a flair. Sin was a business in which he did not have an "in." So, being himself and thoughtful instead of emotional about such matters, he put up bail, hopped the first stage out of town, and was never seen in that particular hell-on-the-border again.

From Fort Griffin, Doc went to Denver and, under the alias of Tom McKey, was soon set up as an expert faro dealer. After flings in Cheyenne and Deadwood, he returned to Denver but business was slow and he decided to move to that talked-about, booming trail town, Dodge City, "where the money was." There, again J. H. Holliday, he registered at the Dodge House and immediately became a regular at Luke Short's Long Branch saloon. Before long, he was on intimate terms with the Mastersons, Ed and Bat, and with Wyatt Earp and his brothers. There, too, Doc met Big Nosed Kate Elder, the beginning of a long and turbulent affair. . . .

Down at the Comique the two warring factions in Dodge (that is, the saloon-gambling-policeman crowd versus their customers) met on an equal footing. By the time the festivities got rolling the heat of the day had worn off, the plains' little evening breeze had sprung up, the stars were out in thick, bright clusters, and the coyotes had started their nightly concert consisting of variations on the theme, "Yap! Grrrr!"

Now the ladies of the evening blossomed, the painted prostitute, the professional dancing partner, the kids out for a good time, the common sporting girl. Doc couldn't bear the sight of pretty little blonde girls with their faces painted and their legs showing. In fact he was so rude to them that he completely gave away his secret attachment to someone who in a way resembled them. One of the faded *nymphs du pavé,* as the *Times* has it, was named Katherine Elder. She was so little faded that you hardly noticed it, being quite young, and was a tall, big-boned, buxom brunette with a nose so determined and handsome that she was known to her cronies in the cribs as Big Nosed Kate. None of that crowd was noted for delicacy of manner, and being no exception herself, Kate didn't let it hurt her feelings. She took one look at Doc and his air of class, the anguish deep in his eyes, and let out a yell of delight. He couldn't fight her off and she drove him to distraction. Every place he went there she was with a hungry look and hands she couldn't keep off of him. His friend Wyatt Earp advised him to belt her one, that was the way he treated these floozies, but Doc only coughed dejectedly. She'd likely cool him off with a right to the choppers if she got the idea she didn't have a chance.

There is a fine story about Doc and Kate, having to do with his killing a man over a game of cards in Fort Griffin and being incarcerated in a hotel room because the town had no jail. Since his victim was quite popular locally Doc was soon nominated by a group of irate miners for the job of becoming trimming on a tree. Before they could find a rope, Kate set fire to the back of the hotel and when everyone rushed to fight the fire she stuck up Doc's guards and rescued him. They hid out in some willows by the river until evening, when a friend brought them horses and clothes.

Well, Doc was wanted in Fort Griffin and would hardly have gone back there just to tempt fate; the town had a very sturdy log jail in which Doc had roomed and boarded long enough to cure him of wanting a return engagement; there were no mines anywhere around, though to be perfectly fair, there could have been a convention of miners meeting in Fort Griffin at the time of Doc's alleged second visit; but a twelve-year-old female child brought up in that area could have tracked the fugitives to their lair in the willows if they had really been there and memorized her Sunday school lesson at the same time. To add to the confusion, I found hints and rumors and half-remembered stories which variously placed the affair in Caldwell, Kansas, Hunnewell, Kansas, and at last, as having happened to a couple of other people.

Kate had certain charms—a true and loving heart, a ready laugh, no brains to perturb her with weighty problems, a fine, healthy body, a marvelous vocabulary of cuss words, and a deep and abiding fondness for cheap whisky. Perhaps the most attractive thing about her to Doc was her very coarseness and vulgarity, a surface quality so different from the memory in his heart that no shameful emotions choked him when he saw her.

One night, they say, he felt so bad that nothing could do him any good. He had to go to bed before his customary dawn. It wasn't that his consumption was worse; it was the black depths of depression that made him feel as if he were losing his mind. The loneliness and despair crushed him. The knowledge of Mattie's prayers and trust could not stop the shaking; whisky only made him sick. It was a violent reaction to his way of life. He lay on his bed staring at hell from the empty blackness of space, it seemed; alone, alone, alone. . . .

Came a knock at the door.

Doc cursed the knocker fluently and coldly.

A succession of blows shook the door in its frame.

Doc went off into a violent coughing spell. His hands jerked so that he could hardly get the lamp lit. The banging on his door continued. Just as he got the chimney rattled back on the lamp and was catching his breath after damn near choking to death, the flimsy lock gave.

Kate bounded into the room, a big Colt gun in her hand, yelling that Doc was a lousy son of a bitch for treating her the way he did and she was going to fill him so full of holes he wouldn't float in brine. Wherewith she punctured the mattress in his immediate vicinity with a .45 caliber slug.

Doc arose in his wrath and a long white night shirt. Fortunately Kate was so blind drunk she couldn't exactly tell where he was but she kept on trying to locate him with a bullet. He clobbered her one aside the head with nearly three pounds of .45-caliber Colt hastily snatched up from beside his bed, and rather put his heart in it.

Kate came to feeling sober and sorry and very fragile—and lying on Doc's bed with a wet towel on her head. The door was braced with a chair and the hullabaloo in the hall was dying down as irate patrons of Deacon Cox's hostelry went back to bed somewhat disgruntled with Dr. Holliday and his friends. Kate snuggled down in bed and grinned at Doc. He stood by the lamp for a long minute looking down at her and then swiftly bent over and blew out the light. . . .

Doc and Kate were not seen again until late the following afternoon, by which time they looked fully as bushed as before, but a great deal happier about everything. In fact, they gave a rosy glow to the dust and shabbiness of Front Street as they walked along the warped board sidewalk. They moved into one of the shanties in Tin Pot Alley, a hotel du dive, as the phrase-coining *Times* put it, supposedly located between 2nd and 3rd. Fortunately one of Kate's redeeming characteristics was a passion for personal cleanliness and a love of neat

surroundings, so their one room, with a lean-to kitchen attached and separate outhouse, was in the best Dodge tradition, ratty outside and cosy inside, and that was all right with
Doc.

This little love nest was a nine-day wonder. Doc had made
plenty of money all summer and while he was usually cautious with his spending, now he proceeded to deck Kate out
like a lady. She was probably scornful of the clothes he had
made for her as being too refined; she would have liked red
satin so she could lord it over the tarts in the red-light district
by posing as a wealthy kept woman.

But dressed or undressed, she was still Big Nosed Kate.
After a while Doc's drink-numbed conscience came to life. He
didn't love Kate and he despised himself for needing her so
badly that he couldn't leave her. He took out on her all the
repressed hatred he felt toward life for killing him so slowly
and disgustingly, for making him a weakling whose manhood
had to hide behind the cardboard demon of homicidal mania.
He would never even have looked at her if she had had any of
Mattie's characteristics, and yet he cursed her for being trash.
He told her what he thought about the flashy gewgaws with
which she cheapened her appearance, about her uneducated
speech, her vulgar mannerisms, about her charming friends
like Hop Fiend Nell and Highpockets and Big Em, and, worst
of all, about her pretensions to gentility. Quite naturally Kate
would get a little upset over such remarks and not having
been brought up to repress her feelings, would let fly at Doc
with anything handy. Their relationship was more inclined
to be off than on. Doc would move back into the Dodge
House until the storm was over, Kate would break up some
more of the furniture and go on a prolonged bat, but before
long they would be back together.

*Somehow, Doc and Wyatt Earp became inseparable friends,
always together; however, when Wyatt pulled stakes for Arizona, Doc stayed put in Dodge, with Kate Elder. He played
his chosen bad-man role to the hilt, running a bartender out
of town, promising to kill him on sight. But the trail-herd
crowd was getting tame, Dodge seemed to be slowing up.
Wyatt wrote from Tombstone, urging Doc to hurry there for*

rich pickings. Bat Masterson and Luke Short were on hand already. As soon as he made a good stake at the poker tables, Doc headed southwest. Kate went with him, having threatened to kill herself and him both if he didn't take her along.

The big news on July 2, 1881, was the shooting of newly-elected President Garfield. Not to be outdone, Tombstone came up with a shooting the following day, a diarist describing it: "Carleton shot Diss, probably mortally . . . all a bad crowd. Diss has bro't it all on himself. Mrs. Carleton the cause." It rained on the Fourth of July, and Doc and Kate had a knock-down, drag-out fight for variation on the usual theme of what to do on a rainy afternoon.

They had had fights aplenty, but this was the worst. This was the end of everything between them, Doc swore. He packed up and moved into the Cosmopolitan, leaving Kate to break up the furniture. But Kate realized that this time he meant it. The fire was out. He looked at her with cold dislike and not the blind rage that would dissolve into one of those cosy affairs of reconciliation to which she was so partial. Instead of breaking up the furniture as usual, she began to tell her woes to anyone who would listen, the while liberally soothing her bruised feelings with a stoneware bottle of gin. One very interested party heard her slobberings and decided to do something to even up old scores.

The *Daily Nugget* for July 6, 1881, carried: "Court Proceedings. United States vs. John H. Holliday. For attempt to rob U.S. Mail at the time of killing Budd Philpot; awaiting examination. Territory vs. John H. Holliday. On charge of murder of Budd Philpot. Continued to July 6, at 9 a.m. Bonds, $5,000." In another column: "Important Arrest. A warrant was sworn out yesterday before Judge Spicer for the arrest of Doc. Holliday, a well-known character here, charging him with complicity in the murder of Budd Philpot, and the attempted stage robbery near Contention some months ago, and he was arrested by Sheriff Behan. The warrant was issued upon the affidavit of Kate Elder, with whom Holliday has been living for some time past. Holliday was taken before Justice Spicer in the afternoon, who released him upon bail in the amount of $5,000, Wyatt Earp, J. Meagher, and J. H.

Melgren becoming sureties. The examination will take place before Judge Spicer at 9 o'clock this morning."

Doc was probably interspersing his cursing with "Hell hath no fury like a woman scorned," as a triumphant Sheriff Behan conducted him to jail. Out on bail he no doubt turned his attentions to Kate again. She explained that she didn't remember what she had done that night; she had just been drinking with Sheriff Behan and that was all she knew. Doc told her what he thought of her loyalty and devotion to his enemies, with the result that the next day's *Nugget* carried, under the court notes: "Miss Kate Elder sought 'surcease of sorrow' in the flowing bowl. She succeeded so well that when she woke up she found her name written on the Chief's register with two 'd's' [drunk and disorderly] appended to it. She paid her matriculation fee of $12.50, took her degrees and departed."

Kate departed straightway for Doc. Her head was splitting six ways from Sunday, but she knew who was to blame for all her troubles. When she got through telling Doc off, he swore out a warrant for her arrest on the charge of threatening to kill him (it was less than two months since a similar charge had been placed against him) and Virg Earp hauled her up before Judge Felter. She was convicted but after due consideration of all points in the case was let go. Kate was evidently a very attractive woman, hangover, rage, tears and all.

"Court Proceedings," in the *Nugget* for July 10, 1881, had: "The case of Territory vs. John H. Holliday was called for hearing yesterday morning at 10 o'clock, the District Attorney addressing the court, said that he had examined all the witnesses summoned for the prosecution and from their statements he was satisfied that there was not the slightest evidence to show the guilt of the defendant; and he therefore asked that the complaint in this case be withdrawn and that the case be dismissed. The Court thereupon dismissed the case and discharged the defendant, and thus ended what at one time was supposed to be an important trial."

After this neither Doc nor Kate wanted to make up. The breach was complete on both sides. After an Earp-Holliday-Elder conclave she agreed to leave town if Doc would give her a fairly large sum of money. This was blackmail, but rather than have the constant possibility of her again getting drunk with Sheriff Behan and swearing Doc's life away, the money was paid. She and Doc parted with a few choice cuss words each had been saving up for a special occasion, and their illicit affair ended on as ungenteel a note as it had begun.

Doc might or might not have been implicated in the stage holdup; authorities differ. He was implicated, up to the ears, in its aftermath, including the famous O. K. Corral gun fight. Wyatt Earp, lusting for fame of the Wild Bill Hickok type, made a clumsy attempt to fasten the guilt for the crime on certain parties so he could claim the credit for their arrest and punishment. He succeeded only in arousing the enmity of the Clantons, "cowboys" whose main occupation was rustling, and their friends. On an October afternoon in 1881, the showdown came, with Doc and three Earp brothers—Wyatt, Virg, and Morg—shooting it out with Ike and Billy Clanton and two friends of theirs, Frank and Tom McLowry. At this time, Virg Earp was city marshal of Tombstone, and Wyatt and Morg and Doc were acting as his deputies. Whether they were acting primarily as peace officers or as interested parties working off personal grudges is open to argument. Whatever the merits of the case, the battle ended with the two McLowrys and Billy Clanton dead or dying, and Virg and Morg Earp wounded. Unscathed were Wyatt Earp and Doc, whose shotgun felled Tom McLowry. Doc and the Earps were arrested but murder charges against them were dismissed, and a drawn-out feud ensued, during which Morg was killed and Virg was seriously wounded, both shot from ambush. Then a group including Doc and Wyatt shot and killed Frank Stilwell in Tucson, Stillwell being the man suspected of the murder of Morg. Later they killed a Mexican who had some connection with their enemies. Now wanted for murder in two counties, Doc and Wyatt and Warren, youngest of the Earps, fled to Colorado.

Pueblo, now grown to a city of about 30,000 in this year of 1882, was booming as an industrial town. Lonely on the plains, the mountains far to the south and west, the smoking towers of Pueblo even then could be seen for miles. It was here, in the gambling district south of the river, around the Santa Fe station, that Doc and Wyatt and Warren came to rest up, take stock of their condition and plan what to do.

Doc was all ready to go to work in some prosperous spot. Pueblo was full of old friends of his from his Denver days and any number of good set-ups were available. But Wyatt and Warren could feel the law breathing down their necks. To Doc's amazement they began to plan for a place in which to lay low until the furor over the murders blew over.

And at last they quarreled. Perhaps Doc accidentally let go some hint that he had known Kinnear's stage was going to be robbed by Bill Leonard and his friends. Perhaps Wyatt now wished he had not taken the law into his own hands after Morg's death and so blamed Doc for sweeping him into two cold-blooded slayings. Perhaps Doc saw Wyatt as a swell-head and a blow-hard, since he was still so puffed up about having been "city marshal" of Dodge. Perhaps Doc saw Wyatt more than himself responsible for Morg's death, since Wyatt had tried so hard for the public renown of catching Leonard, Head and Crane. Perhaps Wyatt saw his friendship with Doc would end up more of a liability than an asset.

Whatever the reason, they parted. Wyatt and Warren sneaked off to the remote Gunnison country which was later to be a fisherman's paradise, but was then isolated rangeland and almost unpopulated. Doc walked the streets of Pueblo unmolested. He and Wyatt never saw each other again.

"I have decided to enter a convent, the Sisters of Mercy, in Savannah," Mattie would have written early in that winter of 1883.

Doc stared at the page, too stunned at first to comprehend what the words meant to him. Mattie went on to explain how she was overcome by a great need to belong, to serve, to do some good in the world. "This is a working order. I shall be a teacher or work in a hospital or do something like that. You mustn't think of me as being lost to life. I have *found* life. This is, to me, the perfect way to a rich and complete life. I am so happy, John, so very, very happy. I shall pray for you every day of my life. Needless to say, Papa is dismayed. . . ."

Perhaps in that moment Doc saw Tom McLowry's face.

Saw Tom's hands grabbing the front of his vest to throw it
open so everyone could see he was unarmed—only Doc had
thought he was going for his gun. Tom had died and many
men had died, and Mattie would never blame anyone.
Only. . . .

Standing in his lonely hotel room, looking down on the
twilight-gray street where suppertime had cleared most of the
passers-by away, he coughed and coughed. Mattie had turned
her back on him—and he knew at last the complete abandon-
ment he had never let himself believe would ever happen to
him. He knew Mattie had not meant to hurt him. Her
prayers, she thought, would be shield enough. "I am so
happy," she had written. *I am so happy*. And at last he understood how it had been for her, all these long years. Her
friends had had husbands and babies and homes, making a
priceless contribution to their world. She had had nothing.
Nothing but love for a man who had at last turned out to be
a killer. And she was too good not to want to make sacrifices
for others—to marry a man half dead, bear his children, and
after his death slave to raise the children herself. She would
have been inexpressibly happy, Doc realized. All of the emptiness of his life swept over him. He had very nearly ruined
Mattie's life in the ruin of his own. He stood there wondering
if he had unconsciously wanted to make her as unhappy as he
was. Well, it was all over. She would be happy, he knew, working as a nun. And for himself . . .

Everything was over.

Doc turned away and lit the lamp. The chimney rattled
faintly but with determination against the bracket in which it
was set as Doc tilted it to get the match at the wick. He replaced the chimney, turned the flame up, and stared at his
white hand. It trembled very slightly, but continuously. His
eyes were cold green-gray in the yellow lamp light. He was
completely alone in the world—Mattie had forsaken him. And
he could not blame her. Now he saw plainly that his constant
drinking was bringing about a slow deterioration of his
physical control. A horrible picture of himself as a drunken,
dirty old bum stood in the center of his vision. He knew the
shameless self-pity which brought that on, and fought the

vision away. He looked down at his finely tailored suit, spot-
less, pressed, neat.

And all alone. The dreadful black pit was right at his heels
—the pit into which stumble the men who know that no one
cares for them, not anyone, anywhere. He walked quickly
over to the table by his bed and poured himself a large drink
of the best Kentucky bourbon. He saw that his hand shook
holding the glass even as he lifted it. He smiled wryly, knowing the net of behavior in which he was caught and how hard
he worked to pull it closer around him, then swallowed the
mellow fire in the glass.

Suddenly the tremor in his hand lessened with the tightening of his fingers around the glass. He was lonely, yes, but he
was also free. He no longer had anyone to consider but himself—he could do anything his slightly warped code of morals
permitted, go any place his health . . .

The coldness in his eyes deepened, the wry smile changed.
He rang for a boy and hauled his little trunk out of the closet
and wiped it off. When the boy came Doc gave him a double
eagle and told him to go over to the Denver and Rio Grande
station and get him a ticket on the early train to Leadville.

"Hey, Doc. You ain't going to Leadville," the kid said,
"coughing like you do?"

"Get!" Doc said. He placed a pile of crisply fresh cotton
shirts in the trunk, then picked his .44 up from under a scarf
in the drawer. The kid still stood in the doorway, staring in
fascination as Doc, a real, sure-nuff killer, spun the cylinder
of the very gun he'd killed all them fellers with. Doc reached
down swiftly with his left hand and came up with a well-
polished boot. The bellboy exploded into the hall and hit
the stairs running.

Doc sat down suddenly. His gun fell on the floor unnoticed.
This was the point where his life reached its climax. From
here on everything is downhill. He sat there trying to justify
his decision to go to Leadville to himself—trying to make it
out anything but what he feared was true, that he no longer
cared what happened to him. Mattie had failed him. Mattie.
He knew that the spark, the something undefinable that gave
zest to his existence was gone. And that his life was over, then,
when Mattie entered the convent of the Sisters of Mercy.

But habit was so deep that he picked up the gun, polished it carefully, and put it away. Then he gave the bourbon bottle an emptying. Ah, well, he had been looking at the gloomy side, making things out as bad as they could be. There were good and logical reasons for going to Leadville.

He opened another bottle and lowered the spirit level.

There were more good reasons than not for going to Leadville.

He finished his packing with his usual neatness, tipped the bellboy a magnificent dime for getting his ticket, had one last good-sized snort, put on his black slouch hat and went out to celebrate his last night in Pueblo. And as he turned down the lamp wick on his way out, he looked at the fine tremor in his hands and it did not bother him in the slightest.

Doc had succeeded in covering up his real reason for going to Leadville to himself, but all his friends thought he was crazy. Leadville is 10,200 feet above sea level, with a climate described as "ten months winter and two months mighty late in the fall." They said it never rained in Leadville, it only snowed, the year around. The tourist guides advised all persons going there to bring a heavy ulster overcoat and be prepared to have colds, catarrh, bronchitis, pneumonia and other respiratory complaints continually, and stated emphatically, "Persons troubled with weak lungs or heart disease should also give the new camp a wide berth. The rare atmosphere accelerates the action of both these organs, and unless they are in perfect condition, serious results may follow."

But Leadville was wide open. Half of the town's population of 10,000 were miners and from having been in Tombstone and Deadwood Doc knew how they loved to gamble. Some of the most famous saloons in the West were there, and many of Doc's friends. He would fit in there, he would get along fine. And he wasn't going to worry about his health, not when he was strong enough to ride all over half of Arizona.

Doc checked into the Clarendon Hotel, next door to Tabor's Opera House and the swankest hotel in Leadville. He couldn't appreciate its splendor; he was too sick. Any unusual exertion caused him to pass out cold. His sole prop, the contents of the bourbon bottle, produced intoxication so acute that he was reduced to walking on his hands and knees and dragging his chin. But no one turned aside from him with disgust and scorn. He was picked up, brushed off, set down in a chair and informed that he was new in Leadville. "It's the elevation. You'll be used to it in a day or two."

The next day, to his surprise, he felt well enough to try to make a trip around the downtown area, just to get his bearings. Harrison Avenue appeared to be the main cow path. The whole downtown area was cut up by oddly-interposed streets which cut some regular city blocks into slivers or uneven-sided rectangles and dead-ended at adjoining blocks. The business section wasn't so big, but it certainly was thick with saloons. Everything had a worn and dingy appearance, the result of the air pollution caused by fumes and smoke from the eight smelters and reduction works, four foundries and a gas works. Almost immediately Doc had run into familiar faces. They showed him the joints and the high spots and introduced him around. "Doc Holliday," was introduction enough; he was known to everyone in his day, not just the sporting world.

Back in Georgia, on October 1, 1883, Sister Mary Melanie Holliday entered the Sisters of Mercy at St. Vincent's Academy in Savannah. It was a Monday, the beginning of a week, of a life, of cheerful and contented work and prayer for others.

"Sister Mary Melanie," Doc said. The name was strange on his tongue and Mattie was a stranger. When he saw some of the Sisters of Charity who operated St. Vincent's hospital in Leadville, he would stare at them out of the corners of his eyes, wondering if Sister Mary Melanie dressed the way they did and looked as busy and at peace with everything and everybody. And then turn away to his loneliness. He had known that he would lose her now, finally and irrevocably, for all that she had yet to take her final vows, but still, when it happened, it was a deeper shock than he knew. Beautiful Mattie in her white dress and veil, to be bound forever in the service of her faith. He came down with some kind of major respiratory infection, the doctor called it pneumonia and let it go at that, which laid him up for several weeks. It was a wonder that it didn't kill him, but the toughness and stamina

which had defied the onslaughts of both whisky and tuberculosis were still holding together in some fashion and he
pulled through.

He was very weak, however, as anybody could see, and was
living close to the thin edge of collapse. The constant, racking
cough kept him so tired that he could never get the rest he
needed to throw off the persistent infection. It took every
nerve he could strain to get through his eight-hour shift at the
faro bank in the Monarch saloon. He managed to forget Mattie's defection for hours at a time, only to find the hurt waiting for him when the last turn had been called. Johnny Tyler
and the crowd of enemies he had made for Doc faded from
Doc's mind. He had too many other worries, the worst of
which was keeping his job, since his concentration and memory continued to get poorer and poorer and he continued to
be so weak and tired.

*Doc got more and more short-tempered, and there were
complaints, but he was kept on as a dealer until he got into
a serious quarrel with a player and was fired. He didn't work
for a long while, went broke, borrowed five dollars and
couldn't pay it back. The man he owed it to swore to lick the
stuffing out of Doc if he didn't fork it over. Doc saw him coming, pulled his gun and shot him in the arm. Doc was tried
and acquitted but ordered to leave Leadville. He went to
Denver, registered at the Metropolitan Hotel and began making the rounds.*

Doc got along fine in Denver, but his friends were all struck
by the change in him: the marked way in which a fine tremor
shook him continually, the way his chest had sunk, giving him
a very stooped appearance, the way in which the white hairs
predominated over the blond ones, the way his accurate judg-
ment had slipped. No one criticized him for his drinking: it
was obvious that he was in constant pain. He was congenial
with his friends and there were a lot of men who wanted to
meet him. "I gambled with Doc Holliday." That was something to tell your grandchildren. A real killer and looked and
talked like a perfect gentleman.

Doc wrote to Sister Mary Melanie far oftener than he had

written Mattie. She wrote that she was praying for his conver-
sion. The two women that he had loved, his mother and
Mattie, stood at the two extremes of Christianity and he was
lost in the middle. He kept on, lost though he might be, loyal,
uncomplaining, brave. And it was hard, now. The alcohol
which padded his nerves against the cruelties of existence was
at the same time breaking them down. His follow-through to
the point of an argument was likely to get side-tracked, his
initiative was fading, his memory was very bad, he found himself with a glib excuse for every discreditable thing he did,
and he was becoming increasingly impulsive and unpredictable. His actions, as his appearance, were those of an old man.
He was thirty-four this winter of 1886.

As spring came on, the Denver *Tribune-Republican* began
a crusade to force the gambling element out of town. There
were anti-gambling-house and anti-bawdy-house laws, the
paper pointed out. Why weren't they enforced? It made such
a stink that all the gambling-house proprietors and prostitutes
were rounded up and fined—and turned loose to go back to
their business.

The Denver *Tribune-Republican* for August 4, 1886:
"The notorious Doc Holliday was arrested last evening by the
police for vagrancy. J. S. Blythe and K. McCoy were arrested
at the same time and on a similar charge. They were locked
up in jail and opposite their names on the prison slate were
marked the words, 'safe keeping.' When asked why such a
charge was preferred, the reporter was informed that if a
charge of vagrancy was preferred the prisoners must necessarily be arraigned in the Police Court in the morning where
the sentence, in all probability, would be a slight fine only."

Doc got his case continued clear out of sight and proceeded
to forget about it. The paper made no mention of it, but
there must have been people around who could put two and
two together. There was a racing meet due soon and a notorious gambler and confidence man was seen talking to one of
the night watchmen at the track. This time Doc was officially
requested to depart and stay departed. He went down to
Pueblo, but things were too easy for him there. He had come
to the point where the only interest in his life was doing
things he wasn't supposed to do and getting away with it.

He was so restless that he didn't know what to do with himself. Everything in his life was shabby and pointless. He felt with dismay that he had outlived his day and the way of life he could get along in. Tuberculosis, gun fights, the eternal drenching in alcohol, the painful altitude of Leadville, losing Mattie, he had survived them all. And for what? To come to emptiness and defeat. He knew that his mind was clouded permanently now from over-drinking; he could only sense things clumsily, fumble dimly and uncaringly for answers to questions that he couldn't put into words. His stay in Leadville had set off the progress of his tuberculosis, largely arrested before, and his dreadful coughing, his painfully collapsed chest and consequently stooped posture, his constant indigestion, all combined to make his life a torment.

It was May of 1887.

He had heard much of Colorado's newest health resort, Glenwood Springs. The hot springs were being boasted as a sure cure for consumption, the vapors being heavily charged with healing chemicals. So Doc had his trunk taken down to Carson's stage and express line, at 106 West 4th, paid twelve dollars for his ticket and got on top of the big four-horse Concord for his last ride.

Glenwood Springs is set in a little valley of the Colorado River, shut in by snow-capped mountains. From Yampa hot spring flow daily six million gallons of water at an average temperature of 140°F, and there are hot-vapor caves and baths besides.

Doc checked into the Glenwood Hotel and began to take the cure. When not breathing the hot, steamy air he hung out in the sheriff's office talking over old times or did his serious drinking in one of the four local saloons. The town had some 400 permanent residents, but as summer came on the population increased enormously. Everyone seemed benefited by the hot mineral waters.

Everyone but Doc.

His chronic pulmonary tuberculosis suddenly developed into miliary tuberculosis, in which the germ attacks not only the lungs but every part of the body, and with vicious force and speed. Doc felt worse and worse, and one day he noticed an ulcer on his chest. He promptly went to a doctor, suspect-

ing syphilis no doubt, and after an examination was informed
that it was a tubercular lesion. Another one was starting. The
doctor told him that he had developed galloping consumption and could expect to live but a few months.

Doc was thirty-five years old this summer of 1887.

He went back to his hotel room and found it marvelously
peopled. The loneliness would never come back. The shadows
were more real, more filled with unfailing companionship
than the crowded saloon he had stopped at on his way from
the doctor's office. He heard so faint and clear his mother's
voice singing, Morg's laugh, the leathery rustle of gun belts
on Frank and Tom McLowry, Billy Clanton, Frank Stilwell,
Florentino. And he was not afraid. He wrote Sister Mary
Melanie a letter to thank her for her prayers. But he was still
Doc and coldly practical, and still an alcoholic to whom truth
was something a lie was dressed up to look like in order to
get you something you wanted. So he went right smack out
and told the Catholic priest, Father Downey, that he had been
baptized a Catholic, and told the Presbyterian minister, Rev-
erend Rudolph, that he had been raised a Presbyterian.

By the first week in September Doc was so weak that he
could no longer get around. His remarkable behavior with
the sky pilots paid off in their unflagging attention to him,
each determined to save the sinner's soul for his own particular heaven—as Doc had intended they should. His sufferings
were so great, and his courage so marked, however, that
others were attracted to his bedside and he would never have
lacked for kindness nor care even without the clergy. He was
rotting away before everyone's eyes, and yet he clung to the
life which had been so grave a trial for him, and whose temp-
tations had so often found in him a ready subject, without
complaining, without blaming anyone else for his troubles.

He died at ten o'clock in the morning on November 8,
1887.

Hill Folk

Whuppin' Holler

BY CHARLES MORROW WILSON

¶ *Mountain people are always interesting, often given to casual violence, sometimes to a perverse logic; suspicious of strangers they may be, but warmheartedly eager to lend a helping hand to those they know and accept. Charles Morrow Wilson found the training of girl-children in one part of his native Ozarks a fascinating but rather puzzling process; and Frank Robertson remembers that the Tennesseans who settled in the wooded mountains of Idaho brought their mayhem-mindedness and readiness to swap lead along with them.*

THAT NIGHT I took lodging in the windowless attic of a cross-roads store. There was no charge and very little sleeping. The space was bare except for a row of dusty wooden churns, a rack of mildewed buggy whips and a feather-stuffed floor pallet covered with a lone and ragged quilt. The pallet was noticeably damp and before midnight I was awake and shivering. At least two chilly hours before dawn I slipped on my shoes and walked out into the waning moonlight.

The sun was all of an hour high before I reached the next crossroad. There I found one slaunched-roofed store which in turn had one window branded with three words all lettered in wavery scrawl: POST OFFICE—EAT. I undertook to purchase a glass of milk and a sandwich. The proprietor slipped down from his high stool and looked me over with great thoroughness. "You ain't in no trouble?" he inquired.

I told him I hoped not. The storekeeper allowed he hoped

not likewise. "You ain't been time-beatin' with ary them Tannehill gals?" my interrogator added darkly. "Onderstand, I ain't pryin' into your business. But ef you don't already know, you're headed into some real tough settlements. . . . Gals come fat and smiley, but menfolks come lean and wicked strong." The storekeeper leered at me. "Mebbe you already know . . ."

I assured him I didn't and asked again of the chances for buying a glass of milk and a sandwich. The storekeeper weighed my query with evident disapproval. "Got no milk. Ole cow died off in Jenewery. Heifer ain't come fresh yit."

"How about water?"

"Yup, how about water?" Begrudgingly, the storekeeper wandered out of sight and after an almost frighteningly long wait returned with a dipperful of water in one hand and an extremely rough-hewn sandwich in the other. The water tasted strongly of sulphur; the sandwich turned out to be two chunks of hard bread propped apart by a roughly hacked chunk of slightly mildewed cheese. I munched at the bread ineffectually, then tasted the rancid cheese, and fed the greater part of both to a beggar hound with eloquent eyes.

When I laid my dime on the table and turned to the open doorway the storekeeper continued to peer at me sadly. "Be careful, feller."

"Any particular reason?"

My counsellor examined the dime sadly. "Case you're headed to southeast, which I figger you be, this here road will take you into Whuppin' Holler. . ."

"So?"

"So if I was you, I'd stay shy of them gals that live down that-a-ways." The old man nodded with vehemence. "They's three broods of 'em all told. Mostly they is purty and fat and trouble bestirrin'. That's how come the neighborhood got named Whuppin' Holler."

The flint-littered roadway seemed to beckon amiably. I followed it for more than an hour without meeting another user. Then as the road dipped into a curving descent, I saw two shapes strolling a side lane of bluegrass. An extremely tall young man in tight-fitting bluejeans and a ragged brown shirt was escorting an exceptionally plump young woman in an

almost skin-tight purple dress. Both were dragging their feet.
The girl's right arm circled the tall man's waist and her free
hand was fondling an immense rip in the back of his shirt.

The young giant stopped abruptly and placed his big left
hand on top of the girl's head which was piled high with red-
brown hair. She smiled up at her escort and bent forward
accommodatingly. The towering young man began spanking
her resoundingly and from all appearances to her complete
satisfaction. As I passed them he grasped the hem of her skirt
and raised it to display leather-brown and extremely plump
thighs.

At that the young woman protested meekly, "We ain't
yet home, Marcus . . . and they's a young man a passin'
by . . ."

"Been too damn many young man's a passin' too damn
close by e'er since I marriet ye last Christmas. 'Fore New
Years I'd seed ye triflin'." The young husband delivered an
echoing smack and turned to glare at me.

I watched his left hand slip into his breeches pocket and
emerge with an oversize knife. He flipped open the Bowie-
length blade and took a long stride toward me. I stooped to
pick up a throwable rock. The extremely tall young man
commanded me to stop. "Tall Shorty," he continued, "I can
throw this here knife a lot quicker than you can pick up ary
a rock . . . likewise I can degut ye in half the time it takes
to spit."

I watched the overweight bride hurrying to stand between
us. She moved with remarkable grace and I noted that her
features were quite pretty. Her oversize husband continued
to glare at me. "You wouldn't be one of them fiddle-playin'
roosters from over aroun' Sulphur Springs?" he demanded.
"You wouldn't be one of them dudey birds that last night
taken out my wife and her fat lil sister and bothered 'em
while me and her pappy was gone 'coon huntin' down on
Henbest branch? You wouldn't be . . ."

I interrupted to deny. "I'm not a fiddle player. I don't live
at Sulphur Springs or anywhere near it. I never saw you or
your wife or her sister before. . . . In fact I never saw your
sister-in-law at all. . . . And I never was in this holler before
now."

"Never was, huh?"

The plump bride was grasping his knife-bearing hand. For a moment he looked down on her with an almost angelic smile, then grasped her nose between two knuckles of his left hand. With a very quick flick of his knife he slashed open the front of her dress, thereby exposing her breasts which were big as medium cantaloupes.

The young woman began to whimper, then ducked free of his hold. "He ain't the one, Marcus. Honest to getout, I never see him before now." She sought vainly to cover her breasts with shreds of what had been her dress front. The young husband smiled down at her.

"So you wasn't triflin' last night?"

She circled his waist with her bare arms. "I already told you I was, Marcus. I already said you could whup me all the much you feel like I should git."

His smile broadened. "You don't sa-say!"

She stroked his right hand. "I done you wrong, Marcus. I'm due a whuppin'. But I want you should give me it at home. If you say so, I'll borry Pappy's braid whup."

The tall young man shook his head as if in disappointment. "Your pap is usin' it on your big fat little sister."

"Rosy's done been corrected, Marcus. I heerd her hollerin' a hour ago whilst you was still searchin' me down. Pappy must of ketched her sneaking in the back door . . ." The erring bride stopped short, then added imploringly, "Marcus, do purty please take me home . . ."

The towering young husband continued to smile. He returned his knife to his pocket. Then with abrupt fierceness he tore off the remnants of her dress and for a moment permitted her to stand naked. Then he pushed down on her shoulders and delivered two sweeping, underhanded spanks.

He turned away from her, took out his knife again, and cut an oversize switch from a roadside cluster of saplings. I heard the switch whack loudly on bare flesh. As I walked along, the tempo of the whacks increased. But the young wife did not cry out.

A mile or so down the road the way forked puzzlingly. I followed the low road which paralleled a youthful and dashing river. Presently the road led directly into the river. I pulled off my shoes, rolled up my breeches legs and waded.

The current was swift and minnows darted at all sides like living arrows. Out of the chilly water I warmed myself on a sunny bank, then replaced my shoes and tramped on. The old road continued to follow the river. From beyond a bend of sumacs I heard merry laughter and a swishing of wet cloth. Then I saw two dark blotches climbing the miniature stone bluff which protruded into a deep pool. The blotches began taking definition as extremely bulgy dresses filled with large female forms.

Next I noted that the young women were protrusively plump and that both sported long and dripping braids of dark red hair. Both had pug noses, plentiful face freckles, full lips and eyes that appeared to be almost as green as the blades of young corn in the field immediately beyond. Both grinned at me and retreated toward the field where they waited for a time, peering about and dripping profusely. Then the taller of the riverside Amazons strolled toward me and inquired if I had seen or heard anything of a black plowhorse. I hadn't.

By way of offering a neighborly exchange of queries, I asked how they found the swimming. Both smiled broadly. Then the larger one answered. "Still right chilly . . . but they's got to be a first time."

The smaller one, who barely missed being six feet tall, took the next line. "We been first-plowin' and first-time hoein' our pappy's corn patch. Sun commenced a-warmin' our backs and so we figgered hit was time to try ourselves a swim. . . . While we was sillyin' around, the old hoss slipped his halter bit and strayed plum off. . . . Now we got to git back that hoss reel quick."

"Maybe he's strayed home," I suggested.

"Shore hope he ain't."

The big one interposed concernedly. "My sister ain't told you maybe. But our pappy don't favor havin' no women folks a-swimmin', perticular whenever they is been told to plow crops. . . . Our pappy figgers womenfolks and hosses is made for to work . . ."

"And to get whupped effin they don't," the smaller sister inserted forebodingly. "Should that hoss git to home afore we do, our pa will be waitin' us with his big mule whup . . ."

The larger sister nodded with enormous solemnity. "Even should he ketch us a-swimmin' our pappy would be shore to leave us settin' on blisters." She rubbed her immense hips apprehensively.

"Begin to see why they call this Whuppin' Holler," I hazarded.

Both of the wet Amazons nodded vehemently. "Hit shore is," the larger one peered down on me. "Our pappy is raised up seben gals of his own and two more adopted. He's wore out enough whups and switches on us to fill up a wagon box."

"Not countin' them bundles and piles of split oak shingles," the less enormous sister confided. She patted her protruding bottom. "But we got 'leven girl cousins . . ."

"Not countin' four adopted," interceded the immense sister.

"They all growed up with blistered tails. . . . Tannehills all calculate as how God put the devil into women and leaves hit to menfolks to whup the devil out of 'em . . ."

The oversize damsels turned at a common urge. I watched them trotting down a fencerow pathway and continued to look on until I saw them overtake the errant plow horse.

The road turned from the riverside and led into a great aisle through a hillside of squatty cedars. It was mid-afternoon before I reached the next crossroad where a solitary store waited paintless-gray and lacking customers. The storekeeper was a plump little man with bristly white hair, large poetic eyes and a violent twitching of the eyebrows. Having purchased a tin of salmon and a handful of heroic-sized soda crackers from an open barrel, I settled myself to self-service on the back counter. When I inquired about business, the proprietor confided there practically wasn't any. When I inquired of the crops, he allowed they were mostly meanness crops.

Then the storekeeper, his white patches of eyebrows twitching wildly, began asking questions. "You new to these parts?"

"Just trampin' through."

"See anything oddish?"

"You might say . . ."

"I might say what?"

"Might say I'm pleased I'm not one of the young girls of these parts."

His eyebrows were twitching again. "Wouldn't do you no great good was you a *old* gal in these parts. This here is Whuppin' Holler. An hit's full up of big ole fat gals—mostly sisters or else cousins. . . . Mostly meaner'n bull nettles in early August." After a cautious pause he settled himself on the counter besides me. "Fust time I come through I was single and afoot, same as you be. I figgered hit was hurtin' hard—anyway on the womenfolks. Kept figgerin' so all the while I was courtin' Violy. . . . She's one of them Tannehill sisters. And she's makin' me a mighty fine helpmeet . . . now that she's my wife woman."

"That's good," I hazarded.

His eyebrows twitched again. "Hit's good, all right. And way I see it so was the way she was raised. . . . Like Violy says herself, she started off 'ornery mean, same as most young gals. Time she was fifteen when I marrit her, her big ole fat pappy had got the meanness purty well warped out'n her. Figger that saved me a mighty sight a troubles." He smiled agreeably. "Wouldn't you say so, too?"

I pondered the question with the knowing gravity of a seventeen-year-old. "Way it looks to me, women are people, same as men. I don't hardly see . . ."

The storekeeper interrupted, "Sweet Jesus, you don't hardly see a-tall, do you?"

Transplanted Tennesseans

BY FRANK C. ROBERTSON

IT WAS INEVITABLE that Father should feel a returning of his old longing for land of his own, but the prairie frightened him and he felt safe only in the timber. He had made the acquaintance of a domineering Tennessean by the name of Ira Lee, who lived a few miles away in what was known as the Zeiglar school district. What Father didn't know then was that the district was inhabited almost exclusively by tough refugees from the law, particularly former moonshiners from the Blue Ridge mountains of the South.

Ira Lee, one of the toughest of them, bragged of having killed a man or two, and was destined to die with his boots on years later after he had returned to his native Tennessee. A poor judge of character and easily flattered, Father was led to believe that Lee's sole interest was in seeing Father established in a home of his own.

Said Lee, "There's a hundred and sixty acres of the finest timber land that I've been achin' to buy, but I'll give up half of it just to have you as a neighbor. We want people like you and your wife in our district."

Father looked the place over. The timber was good—a virgin forest of red and yellow pine, red fir and tamarack. It was only eight miles from a prime market in Moscow. Lee showed him how he could fell house logs right where the building would go up. He pointed out a small clearing of an acre or so grown up to wild strawberries where he could raise a garden.

"Why, man," cried the enthusiastic Lee, "this place is just like a gold mine! When you need a dollar all you got to do is chop a load of your own wood and haul it to town."

To Father, who had chopped many a cord of wood of which the owner of the timber got half, that sounded mighty good.

The real-estate firm of Spotswood & Veach, in Moscow, owned the land. They wanted eight hundred dollars for the eighty Father was to get, but to oblige an old customer—they were the men from whom Father had bought The Forty—they wouldn't require any money down and would give him five years in which to pay.

In his time Father had had many opportunities to make money had he been willing to gamble but he was always afraid of big deals. Yet he had no such terror of debt as obsessed Mother. His trouble seemed to be that he always "saw small."

He made a proposition to the realtors which made even Ira Lee gasp. "I'll take it if you'll let me pay for it in cordwood," he offered. "So many cords delivered in Moscow every year until it's paid for."

The partners looked at each other slyly. "What's wood selling for today?" one of them asked.

"About a dollar and six-bits, but"—

"We can't figure on it staying that high. It might go down to a dollar a cord."

"And it might go up to three dollars," Ira Lee argued.

"It's Mr. Robertson's proposition, not ours," said the partners. "If he will deliver one hundred cords of wood here in Moscow every year for five years the land will be his. That would be approximately a dollar and sixty-six cents a cord."

"I'd rather do that than pay cash," Father said. "Me and my boys can always chop wood, but we can't always lay our hands on a dollar."

They reminded him, of course, that he'd have to haul in a few extra cords every year as interest, and neglected to tell him that if he failed in any payment they could reclaim the land and keep the wood he had delivered. Father agreed. He had made up his mind to have that place. In the end, it was to cost more than double the asking price.

Dread of the impending rumpus was all that impelled Mother to sign the contract. She had hoped for better things for her boys than to have them grow up to be "wood rats," as the men of the timber were contemptuously called in Moscow. She knew that none of the woodsmen made more than a bare living, which was usually helped out by harvest wages in the Palouse country. She couldn't see how we were to live if an extra hundred cords had to be delivered in Moscow each year. Moreover, she saw clearly that each tree that was cut down would decrease the value of the place, there being no market at all for stump land.

When she tried to voice her forebodings he shouted her down. "You never encourage me in anything, you don't want me to have anything! You never recognize me as the head of the house! I should never have come back from Texas!"

"Maybe you're right about that, Will," she retorted. "And maybe I never should have taken you back. But we've got to stick together now, so if you'll only stop your yelling I'll sign your contract."

She signed—but Father didn't stop his yelling. Then, or thenceforth.

Up until now Mother's life had been spent among poor but reasonably peaceful and law-abiding people. Now she was thrown into the society of wild and violent men. Her belief that you could get along with anyone if you did what was right and tried to like them was subjected to a pretty severe test.

Ira Lee was the recognized bull-of-the-woods. A tough fellow but far from illiterate, he could be a charming and engaging talker. He liked to visit with Mother and she enjoyed talking with him, except when he pleaded that if he could have the training of my brother Chauncey for a couple of months he would guarantee that Chauncey could whip anybody of his weight in Latah County. That wasn't exactly what Mother had set her heart on with regard to her oldest son.

In general Ira Lee was a good neighbor, but there were exceptions. It was dangerous to talk about such a man, but Father had never learned to hold his tongue. Once Lee concluded that Father had slandered him, and the only speculation in the district was what form Lee's vengeance would take. Father was frankly scared for he had never been a fighting man and was no physical match for Lee. Father was five feet ten and weighed a hundred and sixty pounds. Lee was only five feet eight, but he weighed a solid two hundred pounds and loved to fight.

He "laid for" Father, knocked him down, and gave him a bad beating. When I came home from school that day and saw Father with both eyes closed and his face bruised and swollen beyond belief I felt sure he was dying. Father hauled Lee into court at Moscow, where the bull-of-the-woods was fined twenty-five dollars and bound over on bail to keep the peace. But Lee held no hard feelings and was soon neighboring with us again.

The next time he got mad at Father his revenge took a different form. He set fire to our timber. Father, Mother and I were paying a Sunday visit to our old neighbors at Tim Bell. On the way home Father saw the smoke from a forest fire, which he quickly decided was on our own place. He whipped the team to a gallop and soon arrived to take charge of the fire-fighting. Chauncey and Obe, closer to home, had got there first and started a back-fire. To me it was a thrilling sight to see that blazing inferno with the flames leaping from treetop to treetop with the mightiest roar I had ever heard.

Thanks to the back-fire, the flames were soon under control and the blackened trees would still make cordwood. Mother and I stayed up until midnight watching, but Father and the boys didn't go to bed at all. Everybody "knew" that Lee had set the fire, but there was no way to prove it.

Just before we moved onto "the eighty," a feud between Lee and a man named Richardson had come to a head. Richardson had come to Lee's place and taken a shot at Lee while he was working in his field. Lee promptly took refuge behind a stump, and shouted, "Wait till my wife can bring my rifle!" Richardson, a true sportsman, obligingly refrained from firing any more shots until Mrs. Lee arrived with her husband's rifle. Then, from behind their respective stumps the two men blazed away at each other until dark when Richardson went home, his honor satisfied.

Another time Lee made the mistake of trying to bully a man named Hart. As he was coming from Moscow he met Hart with a load of cordwood. Lee got down from his wagon and challenged Hart to fight. "Coming," Hart said and, reaching back for his double-bitted ax, started to climb down. When he reached the ground Lee was back on his wagon and driving on. "Can't you take a joke?" Lee called.

One of the stories Lee loved to tell on himself illustrated his peculiar sense of humor. His wife, Reva, was never seen off her own farm, and the Lees seldom had visitors. Once a vicious bull of the neighborhood came into the yard, and Lee sent his wife out to drive it away. When the bull charged her Lee shouted with great glee, "Run, Reva, run! God Almighty'll take care of you!" Relating the incident, he would then add, "If I'd tried to he'p Reva, He'd likely have he'ped the bull."

Lee and another neighbor, Joe Meeks, carried on a feud for several years; because of it neither was ever without his gun whenever there was a chance of their meeting. Meeks, a tall, rawboned Kentuckian who might well have served as an artist's model for Daniel Boone, was a dead shot with a rifle, and had once given the burly Lee the whipping of his life. I was a witness to the ending of this feud.

Father used to "bank out" cordwood on top of a ridge at the edge of our place. Sometimes there would be ricks containing forty or fifty cords. One time when I had gone up there with Father, Ira Lee suddenly came round one end of the rick, and Joe Meeks round the other. Each man had his rifle cradled in his arm; neither had any idea the other was there until they met, with only a few yards separating them. Joe Meeks was my idol, and I remember hoping he would get in the first shot.

Father admitted later that he was scared, but he greeted each man by name. They spoke to him, but not to each other, though Lee nodded to his enemy.

Joe said, "Will, I've got a sick cow and I wondered if you'd know what to do for her?"

Before Father could speak Lee said, "What's the matter with her, Joe?"

Meeks hesitated a moment, then began to list the cow's symptoms. Father joined in the talk, and presently all three men went to look at the cow. The long-drawn-out feud was over.

Lee's fuss with another neighbor, a man named Walters,

came nearer to ending in a murder. Walters, too, a soft-voiced Virginian, had whipped Lee in a fist fight. Then one night in Moscow the two met in a saloon and swore undying friendship. Leaving town with a close friend of Lee's, they started back to the timber, all three riding in the friend's wagon.

A mile from town the quarrel broke out again and they got down to finish the fight. Lee came at Walters with his knife, nearly severing the man's jugular vein with the first swipe, then stabbing him through a lung and laying open his intestines. As he lay helpless on the ground, Lee gave him some more cuts on the arms and legs. So tough were these mountaineers that Walters eventually recovered.

About daybreak the morning after that fight Lee's oldest son came for Father. Father found Lee groaning in bed. He displayed a bruised shoulder where he claimed Walters had hit him with a rack-stake from which he had received internal injuries. As soon as he learned that Walters would recover and that no charges would be pressed, he was sound as a dollar. In the course of time, Walters too became a friend of Lee's.

The fighting wasn't always confined to the men and boys. Two neighbor ladies, one the community termagant, had words about the ownership of a chicken; the other woman scratched her face horribly with the broken end of a shingle. "Just thought I'd curry the old girl's face down a little," she explained to Mother.

In such a community fighting was one of the main topics of conversation and the younger generation readily adopted the tradition of its elders. Fist fights were frequent and bloody. Both Chauncey and Obe had their full share of battles; at times it seemed to Mother that they had interest in nothing else.

I alone showed a complete lack of warlike temperament. For the most part I wriggled out of overtures to combat—not always with credit to myself. I was fortunate in having as my best friend the oldest son of the redoubtable Ira Lee, who constituted himself my protector; it was soon understood that anyone who licked me had to lick Ike. That wasn't easy to do.

I recall how once his father ordered him to lick a much

older boy, an obvious impossibility. Young Ike made a respectable showing, but his father whipped him with a length of barbed wire for having failed. He came to school next day with numerous cuts on his back and legs. Another time, his father threw him into a furrow and plowed him under. Ike, I have heard, became as tough as his father, but I shall always remember him as ambitious, gallant and manly.

One other violent incident remains vivid because I was a spectator. Mother seldom missed a debate, but this particular evening Father and I went without her.

A young man named Pleasant Armstrong lived with a married sister a mile from our house. They were dark-complexioned people, claiming a strong strain of Cherokee blood. I still recall a young unmarried sister of Ples Armstrong as the most beautiful woman I have ever seen.

Ples wasn't often around, but this night it was my luck to have him come in and sit down beside me. Even I knew there was a feud on between him and our neighbor Joe Meeks. There was a sort of unwritten treaty between Meeks and his chief enemy, Ira Lee, that Meeks would stay away from town, and Lee away from the literary and debating society meetings. For this reason Joe Meeks, present this night, was unarmed.

Everyone was uneasy during the exercises, for the violence of Armstrong's temper was well known. Physically he was no match for Meeks, but he always carried the equalizer. Ples didn't even seem to be aware of me crouching beside him. Then, in the customary intermission between the "literary" part of the program and the debate, Meeks came over to our seat and extended his hand.

"How are you, Ples?" he asked courteously.

Armstrong ignored the outstretched hand, and stared straight ahead without speaking.

Rebuffed, Meeks returned to his seat. He appeared to be the most unconcerned person in the room, but his wife sat as if her back was nailed to a board, her face as white as chalk. I glanced at Father and saw that he was licking his lips nervously.

Meeks, one of the evening's debaters, was a great reader and strong in his opinions. I can't remember whether the question that night was whether the cow was a greater boon to mankind than the horse, or if it was resolved that floods had done more damage to the earth than fire; both were favorite subjects for debate. I do know that it must have taken great courage for Joe Meeks to stand there and argue with his usual caustic humor, knowing that within the hour he might be shot to death in the presence of his family. At times he looked straight into the sullen face of his enemy.

The moment the debate was over, Ples left the school-house. The hoodlums in the back seat, including my brother Chauncey, followed him. Meeks waited for his wife to put on the children's wraps. Father said something to him, but Joe shook his head, calling out to his debating partner, "Well, we waxed it to 'em tonight, didn't we?"

Mrs. Meek's movements were stiff and jerky. Her fingers were so awkward that Joe had to button his four-year-old daughter's coat. He lifted the little girl in his arms and said, "Come on, Rosy, let's go."

It was a quarter of a mile to the big sawdust pile where the roads forked. The Robertsons lived on the ridge, the Meekses in the holler. Father and I walked along about fifty feet behind Meeks and his family. Ordinarily, Father was a fast walker, but this night he sauntered—because the folks ahead of us sauntered. There was none of the usual good-natured bantering back and forth. It was almost as if we were walking in a funeral procession.

Suddenly, Ples Armstrong stepped from behind a bush half-way between us and the little group ahead.

"Joe Meeks, you're a dirty, yellow, lowdown Kentucky son-of-a-bitch, and I'm going to kill you!" he yelled.

Meeks and his family kept on walking.

Ples waved a six-shooter in his hand. "Turn around, you bastard, so I won't have to shoot you in the back!"

Meeks continued his slow, even pace, and Ples got closer and closer as he waved the gun and continued his abuse. To make matters worse young Claude Walters ran past us all and, in sight of Armstrong, stuck a six-shooter in the pocket of Meeks's overcoat.

"You've got a gun now, you coward, turn around and use it," Ples shouted, but Meeks marched straight ahead.

We had to turn off, and so long as we could hear, Ples was still trying to taunt Meeks into turning around.

Mother was still up when we got home. Father was telling her about the trouble, wondering if Joe Meeks was still alive, when there came a knock at the door. Ples Armstrong stood there, pale and wild-eyed. "I'd like a drink of water," he said. He drank two big dipperfuls, muttered, "Good night," and vanished into the darkness.

He hadn't killed Meeks for fear of hitting the little girl in Joe's arms, he said later. He had come back by our house for fear Meeks would get his rifle and ambush him. Meeks told Father later that he had got his rifle and run headlong through the timber to head off his foe before Ples got home. "But I wasn't going to kill him," he maintained. "I was just going to cram that damned sixgun down his throat."

That was the kind of thing that very often broke the monotony of living in the Moscow mountains.

Harbor Hamlet
to Boom Town

The Village of Yerba Buena

¶ *The metemorphosis of the Old Southwest from good-natured Lat'n easy-goingness to buzzing Anglo busy-ness is well illustrated by the following two selections. Within a few short years the California gold excitement changed tiny, sleepy Yerba Buena into sprawling, roaring San Francisco, a fitting locale for one of the wilder manifestations of Know-Nothingism, the anti-alien, anti-Catholic political movement that swept through America in the decades before the Civil War.*

Dusty, fleabitten little Yerba Buena was in 1835 an insignificant outpost long frequented by roving seafarers, Russians, and a few nondescript traders who smelled of hides and tallow. But for four redwood posts covered with a ship's foresail which De Haro's harbormaster, William Antonio Richardson, erected on "La Calle" in 1835, San Francisco's original site was little more than a waste of sand and chaparral sloping down to a beach and a small lagoon. *El Parage de Yerba Buena* (The Little Valley of the Good Herb) it had been named long before, because of the aromatic vine (*Micromeria Chemissonis*) found in the underbrush there.

Richardson, young master mariner who had deserted the British whaler *Orion* in 1822, was appointed Captain of the Port of San Francisco by Governor Pablo Vicente de Sola in 1835 when the Bay was declared a port of entry. Stocking his huge tent with wheat, hides, and vegetables, trader Richard-

From *San Francisco* (American Guide Series). Copyright 1940 by The City and County of San Francisco; 1947 by Hastings House, Publishers, Inc.

son soon supplemented his official duties by raising two sunken schooners which he put into service transporting rancho products from one end of the Bay to the other at somewhat exorbitant rates.

Democratic self-government, of the bureaucratic sort decreed by the Mexican Republic, came to Yerba Buena before the town itself arrived. Citizens of the *partido* (civil district) of San Francisco, on Governor Jose Figueroa's orders, assembled in the Presidio on December 7, 1834 to choose electors for the *ayuntamiento* (district council). On the following Sunday Don Francisco de Haro was elected to the *ayuntamiento* as *alcalde* for the projected *pueblo* of Yerba Buena. As a gesture toward establishing the town, Don Francisco marked out on the ground, from the site of Yerba Buena to the Presidio, *La Calle de la Fundacion* (Foundation Street) and retired thereafter to Mission Dolores to look after private matters.

Richardson, on July 1, 1836, suddenly acquired a neighbor as resourceful as himself—one equipped to do business in really sumptuous style. Jacob Primer Leese, Ohio-born partner in a Monterey mercantile firm, sailed into the cove aboard the barque *Don Quixote* with a $12,000 cargo of merchandise, a six-piece orchestra, and enough lumber to erect a mansion. By July 4, on a lot adjoining Richardson's property, the amazing Mr. Leese had thrown up a frame house 60 feet long, and 25 feet wide. Borrowing two six-pounders from the Presidio and decking his domestic barn with bunting from ships in the cove, Leese summoned all leading Mexican families north of the Bay to an Independence Day celebration—which lasted two days and a night.

Among the guests at Leese's patriotic housewarming had been Captain Jean Jacques Vioget, of the Peruvian brig *Delmira,* who was also a surveyor and a lively man with a fiddle. In the autumn of 1839 this versatile Swiss was commissioned by *Alcalde* de Haro to make the first survey of Yerba Buena. By 1840 on the west side of Montgomery Street, between Clay and Sacramento Streets, next door to the new Hudson's Bay Company's post and saloon he was serving ship's captains, supercargoes, merchants, and clerks in a tavern.

Thirty families, in 1841, comprised the village population. The most impressive house was that of Nathan Spear, who was running the Bay area's only flour mill. Jacob Leese had now transferred his business to Sonoma. Richardson was living across the Bay on his huge Rancho Saucelito, where he continued to collect customs and pocket the funds, claiming that his salary as harbor master was not paid and that he had no other source of income.

Governor Juan B. Alvarado's decrees, restricting trade with foreigners after 1841, drove the American whalers from San Francisco Bay to a new headquarters in the Sandwich Islands; and by 1844, outrivaled by the port of Honolulu, Yerba Buena had fallen back into obscurity. Though that same year saw the election of its first American-born *alcalde,* William Sturges Hinckley, the village continued to languish.

The mock-heroics of "Pathfinder" John Charles Frémont's raid on the Castillo de San Joaquin were Yerba Buena's first warning of impending change. Slipping over from Sausalito on July 1, 1846, the Yankee adventurer spiked the dismantled guns of the old fort. ("So far as can be known," says Hubert Howe Bancroft, "not one of the ten cannons offered the slightest resistance.") Thereafter, for a week, the habitues of Vioget's hangout gave themselves up to warlike gossip, forgetting to play billiards.

Suddenly, on July 9, the U.S.S. *Portsmouth* quietly dropped anchor in Yerba Buena's cove. The villagers—unaware of Commodore Sloat's flotilla off Monterey—were disturbed at breakfast by a roll of drums and a flurry of fifes. When they rushed to the Plaza, Captain John B. Montgomery's 70 sailors and marines were running up the Stars and Stripes on Mexico's flagpole atop the adobe Custom House. Down in the cove the *Portsmouth's* 21-gun salute rumbled into history across San Francisco Bay.

Captain Montgomery on August 26 appointed Lieutenant Washington Allen Bartlett first *alcalde* of Yerba Buena under the American flag. On September 15 Bartlett was confirmed in office by popular vote, with the same powers enjoyed by his Mexican predecessors. His first important decree ordered revision of Vioget's survey, which had served to locate building lots since 1839. Jasper O'Farrell, civil engineer employed for the job, discovered in 1847 that the Swiss tavern-keeper's streets intersected at two and a half degrees from a right angle.

His prompt correction of this error, known as "O'Farrell's Swing," left building frontage and vacant lots projecting somewhat beyond the theoretically proper lines of nonexistent curbstones.

On the last day of July 1846, Samuel Brannan, the bombastic Mormon Elder, sailed in through the Golden Gate aboard the *Brooklyn* with his well-armed flock of Latter-day Saints, a hold crammed with farmer's tools, two flour mills, and a printing press. The Mormons provided all that was necessary to pull Yerba Buena out of its rut once more. Within a year that place which had baffled the urbane and mystical Spaniards for three-quarters of a century would appear on the map of Alta California. Two years later the name of San Francisco would be blazoned in gold on the map of the world.

The Native Sons of Golden California

BY CARLETON BEALS

THE FIRST Native Sons were the Indians; by all accounts, probably prejudiced, they were a shiftless lot, although they gave the first Spanish missionaries some bad moments.

The second Native Sons were the Mexicans, who arrived several centuries before the Anglos, founded missions, presidios, and landed estates, and established a frontier society that, whatever its worse aspects, had leisure and grace.

There was neither grace nor decency in the greedy swarms who came to win fortunes—not merely the gold hunters, but

the saloonkeepers, gamblers, desperadoes, ex-convicts, speculators, and fancy females. The newcomers were mostly Americans, but Chileans, Peruvians, Europeans, Australians, Japa-
nese, and Chinese came also. Overnight San Francisco grew
into a filthy town among the masts of abandoned ships, mostly
tents and shacks, a few flimsy wooden structures, and some
solid Spanish-American buildings. At night, when lamps were
lit, and showed through the semi-transparent canvas and
burlap, the city on its hills resembled cubes of sunlight
stacked up like gold bars. Gambling hangouts, saloons, dance
halls, whore houses ruled nearly every street and Portsmouth
Square—to this day known as the Uptown Tenderloin. There
were no sewage facilities. The streets, even Market Street, the
main thoroughfare, were so deep with mire that they were
"not even jackassable," so one humorous sign warned. Drunks
who fell in suffocated before they could be rescued.

From the start there was hostility by the Anglos toward all
foreigners, particularly toward the Mexicans, whose proper-
ties were being stolen as rapidly as possible. Often they were
killed and their women raped. The Chileans and Peruvians—
who brought to Frisco its permanent heritage of "Pisco
Punch"—were subjected to raids, arson, and murder. Such
was the backdrop of Know-Nothingism in the Golden State:
heartless persecution, abetted by the authorities and by General Persifer F. Smith, United States Army commandant, of
Spanish-American "greasers" in the gold fields, on their
ranches and in cities and towns. They were driven from their
claims, their farms, and homes, and he who refused to evacu-
ate was strung up pronto. At Downieville, the Anglos made
a carnival of lynching a Mexican girl for stabbing an American miner who broke into her cabin to rape her.

A San Francisco alcalde, one of the first elected Americans,
who hated cigarette smoking, tried a Mexican accused of
horse stealing:

> JUDGE. "Do you smoke cigarettes?"
> PRISONER. "Sí, Señor."
> JUDGE. "Do you blow smoke through your nose?"
> PRISONER. "Sí, Señor."
> JUDGE. "Constable, take this fellow out and shoot him. He stole
> the horse sure enough."

This sort of brutality was aggravated first by the OUA (Order of United Americans), set up in 1850; later, by the SSSB (Supreme Order of the Star Spangled Banner). From the start, the Nativists were backed by newspaper editors, who berated the original Mexicans and the Chilean immigrants as trespassers on the public domain. The public domain was anything not owned by an Anglo-Saxon.

Such brutalities produced counter-violence. Daring eighteen-year-old outlaw Joaquin Murieta (alias Carrillo), a circus horse trainer, and his wife Rosa Felix, who rode with him in male attire, hair cropped close, performed exploits soon celebrated in Spanish, even English, ballads. They were the terror of all "white" land thieves, and Murieta considered himself a true patriot, called to free his "native" countrymen. He was the futile Aguinaldo, the Sandino, of the raped province of the West. He was finally betrayed for a few hundred dollars, by his friend, gambler William Burns.

The race-hating Nativists were the Hounds, "The Regulators," who proclaimed that California had been "preserved by Nature for Americans only, who possess noble hearts." They beat Spanish-Americans, robbed them, stabbed them, killed them. They broke into their homes, raped their women, time and again burned down their tents, cabins, and houses and, on occasion, half the rest of the city besides.

"With the coolest impudence," wrote Bancroft, "the Hounds asserted their determination to protect American rights against Spanish-speaking foreigners, and sometimes claimed to have instructions from the alcalde to extirpate the Mexicans and Chileans." The Mexicans were, of course, theoretically American citizens.

The Hounds were mostly Colonel Jonathan D. Stevenson's regiment of New York volunteers—originally Plug Uglies, Bowery and Atlantic Boys, "true Americans" all—recruited in the war against Mexico and stationed in California. Most of these patriots had been well trained in stealing and brawling as members of New York volunteer fire companies and Know-Nothing gangs, hence were well schooled as spread-eagle Americans for street forays. So began the tradition that persisted in California for half a century—the worst New York Bowery riffraff running the great commonwealth.

Stevenson's regiment was discharged on the scene, October 1, 1848—all who had not already deserted to the gold fields. They caused trouble in every mining camp, town, and city.

In San Francisco, Sam Roberts, a private in Stevenson's regiment, assumed the rank of full lieutenant and wore regimentals and organized his fellows for action against the "foreigners." They continued to wear army uniforms or more outlandish uniforms. Mostly they hung out in the Shades Saloon on Kearney Street. Their official headquarters, a large tent at Kearney and Commercial streets, near the later Barbary Coast, was called Tammany Hall. A big drum called them together for hoodlum forays.

They drilled regularly with muskets and swords and paraded each Sunday with fiddle, fife, and drum. Usually the day ended in a brawl in Chilean town on Telegraph Hill or in the Portsmouth Square whore houses. Pets of Nativist politicians, the Hounds were used for controlling voting booths and were employed by steamship companies to shanghai crews.

The big voice behind the Nativists was political boss David S. Broderick, a former New York saloonkeeper and Tammany hireling, who received a 50 per cent kickback on all fees and municipal salaries. Typical was his henchman, Charles P. Duane, who shot A. Fayole, owner of the French theater, for not letting him in free.

Growing bolder, the Regulators demanded support from merchants. Those who refused were smashed up and robbed. In taverns and restaurants they left without paying, telling the owner "to collect from the city." If he objected, they smashed up his place or set it on fire. They pushed men and women off the sidewalk. One Negro, who accidentally jostled one, had his ears cut off. A Mexican pedestrian who failed to obey an order in a servile manner had his tongue torn out.

On July 15, 1849, the Hounds descended en masse on the Chileno tents and shanties and displayed their "noble American hearts" by plundering them, beating the occupants with sticks and stones, and knifing them. Recklessly they fired into the homes amid the shrieks of terrified women, one of whom was murdered, and the groans of wounded men.

This occurrence was too shocking to be ignored. Sam Brannan and Captain Bezar Simmons laid down the law to the alcalde, T. M. Leavenworth, and obliged him to issue a call for a citizens' mass meeting in Portsmouth Square.

Big Sam Brannan, California's first millionaire, was one of the most extraordinary characters of his time. A Mormon elder, Brigham Young's New York representative, he had grown embittered by official and private persecution of the Mormons. On February 15, 1846—the same day Young led his Mormons out of Nauvoo, Illinois, on their long march to the promised land of Utah—Brannan set sail from New York on the *Brooklyn* with another band, about three hundred—to set up a colony on the Pacific Coast where the United States would have no jurisdiction. Ironically, the *Brooklyn* sailed through Golden Gate three weeks after Captain John B. Montgomery and sailors from the U.S.S. *Portsmouth* ran up the Stars and Stripes on Mexico's flagpole atop the adobe customhouse on Yerba Buena's main square—at once re-named Portsmouth in honor of the American sloop of war and soon to become the focus of a brawling tenderloin. That flag was the first thing Brannan saw when the *Brooklyn* moved toward the Embarcadero. Enraged, he hurled his hat to the deck and yelled, "There's that damned rag again!"

After settling his flock in tents and adobe houses near Yerba Buena cove, Brannan went to Utah to try to persuade Young to bring the rest of the Mormons to the beautiful Eden of California, but Young refused to settle in a rich area that was bound to attract other, non-Mormon settlers. Brannan returned to San Francisco and told his band they'd be fools to go to dreary Utah. With numbers of his followers, he settled near Swiss John Sutter's fort in the Sacramento Valley, and there started a store near the big log blockhouse. When gold was discovered on the American River, he went and personally led all but seven of San Francisco's 900 inhabitants off to the foothills.

Sutter was overwhelmed by the rough, mad rush, but not Brannan. He had his store and he was still collecting tithes from his Mormon followers, and he made a quick fortune by selling supplies to the horde of invading gold seekers. Furthermore, he installed a scales and a safe and bought gold

dust at discount with drafts on eastern banks, and lo, he became a banker.

But Brannan is better remembered for his leadership of
the Vigilantes than for his piled-up gold. At the big Portsmouth Square rally, his great whiskers rattled and his booming voice rolled forth from the rooftop of the alcalde's building in invective of the Hounds. His "vigor of vituperation
. . . had rarely been equaled." He enumerated the killings
and burnings in the city: he pictured the horrors of the as-
sault on Telegraph Hill and the plight of the Chileno families and called for contributions to help the destitute. Sacks
of gold dust and gold nuggets and gold slugs overflowed the
hats. Two hundred and thirty volunteers were armed to extirpate the Hounds.

Most of the Nativist desperadoes took to their heels, fleeing to the interior or frantically taking to the bay in small
boats. Some twenty were captured—including Roberts—on
the road to Stockton. The prisoners were lodged in the brig
of the warship *Warren,* and two days later were tried by the
mayor and two Vigilante judges. Roberts and another were
sentenced to ten years at hard labor, the rest for shorter terms,
and heavy fines were imposed. But within a few days politicians quietly released them, and they left the city.

The Hounds' role of terrorism was taken over by the Sidney Ducks, deported or escaped British and Australian criminals who had settled on Kearney Street, on the Devil's Half
Acre, later known as the Barbary Coast. They, too, were used
by politicians at election time and by shipowners. Sidney
Town became the chief center for whore houses, lodging
houses, gambling joints, dance halls, saloons, "hives of dron-
ish criminals," shabby little dens with rough, hangdog fellows
lounging about the doorways. If an arrest had to be made,
the police never ventured there without a small army. "Little
better than the Five Points of New York or Saint Giles of
London," said the leading daily, the *Herald,* a paper that
later sold itself to underworld politicians. "Unsuspecting
sailors and miners are entrapped by the dextrous thieves and
swindlers . . . always on the lookout." Often victims were
drugged. "These dance groggeries are outrageous nuisances
and nurseries of crime." Drunkenness, fornication, robberies,

fights went on day and night. For a pinch or two of gold dust, the whores would stage indecent exhibitions. Herbert Asbury tells of the "Bear's Head," where a regular feature consisted of copulation by a boar and a woman, and of the "Fierce Grizzly," where a live female bear was used in sexual shows.

A criminal, "English Jim," and a companion—both Sidney Ducks—blackjacked a Montgomery businessman and stole $2,000 in gold. That was killing too close to home for Brannan's comfort, and he aroused 8,000 Vigilantes to take action. To the assembled crowd he roared out, "I'm . . . surprised to hear people talk about grand juries or recorders or mayors. I'm tired of such talk. These men are murderers, . . . and . . . I will die or see them hung by the neck."

Unfortunately, the Vigilantes convicted the wrong men.

In May, 1851, a Sidney Duck set fire to a paint shop on Portsmouth Square. As the flames spread, devouring three fourths of the city, the ruffians swarmed over the hills looting and shooting. DeWitt and Harrison on Commercial Street saved their establishment by dousing on 80,000 gallons of vinegar.

Sam Brannan called a meeting at his office and again aroused the Vigilantes. A few days later, they seized a thief and after a summary trial, hanged him at two in the morning from the gable of the customhouse on Portsmouth Square. It was a moonlit night.

Then in July they caught the real "English Jim," who "confessed." Although somewhat stunned by their previous mistake, the Vigilantes hanged him from a gallows on Market Street Wharf. A few weeks later, balked by the sheriff from lynching two more Sidney Ducks, the Vigilantes burst into jail and strung them up from two redwood beams stuck out the windows of their headquarters at Battery and Pine streets. A vast crowd sent up a paean of rejoicing.

But the real crescendo of criminality, corruption, and vice was to recur under Know-Nothing rule—and remedial action was taken by the Second Vigilante Committee. Out of such disorders, Know-Nothingism—one piece with the aims and operations of the Hounds if not always the Sidney Ducks— emerged with the false slogan of "Reform."

The OUA was started in 1850 by Robert D. Hart, W.

Ackerman, and Charles M. Yarwood. By 1857 it had nine chapters. The first SSSB organization, according to *Alta California,* appeared in May, 1854, and headquarters for a "Native American party" were set up on Sacramento Street. The *Chronicle,* practically a Know-Nothing sheet, reported in June that rules and regulations were expected by the next ship. If the Know-Nothings would be able "to stop drunkenness and fighting at elections" they would deserve credit. The paper was pleased that the order had also appeared in interior towns.

On August 5, 1854, the Stockton *Argus* wrote: "Where are they?" They were meeting every night and increasing in numbers. But "nobody seems to know where their headquarters are. How the devil do they increase their numbers so fast when nobody can find the right door to knock at?"

That same month the *Alta California* commented that the administration had "stirred up the political cauldron in all the states" until it had "bubbled and boiled over," and that the Know-Nothings in California had their candidates ready to be launched at the opportune moment. They had "a good chance" to win, for the Whigs had little strength, and the Democrats were fighting over spoils—a split between "Tammany" and "Chivalry," a hint of sectionalism that might become decisively destructive.

The two Democratic groups were also known as the Electionists (the ins) and Anti-Electionists (the would-be-ins). From the latter, two more factions split off, the "Bone and Sinew" and the "Rose Waters." Thus five tickets would enter the mayoralty race. More would soon appear. For the electoral situation was incredibly confused. There was disaffection because public officials were stealing right and left and doing little to provide the necessary improvements and services needed desperately by the fast-growing city. Nor did they provide adequate law and order, because they were tied in with the worst ruffians and criminals.

The Know-Nothings branded the whole caboodle as "riffraff candidates" and called for a "Citizens' party"—men who would "administer the government with economy and a desire for the welfare of the people." But according to historian Bancroft, the Know-Nothing lawyers, judges, and fire-eating politicians were the scum of the state—"thieves, gamblers, murderers, some . . . living on the proceeds of harlotry." The president of one Know-Nothing convention was the leading racetrack owner. The Know-Nothing "Citizens' Reform" ticket was named in secret convention and disclosed four days before the election, September 2.

Two days later, the membership refused to ratify the choices, chiefly because names had been put on the ticket by "the same corrupt mode of bargaining, selling, and swapping" as on other tickets, and the candidate for mayor, Lucien Hermann, was a Roman Catholic. The day before elections an open nominating convention met in Metropolitan Theater, 760 members present, and put up a new ticket headed by S. P. Webb for mayor.

The discarded Hermann roundly denounced "the bigotry and intolerance" of members of the order who had opposed him "because of his religious faith." He remained in the race at the head of an independent "Cuidado" ticket, with a platform of "equal rights to all . . . no proscription on account of country, religion, or politics." By then an amazing number of tickets popped up—not to mention various candidates running on no ticket. The list included: Electionist Democrats; Anti-Election Democrats; Rose Water Democrats; Anti-Election Bone and Sinew Democrats; Citizens' Reform (Know-Nothing); Cuidados; Anti-Slavery; Independents; Y. I.'s Pine Tree Club; Independent Citizens; Anti-Anti Know-Nothings; Know-Somethings; and Independent Union.

To keep order, Mayor C. K. Garrison, running for reelection, reinforced the police by sworn-in citizen deputies, chiefly recruited from the Sidney Ducks. Ironically, most had been bought off by the Know-Nothings with cash, promises, and guarantees of protection.

The *Chronicle* described Montgomery Street election-day scenes: bankers passing out slugs (fifty-dollar gold pieces); newsmen stealthily taking notes; the bars and billiard rooms jammed with a host of gentlemen and seedy loafers, 200 candidates and their multitudinous friends. All day long they drank and smoked, chewed and spat, and drank again. Everybody "speculated" and "nearly everybody belched forth perpetual volleys of oaths which like the discharge of unshotted guns meant nothing save impotent fury." Noise! Smoke! Stench! At least half of those electioneering were passing out Know-Nothing ballots.

Things went fairly peacefully until near closing time, when in the First Ward "shoulder strikers" tried to steal a ballot box. The Know-Nothings fought them off, wounding three and killing one. In the Second Ward, where a judge was absent, the Irish were shouting "No Know-Nothings!" until a wedge of SSSB thugs hit them. Police Captain North lost his gold star and was badly cut on the head. The roofs were black with spectators.

Twenty cops and armed Know-Nothings kept perfect order in the Third and Fourth wards. There was a fist fight in the Fifth, where a tax collector tangled with special cops and Irishmen "Do-Nothings." In the "Bloody Sixth," Mayor Garrison angrily tore off the badge of one of his police, who was "electioneering" for the Know-Nothings, but the SSSB thugs sent up their "Ay Ay Ay," for help, and the mayor got badly roughed up when 300 men poured in. The Second Ward "Mulligans" (Know-Nothings) marched in a body to the Sixth Ward where, the *Chronicle* remarked mildly, "they did not contribute to peace"—at least immediately. The Know-Nothings kept the Seventh Ward deadly quiet. In the Eighth, controlled by the mayor's crowd, there was one interesting dogfight and one less interesting human scuffle.

The Know-Nothings won easily. The vote from the First Ward was never counted, and the returns from the mayor's strong Eighth Ward—800 ballots—were held up for a week. But no doctoring could cut down Webb's lead, 47,739 to only 4,200 for incumbent Garrison, mostly from the Eighth. All the new aldermen were Know-Nothings, except those from the First and Eighth wards.

It was immediately after this Know-Nothing success that Alderman Henry Meiggs fled to Chile, leaving the banks holding $800,000 in forged city warrants, and businesses and banks began folding up, leading up to the terrible Black Friday of February 13, 1855.

In March, Mayor Webb informed the city that when the Know-Nothings took over they found an $840,000 deficit—

more or less the total of Meiggs' stealing—and an accumulated debt of $2,000,000 created since 1851. By legislative act, the entire debt was scaled down to $300,000, an easy solution but one that hit the banks and honest creditors, not the thieves, and aggravated the financial crash.

After Brannan's 1851 Vigilante activities, which had lashed at Nativist elements, crime and violence had been relatively muted. Now, under the Know-Nothings, it rose to a new crescendo, first under Webb, then under his successor, James L. English. Between 1849 and 1856 1,000 murders were committed in San Francisco, few of them ever solved. The Know-Nothings retained Sheriff David S. Scannel, a Broderick man and a former Bowery saloonkeeper; and his assistant jail keeper was none other than little Billy Mulligan, the Bowery thug, ex-convict, killer, and ardent patriot who had chased big Morrissey with a billiard cue. He ran a bunch of thugs for Broderick to control elections in the various wards, at the service of the Know-Nothings.

In March, 1855, a Know-Nothing Grand Council for the state met in San Francisco with 200 delegates; every county was represented except Los Angeles and Siskiyou.

The Democratic convention May 3, 1855, had denounced Know-Nothingism and secret organizations. "The Democracy of California abhors and repudiates as un-American and anti-republican the proscription of a man for the accident of his birth or for his religious opinions. . . . Universal democracy is a doctrine of equal rights to all under the constitution and the laws." The Sacramento *Journal* (anti-Know-Nothing), opposed to the *Tribune* (pro-Know-Nothing), called the movement a hoax, and dubbed the Know-Nothings "Hindoos." (It was being charged that the "American-born" Know-Nothing New York gubernatorial candidate had been born in India.) The paper brooded over the cryptic utterance of the initiated, "Sam is out; the Gayascutus is loose." Already there were signs of northern Know-Nothingism with its Abolitionism, and southern Know-Nothingism with its anti-Catholicism. The dilemma of sectionalism could not be sidestepped even in California. "God is with Democracy," concluded the paper.

All during June, parades and meetings were held throughout the state. Turnouts in Duane Springs and Placerville were notable and boisterous. A monster Know-Nothing campaign meeting was held in Sacramento on June 24. It was addressed by Senator Wilson D. Flint, a wealthy warehouse commission man; famous David S. Terry, Supreme Court justice, a close friend of Boss Broderick; and former Governor Henry S. Foote of Mississippi. The Democrats were "unmasked."

Special Know-Nothing conventions were also held June 30 and August 22 to take a stand against Mexican land grants and in favor of "native born"—i.e., non-Mexican—settlers who were stealing land from the Mexicans. The nominating convention was held on August 7 at the First Congregational Church on Sixth Street in Sacramento, after a big mass meeting in front of the Orleans Hotel. Three hundred and seventy delegates were present. The permanent president was James W. Coffroth, owner of the Tia Juana race track.

The platform adopted included "Union" and "Constitution and Law," revision of naturalization statutes, universal religious toleration but no union of church and state, and "inflexible opposition" to the "appointing or election of officials acknowledging allegiance to any foreign government" —indeed, the election of only persons born in the territory of the United States. It called for an end of sectionalism, of high costs of government, of fraud in government, for ballot-box purity, and a railway from the Pacific Ocean to the Mississippi. It wanted a liberal legislature of "settlers," meaning one that would uphold Anglo land steals. Voters were urged to disregard party labels and judge candidates according to their principles. The criterion should be: "Is he capable? Will he support the Constitution?" Just how voters could ascertain this when Know-Nothing candidates were usually presented on election day was not explained. The *Journal* observed that the platform was clever pussyfooting, arranged by the former Whig, Henry V. Crabb, to sidestep Catholic and slavery issues and to focus on "good government."

John Nealy Johnson, president of the previous year's Whig convention, was put up for governor. A grand public ratification rally was held in front of the Orleans Hotel on August

9. A Supreme Court judge was attacked for upholding Mexican land titles.

At the September 5 election, Johnson and the entire Know-Nothing ticket were elected by a 5,000-vote majority, along with a K-N majority in the legislature. The Know-Nothing state treasurer Henry Bates promptly stole $124,000, a feat discovered by a later Democratic legislature, which convicted him.

The following year, a secret anti-Know-Nothing order, Freedom's Phalanx, which admitted naturalized citizens, held a mass meeting in the United States Hotel in San Francisco and put a ticket into the field to fight "the Yankee Mackerel-Snatchers." The municipal Know-Nothing ticket was given out on April 2, the morning of election day. Whigs and Democrats began withdrawing, and the Know-Nothings easily elected James L. English mayor; they lost only one alderman's seat.

Prior to that, a full delegation was sent to the February 22, 1856 Know-Nothing convention in Philadelphia, which nominated Fillmore. The national candidates and platform were endorsed by a Sacramento reunion of 140 delegates from twenty-five counties on May 13. A pro-slavery view prevailed. The Republican party was denounced.

A few days later, Governor Johnson was embroiled in the second Vigilante fracas in San Francisco, which resulted from the shooting of James King, editor of the *Bulletin,* by Johnson P. Casey, editor of the *Sunday Times,* a protégé of various Know-Nothing politicians and particularly of Boss Broderick. King, who started his paper October, 1855, fought crime and political corruption and was a thorn in the flesh of the Know-Nothing administration. King exposed the fact that Casey had served a term in Sing Sing for grand larceny. After an extremely savage attack by King, on May 14, Casey lay in wait for him at the *Bulletin* doors. King came out at five o'clock when the streets were full of people, and Casey shoved his pistol against his chest and left him writhing in blood on the steps.

Casey was lodged in the county jail, and by 7 P.M. an angry lynch mob of 10,000 people howled outside the stone walls and kept it up all night. They were held in check by the entire police force and two hastily mobilized militia companies. The morning newspapers called for a citizens mass meeting at the former Know-Nothing headquarters on Sacramento Street. Tom Coleman, right-hand man of Brannan in the first Vigilante efforts five years previous, was made head of a new Vigilante committee. Coolheaded, energetic, by noon he had assembled 1,000 armed volunteers. (Twenty years later, he headed a third Committee of Safety to put down the terrible anti-Chinese riots, instigated by the latter-day ruffians of the Nativist White Caucasian League, the Native Sons, and the Sand Lots Labor elements.)

Events now took a strange turn. The militia companies resigned and marched out to join the Vigilantes. Other mass meetings in half-a-dozen interior towns denounced the shooting of King and offered armed help.

Nearly all the politicians, especially the Know-Nothings, were against the Vigilantes, but many responsible citizens also deplored mob usurpation of justice. The citizens who had failed to use their energies and votes to clean up the long-standing mess, now roared into the streets over a shooting between two editors.

Boss Broderick had no love for the Vigilantes—Casey was his man—but, a wise politician, he slipped out of town and took the occasion to build up his fences for future control of the entire state. Secretly, however, he gave considerable money to a rival Law and Order group, and subsidized the leading newspaper, the *Herald,* to support them and attack the Vigilantes. The Law and Order force, among whom was Supreme Court Justice David S. Terry, a famous and fearless duelist and a prominent Know-Nothing, was organized to uphold the constituted courts and the authorities against Vigilante "mob law."

For several days, while King lingered between life and death, thousands waited in front of his home and mobs continued to threaten the county jail. The Vigilantes bought up every gun in the stores, seized all rifles, pistols, swords, two cannon, and much ammunition from the state armory on Grant Street and began drilling.

Governor Johnson hurried down from Sacramento and parleyed with Coleman and the Vigilante committee. He

agreed to allow a small Vigilante contingent to camp inside
the jail walls, and so instructed Sheriff Scannell. They feared
that Casey's friend, jail keeper Billy Mulligan, would arrange
for his "escape."

At the same time Scannell served court orders on citizens
in the streets to appear at the jail and resist the expected
Vigilante attack. Only 50 obeyed the summons, and these
were mostly Broderick lawyers and henchmen who felt safer
inside the jail than out.

At nine o'clock Sunday morning, May 18, the bell at Mon-
umental Fire Engine House on Washington Street on the
north side of Portsmouth Square near the city's first theater,
Washington Hall, called the Vigilantes to assemble there.
Guns were passed out to all who showed up; by noon, there
were some 2,600. Coleman surrounded the jail with them and
demanded the surrender of Casey and the gambler Charles
Cora.

The previous November 18, 1855, Cora had killed United
States Marshal General W. H. Richardson in the Blue Wing
Saloon after the general had abused him for bringing his
mistress, who passed as Bella Cora, and Madame Arabella
Ryan, keepers of a super-fashionable Pike Street whore house,
to a public performance of *Nicodemus*. Arabella, the daughter of a Baltimore clergyman, was now providing the most
beautiful and most highly skilled girls at premium prices. At
his wife's instigation, the general ordered the theater owner
to throw the two girls out but the man refused to do so. Cora
and the general bumped into each other at various bars and
quarreled. Richardson threatened to kill him on sight. When
he came into the Blue Wing, where Cora was drinking at the
bar, however, the gambler drew his gun first and shot the
general. Cora had powerful backing and was defended by a
battery of first-rank lawyers. He might have gone free, except
for King's constant demand, in the pages of the *Bulletin,* that
he be hanged. Rumors spread that the jury had been bribed
with $40,000, also that his escape was being engineered by his
friend, jail keeper Billy Mulligan. "Look well to the jury,"
warned the *Bulletin.* "If the jury is packed, either hang the
sheriff or drive him out of town. . . . If Billy Mulligan lets
his friend Cora escape, hang Billy Mulligan or drive him out

of town." He kept this up every day: "Hang the sheriff . . .
Hang Billy Mulligan!"

The trial two months later resulted in a hung jury after
forty-one hours of deliberation. The *Bulletin* stated baldly
that crooked men had been put on the jury . . . "depravity
. . . crime . . . cannot be prosecuted in San Francisco. He
[Cora] may go through the farce of a trial [again], but nothing
more." At the time King was killed, Cora was still waiting for
his second trial.

The sheriff, now facing Coleman with less than one hundred men, was obliged to hand over the two prisoners. They
were taken handcuffed to hastily improvised cells at the Sacramento headquarters, where 300 men maintained guard
around the clock.

King died on Tuesday. Twenty thousand men and women
participated in his funeral and the burial, in Calvary Ceme-
tery on Lone Mountain (Laurel Hill), a sand-dune graveyard
set up the previous year. That same day, Casey and Cora
were "tried," condemned to death, and hanged. Cora was
given an hour's reprieve, at the request of the attending
priest, to marry Bella.

The Vigilante Committee continued to parade and patrol
the city, arms in hand. Governor Johnson proclaimed the
metropolis in a state of insurrection and ordered the Vigilantes to surrender their arms and disband. He appointed
William T. Sherman, who had a heroic Mexican War record,
to be major general of the nonexistent militia, and called all
local units to duty.

Defying the governor and Sherman as well, Coleman moved
his Vigilantes to quarters near the water front, where they
installed cells, a guardhouse, courtrooms, and fixed up a flag-
decorated meeting room. A stone wall was hastily built in
front, and beyond that, sandbag breastworks ten feet high
and six feet thick. The two cannon were mounted on the
roof and manned night and day. So was Fort Gunnybags
created. Only artillery could dislodge the Vigilante force, and
there was none except at the federal presidio and at Mare
Island Navy Yard. The governor and the Law and Order
leaders called on the federal forces for aid, but this was refused, and the refusal was upheld by President Fillmore.

Less than one hundred men responded to the governor's mobilization orders. Sherman garrisoned them in the state armory and at strategic points. But when no more help was forthcoming by the end of the week, he resigned. The governor replaced him with Volney E. Howard, a former Texas congressman, and sent Reuben Maloney, a Broderick henchman, with a large quantity of arms and ammunition on a flatboat down the Sacramento River to Howard and the Law and Order party. The Vigilantes boarded the vessel and also intercepted another shipment hidden under bricks on a small schooner. They toted everything to Fort Gunnybags.

A Vigilante deputy, Sterling A. Hopkins, and two assistants were sent to arrest Reuben Maloney, whom they found accompanied by Judge Terry in the office of Dr. H. P. Ashe, a United States naval agent. Terry and Ashe refused to allow Maloney's arrest, and all three left for the state armory to put him under Law and Order protection. A block from there they were overtaken by Hopkins, reinforced by more Vigilantes. In the ensuing brawl, Terry stabbed Hopkins in the throat with his bowie knife and got Maloney to the armory. Ashe returned to his office.

The Fort Gunnybags bell rang. Within an hour 2,000 armed Vigilantes surrounded the armory, and the Law and Order group surrendered. The Vigilantes seized all arms, then released everyone except Terry and Maloney, who were lodged in cells at Fort Gunnybags.

Maloney was deported from the city. Terry was held for a week, till Hopkins recovered, then put on trial for stabbing and other alleged affrays. The trial lasted seven weeks. Broderick secretly paid *The Herald* $200 a week to defend Terry and blast the "lawless Vigilantes." They burned the papers and terrorized businessmen into withdrawing their advertisements. Within a month the paper had to suspend publication.

After hearing 150 witnesses, the Vigilantes declared Terry guilty on three counts, and demanded he resign as Supreme Court judge. This he refused to do. The Vigilante court then announced that the "usual punishments" in their power to inflict were not "applicable in the present instance," and he was released.

On July 29, 1856, after a quick shotgun trial, two other

men involved in shooting affrays were hanged. One went insane two days before his execution, which he faced with blood-curdling shrieks. The committee deported twenty-six persons from the city. On August 18, they marched through the city, 8,000 strong, deposited their arms in Fort Gunnybags, and disbanded. On September 1, the sandbags were removed, the flag lowered, and the last guards left. On the 3rd of November the weapons were formally surrendered to the governor, who withdrew his proclamation of insurrection.

Know-Nothing rule of state and city had become one big uproar, and the end for the patriots was in sight. In the 1857 state election the Know-Nothings fell to third place, pulling fewer votes than the Republicans.

Fact and Legend

The Cannibal

BY HOMER CROY

¶ *In the Old West story, history vies with legend. Sometimes the two are intertwined, truth furnishing the core of
some far-ranging concoction of the imagination, or legend
garnishing the salad greens of fact. Unadorned, though, is
the grisly story of Jacob Keseberg, member of the heroic
Donner party of westing pioneers, winterbound, waiting and
hoping for rescue. Many have been reluctant to believe this
story, but it is, unfortunately and indubitably, true.*

AFTER REED had left that day, Tamsen was hopeful, for still
at the camp with her were Cady and Stone. They must be
noble men, so much had they suffered. She was pleased to see
them willingly cut wood and seem to want to do what was
necessary. Now and then they engaged her in conversation;
most people going to California took along valuables, they
said. They slept that night in the hut. During the night the
storm broke. Snow. Snow. Would it never cease? That afternoon, Tamsen heard the men coming down the steps talking
and, when she went to the door, there was a strange man with
them. He was introduced as Mr. Clark. When she asked him
if Mr. Reed had sent him he said No, he had decided to come
and see if he could be of help. It seemed strange that three
men, in addition to Bapteeste, would be needed to take care
of the depleted huts, but they were there; maybe it was all for
the best. The new man said that he had found bear tracks and
that he would go and see if he could "get some meat." Shoul-
dering the rifle he had brought along, he started out.

After he had gone, the other two walked off by themselves

to cut wood, or so they said. When Bapteeste approached, they waved him away.

After a time the two came back. Tamsen had made her decision. She would, she said, pay them to take her girls out.

"How much?" one asked.

"Five hundred dollars."

The men glanced at each other.

"The snow is deep."

"The little ones would have to be carried on our backs," said one. "It's a long way to Sutter's Fort."

"The snow is deep."

"If you have jewelry and valuables we could carry them out for you."

"You could claim them when you get to the Fort," said Cady.

At last the bargain was struck. She told them to go out and she would get the girls ready. When the last wagon could no longer travel, she had brought down into the hut a chest which contained clothes the girls were to wear when they reached California, and now she dressed them in their best and combed their hair, looking, as she did so, into their little pinched faces. "Tell your father good-bye and that you will wait for him in California."

George Donner looked at the three gathered around his bed. "Good-bye, girls," he said.

Tamsen got the money from its hiding place and took the girls to the top of the snow pit. The men counted the money greedily, then demanded the silver knives and forks and family valuables that Tamsen had brought. She got them out.

Eliza lacked a week of being four. Georgia was five. Immediately it was seen the two could not walk and the men put them in slings on their backs. Frances was six years and eight months and could walk.

"Good-bye," said the men casually and moved off.

Frances was in the rear and stepped in their tracks.

Tamsen watched them, thankfulness in her heart. Her daughters had been entrusted to strangers, but the men would take good care of them. And then she saw the men stop, put the children on the snow, walk off a short distance and talk. Some kind of argument was going on; they kept glancing at the girls. After a time the men came back and picked up the two and started on again, with Frances following. Soon they were out of sight.

Even after they were gone Tamsen still stood looking in the direction they had gone. Finally she turned and went down the steps. George was lying quietly in the dark. "Have they gone?" he asked weakly.

"Yes. The men are carrying Georgia and Eliza, and Frances is following behind in their tracks. She is surprisingly strong."

"She was always the strongest one of the three." There was a wait, then his thin voice again. "They'll soon be with Elitha and Leanna."

"Yes, at Sutter's Fort. They'll all be there together," she assured him.

After a time she heard someone coming down the steps and when she peered out she saw Clark. He looked here and there in the gloom, announced that the bear had got away, then said, "Where are they?"

When she told what had happened, anger came into his voice—he had been deserted by his sly friends. But it was too late to do anything about it, for night came and the storm descended and the whiteness became whiter.

Her girls were being taken out by a rescue party. The rescue party might have trouble in going over the Pass, she thought, but each day, after they had achieved the Pass, the snow would be less. Thank God for that. The dreadful, pitiless, unending snow. The dazzling whiteness which blinded one. How could she stand it any longer? But she would. She would never, never give up. She had got her five daughters out. She would get out herself when George was better. . . . What a fine character he was. He had always been kind and gentle and even now, in his distress, tried to make it as easy for her as he could.

She must do all she could for her sister-in-law who was not as strong as she was. Four of Elizabeth's children had been taken to the camp by the lake and had been carried out by rescuers, but two still remained. Lewis Donner, her youngest, was steadily growing weaker. In addition there was Sammie who was stronger and who did not cry so much. Also in Elizabeth's tent was another problem. Bapteeste would cut hardly any wood; he preferred to sit around all day in the chill and damp rather than work, for he was that kind.

Nick Clark was in Tamsen's hut and he, too, lost interest in cutting wood and keeping the fire going, and would not hunt for ox skins, or carcasses. Now and then he and Bapteeste went out of hearing and secretly talked together.

One day Elizabeth came hurrying down the steps. Would Tamsen come? Tamsen put on clothes and got to the tent as quickly as she could. There, on the rough stake-bed, was little Lewis. It was hard for Tamsen to comfort Elizabeth, after he was gone. The two women sat in the gloom, suddenly tender toward each other. Why! it was such moments as this that made life worth while. After a time the two, feeling strengthened, wrapped the body in a sheet and took it out and buried it in the snow. Clark and Bapteeste were off at a distance, talking.

One day Bapteeste came hurrying to Tamsen's tent. "Cub queeck," he said and when Tamsen got to the hut she found her sister-in-law lying on the fatal stake-bed and in a few minutes Elizabeth was dead. With what grudging assistance she could get from Bapteeste she put Elizabeth in a sheet and took her out and buried her in the snow. Sammie was the only one left and he was so weak that she took him to her own tent and, for warmth, put him in bed with his Uncle George.

The food Reed had brought was running low. Surely, by this time, another rescue party must have got through; she would go and see if she couldn't get food.

She asked Clark if he would stay with her husband; he grudgingly consented. She got her money belt, for she did not want to leave it in the hut with these two shifty men coming in and out, and, finally, March 12, started—a small figure among the towering trees in the vast white silence.

The snow had melted so that the tops of the cabins were visible. A scarecrow figure was tottering across the snow; it turned, when she called, and looked at her in a daze, then, without speaking, went floundering on.

At last she reached Donner Lake. It was a vast snowy plain, with, here and there, white hummocks of ice—cabins, she knew them to be. She approached the Murphy-Eddy cabin which had been built against a black rock. (On this rock to-

day, on a bronze tablet, are the names of the members of the
Donner Party.) She edged down the steps to the cabin and
pushed open the door, but in the gloom she could not see, for
her eyes had been adjusted to the glare of the snow. She was
shocked to see her three daughters. They had been abandoned
by Cady and Stone, who had left them in Lavina Murphy's
cabin and had set out to get over the mountains before a
threatened storm. The noble men did not want to have to
suffer privation and cold in the mountains, for they were
carrying the jewelry, silver and silk dresses they had stolen
from Tamsen's hut. This added considerably to the weight
they must pack in all that deep snow.

Lavina Murphy had taken care of the children as best she
could; indeed she had gone without food herself so they could
live. She had gone out across the snow trying to gather sticks
which would serve as firewood. The strain on her eyes had
been too much, and now she was half blind. Her mind had
become so affected that part of the time she did not know
what she was doing. Then her mind would clear; the first
thing she thought of, then, was the children.

Tamsen put her arms around the girls, kissed them and
began talking to them tenderly. Then she heard someone in
the gloom and looked and there, lying on a crude bed, was a
man with a great mass of tangled hair. "You come here?"
grunted Keseberg. "Die kinder cry," he added sharply.

She was so terrified by his threatening voice and by his
hollow eyes that, for a moment, she could not speak. Finally
she said, "They will do better now."

"Dey besser." There was a silence, then he said in the same
threatening tone, "Ve haf no foodt."

After a time he got up and slowly climbed the icy steps.
Tamsen and the girls watched, not speaking, such terror had
the sinister man cast over them.

After they had talked a few minutes and reassured each
other of their love, Tamsen was able to piece together what
had happened. When the girls had been set down on the
snow, they had known by the actions of the men that something was wrong, for the men had kept looking at them and
talking in low voices. Then Frances had said to her sisters,

"If they go off and leave us, I can follow the tracks back to Mama and she can come and take you back."

The men had picked the girls up, started on again and finally had arrived at the Murphy cabin where they had taken them in, and with hardly a word of explanation, had left them with Lavina Murphy. The first person the girls saw was Keseberg on a quilt near the fire. As their eyes became adjusted, they saw other people lying in beds, all of whom resented the new burdens that had been thrust on them.

One of the children began to cry. "Shut up or I vill kill you," said Keseberg.

At last supper time came and the people began doling out strips of ox hide. But no one offered the girls any. Then little Patty Reed gave them some of the biscuits that had been allotted to her. The three girls divided them. When bed time came they lay down on a bed of branches and put their arms around each other. A new storm broke; the wind howled and the cry of the wolves came to them. Morning came and they shook the snow off and lay quietly, watching the people, afraid to move.

One of the children in the miserable hut was little Georgie Foster, four years old, the grandchild of Mrs. Murphy. The cold and the suffering was too much for the child and he cried almost continuously. Keseberg shouted at him and told Mrs. Murphy to make him stop crying.

Finally he said in an ingratiating voice that if the child slept with him, it might get warm and stop crying. Mrs. Murphy moved the child to Keseberg's bed. The next morning the child was dead. When the grandmother discovered this, she picked the child up in her arms and began to wail. Keseberg came and took the child from her, put a rope around it, hung it up inside the cabin and told her not to go near it. She sat a little distance from it, looking at it and sobbing.

Another of the children was little Jimmie Eddy, son of Will Eddy. Little Jimmie had died and had been taken outside and buried in the snow. After a time, Keseberg had gone up the steps; he came back with some strips of flesh which he roasted over the fire and ate.

Tamsen listened, appalled at what had happened. What should she do?

She could not take the children back and, seemingly, they could not be sent over the mountains. Then she and the others in the dark cave heard a shout and when Tamsen went up the steps, there was Will Eddy, who had arrived as a member of a rescue party.

They climbed the steps as best they could and gathered around Will Eddy, laughing and sobbing. He stared at the gaunt figures, hardly able to speak, so affected was he. Finally he said, "Where is Jimmie?"

"He died," said one of them but did not dare to tell what had happened.

A bit later, however, some one did tell him. Eddy was overcome, but finally gained possession of himself. He would kill Keseberg, he decided, but he would wait till Keseberg got to Sacramento.

Food was distributed; the people ate like animals. Eddy was so touched by the sight of the ravenous creatures that he himself sobbed. When they had eaten what he had allotted, they begged for more. He had to be firm, for he knew what might happen. At last, all the people in the camp had been given food; and now, with the men he had brought along, he could take a number of the people out.

Tamsen watched the preparations, with hope rising and falling. Then she found that her children were not to go; they were stronger than the others and would have to wait till another rescue party arrived. Eddy was busy getting the people ready. Lying on his bed, as he always seemed to be doing, was Keseberg with his bushy beard and hollow eyes.

"Will," she said, "I want you to take my girls out." She told how Cady and Stone had deserted them.

"I'd like to, Tamsen. But every one wants to go and we can't take them all."

"I have fifteen hundred dollars here," she said, indicating her money belt, "and I will give it all to you, if you will take them out."

"I couldn't carry that much money, Tamsen, with the loads I will have to pack. I don't want to add even a silver spoon to the weight. But they do deserve it, and I will take the girls out." He paused and looked at her carefully. "You're strong,

Tamsen. You come with me and help take care of the girls.
We will start in the morning while the snow is still hard."

"I can't, Will. I must go back to my husband," she said.

"You don't want them to arrive in California as orphans,
do you?" he said, admiring her and, at the same time, thinking how short-sighted she was.

"Of course not, Will. I must stay."

"Well, you've made your choice," he said shortly.

"Can you wait while I go back and see my husband? . . .
maybe he'll be better. The men can bring out Sammie. Will
you do that?"

"I can't, Tamsen. That would take a day. We have to start
early in the morning."

She began getting the girls ready, although there was little
to do and they would not leave till morning. It was growing
late and she must start back to her husband on Alder Creek.
The girls came to the top of the icy rim. Tenderly she kissed
them good-bye and started through the snow without letting
herself look back.

What thoughts must have been in her mind as she struggled through the vast expanse of white. Why! it had been
eleven months since they had started from Springfield. Keseberg! What a monster he was. But in the morning the girls
would be taken from his presence. Soon they would be at
Sutter's Fort with Elitha and Leanna. As soon as George got
better, she would go, too. . . .

At last she saw the tops of the huts sticking out of the snow.
But no smoke was coming from the vent in Elizabeth Donner's brush tent. The feeling in her grew stronger that something was wrong. She hallooed, but there was no answer in
the white silence. When she went down the steps of her tent,
George told her that Clark and Bapteeste had deserted. She
found, on examination, that they had taken out booty of silver spoons, silk and two guns. She sat down, overwhelmed.
But, after a time, her courage plucked up. She would succeed
yet.

She told George how she had found the girls there, and that
they would be taken out in the morning.

At the good news, George revived a little. "It makes it
easier," he said. She did not mention Keseberg.

Little Sammie continued to grow worse; when he died she carried him up the steps, and buried him in the snow and returned to her husband. He, too, grew weaker. She continued to heat water and to bathe his feverish arm. The end came, and again she struggled up the steps. And now she was alone in the camp that had sheltered, the first night they had camped, thirty-one persons.

She would go back to the camp by the lake and wait for the next rescue party. The snow was clearing away; signs of spring were everywhere; geese were honking north; wolves were not heard so often. She would get to Sutter's Fort and there would be her five girls. Some of the people she had known so long, and had traveled with so far, would be there. But also some wouldn't. There was the matter of how starvation and death had brought out their character. Some had proved to be heroes; some little above animals. Was it only when strain came that one's true character showed? But none had given up. What a strange circle she herself had moved in: life and death. But all life was a mystery. And death, too. The girls would want to know how their father had died . . . she would soften that. She must bring them up to remember him with reverence.

She set about packing the things to be taken out when the rescuers came. When the things got to Sutter's Fort they would be valuable and would help her start their new life. Her school. Had that been an idle dream? No, it had not. She would, somehow, manage it alone.

She came out of her musings with a start; someone was coming down the steps. The rescuers had arrived! On second thought this seemed strange, for people arriving at a hut always hallooed.

Across the opening, which served as a door, was an ox hide; it was slowly pulled back and a hairy face showed. Hollow eyes stared at her in the low light, then a voice said ingratiatingly, "Can I come in?"

"My husband is dead. What is it you want?"

"Is deadt? Ah! it is badt. I vill come in, please."

"What is it you want?" she repeated.

"Yoost to come in."

He moved slowly in and seated himself on the edge of a

stake-bed. "It is badt about your husband. I am sorry. I have him alvays liked. It is badt." He blinked as his eyes adjusted themselves. "De whole trip is badt. Many horrible deat's. But now mercy comes and ve can go. I have come to help you oudt."

"I don't need you, Mr. Keseberg. I can get out myself."

"Many t'ings to carry, you have. De money . . . vere is it? I vill help you. Ve vill be friends, is it not so?"

"Please go, Mr. Keseberg."

She tried to edge toward the skin door, but he moved between her and the opening and glared at her with his sunken eyes.

"I have no money," cried Tamsen.

"*Hein!* De money belt, vere is it? You vill not give it me, *heh?* Ve vill see." Seizing a stick from the fireplace, the enraged, half-demoniacal man advanced toward her . . .

In a moment it was over. Tamsen was on the floor and Keseberg, exhausted from the struggle, again sat down on the stake-bed. He rested, panting, and looking at the crumpled body. Finally he got up and started to ransack the hut.

After a time he came back and stood looking down at the body. Then he found the axe used to cut firewood and methodically began to chop up her body. He started the fire going more brightly, arranged an iron kettle and put parts of her body in it. Then he sat down to rest, as the exertion and the walk over from the main camp had tired him.

The Lost Dutchman Mine

¶ *Tall tales and legends abound in Arizona, many of them about fabulous treasures and lost mines. It has been said that the mines men find are never as rich as those they have lost. The Lost Dutchman is no exception to the stated rule. Of all the hidden-treasure yarns, it is the best known; almost endless variations of it have been related at one time or another.*

THERE IS A SAYING in the Southwest that "the mines men find are never so rich as those they lost." To prove it, Arizona's folklore is filled with stories of fabulous deposits of precious metals found, and then lost, and searched for diligently through two or three generations. Every section of the state has its share of lost mines, but probably the most famous one is the Lost Dutchman Mine in the Superstition Mountains about thirty-five miles east of Phoenix. The long series of very interesting legends dealing with this rich gold mine begins with a young Mexican lover fleeing the wrath of his sweetheart's father and seeking refuge far north in the forbidding Superstitions. He is supposed to have found the great gold deposit when its location was still a part of Old Mexico, but the Gadsden Purchase was about to take place, so the young man's entire Mexican community formed a great expedition and made the long march into the Superstitions. There they mined as much of the gold as they could carry and set out jubilantly for home. But the Apaches ambushed them, and

From *Arizona, A State Guide*. Copyright 1940 by The Arizona State College at Flagstaff; 1956 by Hastings House, Publishers.

killed the entire party—four hundred men—except two young boys concealed under a bush. These two children found their way back home, and grew up with the knowledge that they alone knew the location of the mine. When they were old enough they took a third partner and went to the Superstitions, finding the mine without difficulty. They had hardly begun to dig, when the Dutchman came along.

The Dutchman was a prospector with a long white beard, and his name was Jacob Wolz, or Walz. He had been prospecting in the Superstitions, and a band of Apaches had driven him into a part of the mountains he had never seen before. He stumbled into the camp of the Mexican boys and became friendly with them and they told him about their mine. Wolz killed the three Mexicans and from about 1870 until his death the mine was his.

As stories of the Dutchman's gold ore spread around Phoenix and Florence, many prospectors tried to trail him into the mountains but he outwitted them, or killed them. Wolz is said to have admitted killing eight men because of the mine, including his own nephew. He died in Phoenix in Oct. 1891, with a shoe box of the beautiful ore under his bed. Almost with his last breath he gave a friendly neighbor directions to the mine, saying they must be followed exactly as the mine entrance was concealed under ironwood logs covered with rock. Unfortunately the most important landmark in Wolz's directions, a palo verde tree with a peculiar pointing branch, could not be located then or later.

Since then, literally thousands of prospectors, both professional and amateur, have searched for the Lost Dutchman Mine, and their luck has been uniformly bad. Some have never come back at all, others have returned with pieces of human skeletons and accounts of almost dying of thirst, and still others have been mysteriously shot at in the wild canyons. The tragedy and violence connected with the Lost Dutchman have added to the strong conviction of Arizonans that the Superstition Mountains are cursed. Some people say that pigmies guard the mine; some think it possible that a few wild Apaches still live up there; and others believe that some prospector has found the Lost Dutchman and shoots to kill any who approach the bonanza. Of course, there are some who say Dutchman Wolz "never had nothin' up there no-how," but judging by the number of prospecting expeditions into the Superstitions annually, these skeptics can never command as large an audience as exponents of more exciting theories.

⟨⚬⟩⚬⟨⚬⟩⚬⟨⚬⟩

The O.K. Corral Fight

¶ *On October 26, a gun battle took place in Tombstone, Arizona. On one side were Virgil Earp, then the city marshal; two of his brothers, Wyatt and Morgan; and Wyatt's crony, Doc Holliday (Virgil had deputized the other three to act as special policemen). On the other side were Ike and Billy Clanton, brothers, and Frank and Tom McLowry, brothers. The McLowrys were cattlemen; the Clantons, although reputedly rustlers, were friends of the McLowrys and all four were associated in a pending business deal. That morning, Tom McLowry and Ike Clanton had been disarmed by the Earps, hauled into court, and fined for carrying concealed weapons. Later in the day, Tom and Ike and their brothers were confronted at the O.K. Corral and ordered by Marshal Earp to throw up their hands. A gun fight ensued, in which Billy Clanton and the two McLowrys were killed and Virgil and Morgan Earp were wounded.*

So much is certain. What is less clear is the reason for it. The two groups had been hostile toward each other. The Clantons and McLowrys and others in the "cowboy faction" supported or favored Sheriff John Behan and his deputies, who were political opponents of the Earps. The Earps be-

From *Arizona: The Last Frontier*, by Joseph Miller. Copyright 1956 by Hastings House Publishers, Inc.

lieved the cowboys had knowledge of some recent stagecoach robberies, and Wyatt had tried unsuccessfully to get Ike Clanton to testify against certain suspects. Anyway, "bad blood" existed between the two groups and, with their four enemies in town, the Earps clearly decided to (a) force a fight and settle things for good, or (b) drive some "undesirable characters" out of town—whichever way one chooses to look at it. Some eyewitness testimony maintained that Tom McLowry and Billy Clanton raised their hands and tried to surrender before the shooting started, but that was contradicted. Ike Clanton ran away when the bullets began to fly; it is probable that he still did not have a gun. The newspaper account below, as it appeared in the Tucson Citizen from a Tombstone Nugget report, has Billy Clanton firing the shots that wounded both of the Earps; but some authorities maintain it was Tom McLowry who put the bullet into Morgan—if so, Tom had replaced the weapon confiscated from him earlier in the day. The Earps were arrested for murder following the fight, but discharged on the ground that they were "doing their duty" as officers of the law. Later, Morgan Earp was killed and Virgil Earp was seriously wounded by shots fired from ambush; and the Earp crowd shot and killed Frank Stilwell, who was believed to have been involved in the attacks on Morgan and Virgil.

THE 26TH OF OCTOBER, 1881, will always be marked as one of the crimson days in the annals of Tombstone, a day when blood flowed as water, and human life was held as a shuttlecock, a day always to be remembered as witnessing the bloodiest and deadliest street fight that has ever occurred in this place, or probably in the Territory.

The origin of the trouble dates back to the first arrest of Stilwell and Spence, for the robbery of the Bisbee stage. The co-operation of the Earps and the Sheriff and his deputies in the arrest caused a number of the cowboys to, it is said, threaten the lives of all interested in the capture. Still, nothing occurred to indicate that any such threats would be carried into execution. But Tuesday night Ike Clanton and Doc Holliday had some difficulty in the Alhambra saloon. Hard

words passed between them, and when they parted it was generally understood that the feeling between the two men was
that of intense hatred. Yesterday morning Clanton came on
the street armed with a rifle and revolver, but was almost immediately arrested by Marshal Earp, disarmed and fined by
Justice Wallace for carrying concealed weapons. While in the
Courtroom Wyatt Earp told him that as he had made threats
against his life he wanted him to make his fight, to say how,
when and where he would fight, and to get his crowd, and he
(Wyatt) would be on hand.

In reply, Clanton said: "Four feet of ground is enough for
me to fight on, and I'll be there." A short time after this Billy
Clanton and Frank McLowry came in town, and as Tom
McLowry was already here the feeling soon became general
that a fight would ensue before the day was over, and crowds
of expectant men stood on the corner of Allen and Fourth
streets awaiting the coming conflict.

It was now about two o'clock, and at this time Sheriff
Behan appeared upon the scene and told Marshal Earp that if
he disarmed his posse, composed of Morgan and Wyatt Earp,
and Doc Holliday, he would go down to the O.K. Corral,
where Ike and Billy Clanton and Frank and Tom McLowry
were and disarm them. The Marshal did not desire to do this
until assured that there was no danger of an attack from the
other party. The Sheriff went to the corral and told the cowboys that they must put their arms away and not have any
trouble. Ike Clanton and Tom McLowry said they were not
armed, and Frank McLowry said he would not lay his aside.
In the meantime the Marshal had concluded to go and, if
possible, end the matter by disarming them, and as he and
his posse came down Fremont Street towards the corral, the
Sheriff stepped out and said: "Hold up boys, don't go down
there or there will be trouble; I have been down there to disarm them." But they passed on, and when within a few feet
of them the Marshal said to the Clantons and McLowrys:
"Throw up your hands boys, I intend to disarm you."

As he spoke Frank McLowry made a motion to draw his
revolver, when Wyatt Earp pulled his and shot him, the ball
striking on the right side of his abdomen. About the same
time Doc Holliday shot Tom McLowry in the right side,

using a short shotgun, such as is carried by Wells-Fargo & Co.'s messengers. In the meantime Billy Clanton had shot at Morgan Earp, the ball passing through the point of the left shoulder blade across his back, just grazing the backbone and coming out at the shoulder, the ball remaining inside of his shirt. He fell to the ground but in an instant gathered himself, and raising in a sitting position fired at Frank McLowry as he crossed Fremont Street, and at the same instant Doc Holliday shot at him, both balls taking effect, either of which would have proved fatal, as one struck him in the right temple and the other in the left breast. As he started across the street, however, he pulled his gun down on Holliday saying, "I've got you now." "Blaze away! You're a daisy if you have," replied Doc. This shot of McLowry's passed through Holliday's pistol pocket, just grazing the skin.

While this was going on Billy Clanton had shot Virgil Earp in the right leg, the ball passing through the calf, inflicting a severe flesh wound. In turn he had been shot by Morgan Earp in the right side of the abdomen, and twice by Virgil Earp, once in the right wrist and once in the left breast. Soon after the shooting commenced Ike Clanton ran through the O.K. Corral, across Allen Street into Kellogg's saloon, and thence into Toughnut Street, where he was arrested and taken to the county jail. The firing altogether didn't occupy more than twenty-five seconds, during which time fully thirty shots were fired. After the fight was over Billy Clanton, who, with wonderful vitality, survived his wounds for fully an hour, was carried by the editor and foreman of the *Nugget* into a house near where he lay, and everything possible done to make his last moments easy. He was "game" to the last, never uttering a word of complaint, and just before breathing his last he said, "Goodbye, boys; go away and let me die."

The wounded were taken to their houses, and at three o'clock next morning were resting comfortably. The dead bodies were taken in charge by the Coroner, and an inquest held. Upon the person of Tom McLowry was found between $300 and $400 and checks and certificates of deposit to the amount of nearly $3,000.

During the shooting Sheriff Behan was standing near by commanding the contestants to cease firing but was powerless to prevent it. Several parties who were in the vicinity of the shooting had narrow escapes from being shot. One man who had lately arrived from the East had a ball pass through his pants. He left for home this morning. A person called "The Kid," who shot Hicks at Charleston recently, was also grazed by a ball. When the mine whistle gave the signal that there was a conflict between the officers and the cowboys, the mines on the hill shut down and the miners were brought to the surface. From the Contention mine a number of men, fully armed, were sent to town in a four-horse carriage. At the request of the Sheriff the "Vigilantes," or Committee of Safety, were called from the streets by a few sharp toots from the whistle. During the early part of the evening there was a rumor that a mob would attempt to take Ike Clanton from the jail and lynch him, and to prevent any such unlawful proceedings a strong guard of deputies was placed around the building.

That evening Finn Clanton, brother of Billy and Ike, came to town, and placing himself under the guard of the Sheriff, visited the morgue to see the remains of his brother, and then passed the night in jail in company with the other brother.

Shortly after the shooting ceased the whistle sounded a few short toots, and almost simultaneously a large number of citizens appeared on the streets, armed with rifles and a belt of cartridges around their waists. These men formed in line and offered their services to the peace officers to preserve order in case any attempt at disturbance was made, or any interference offered to the authorities of the law. However, no hostile move was made by anyone, and quiet and order was fully restored, and in a short time the excitement died away.

At the morgue the bodies of the three slain cowboys lay side by side, covered with a sheet. Very little blood appeared on their clothing, and only on the face of young Billy Clanton was there any distortion of the features or evidence of pain in dying. The features of the two McLowry boys looked as calm and placid in death as if they had died peaceably. No unkind remarks were made by anyone, but a feeling of unusual sorrow seemed to prevail. Of the McLowry brothers we could learn nothing of their previous history before coming to Arizona. The two brothers owned quite an extensive ranch on the lower San Pedro, some seventy or eighty miles from this city, to which they had removed their cattle since the recent Mexican and Indian troubles. They did not bear the reputation of being of a quarrelsome disposition, but were known as fighting men, and have generally conducted themselves in a quiet and orderly manner when in Tombstone.

—Tucson *Citizen,* 1881

The Hermit of the Superstitions

BY JOSEPH MILLER

¶ *"Old Man Reavis" was a remarkable member of the Southwest's generous legion of colorful characters. Perhaps he first went into the Superstitions to hunt for the Lost Dutchman mine, as some have said. He stayed there to hunt, to grow prize vegetables, to read good books, and to mind his own business.*

"OLD MAN REAVIS, the Hermit of the Superstitions," is dead! His body, half eaten by coyotes, was found near his hut in the Superstitions. This was the startling and gruesome message carried in some of the Arizona newspapers in mid-May of 1896. Whether death was natural or violent was only a matter of conjecture, also the time when it might have occurred, for the hunger of the wolves had not left enough evidence upon which to base an opinion.

From *Arizona: The Last Frontier,* by Joseph Miller. Copyright 1956 by Hastings House, Publishers, Inc.

Word was brought into Florence by Bud Neighbors of the finding of the decomposed body on the trail about four or five miles from the Reavis ranch. James Delabaugh, a prospector, was at the Reavis ranch on the 20th of April, when the hermit was about to start out for Mesa to procure some seed potatoes. Being at Fraser's ranch on the 6th of May, and finding that Reavis had not passed that way, as he would necessarily be compelled to do, Delabaugh became alarmed and went back on the trail to learn the reason. He found the body of the old hermit near the trail. His burros were tied near by, half starved from their fast of several days, and his two big mongrel dogs were hovering near the body of their dead master, and had evidently destroyed a portion of his body. [*It seems doubtful that these dogs would allow any varmint to approach the body of Reavis and mutilate it as some of the stories have it. It seems logical that they, sensing death, tugged at their master's body, causing the damaged state in which it was found.*]

Of all men so widely known there was none in Arizona of whom so little was known as "Old Man Reavis." Much had been written about him by the few who had visited him in his mountain home, but what was written was generally produced by the imagination of the writers. It is said that the old recluse was driven into exile by a disappointment in love, but he never said so and nobody else has been found who could have said so. It is only known that he settled in the Superstition Mountains in the early seventies, and while he may have been hunting for the "Lost Dutchman" mine, nothing was ever mentioned about it. He never told anybody where he came from, in fact he never told anybody much of anything, except an interesting story now and then of his adventures.

The Apaches were roaming the hills in those days, but they soon learned to shun the cabin of the hermit whose unerring rifle first inspired respect, and then a sort of superstitious terror. The old man spent the most of his time in hunting and raising vegetables and fruit which were carried by burro train to the various mining camps in the area, among them Silver King, Goldfield, Globe and Pinal, as well as the towns of Florence, Mesa and Tempe.

The Reavis ranch of some fifteen acres, located in an almost inaccessible part of the Superstitions, was about fifteen miles northwest of Silver King and some forty miles east of Phoenix. There was always plenty of wild game in the area, and for many years the Apaches hunted both man and beast throughout this area. A never failing stream of pure water flowed there which was used to irrigate the land. The elevation, about five thousand feet above sea level, provided an excellent climate where all kinds of deciduous fruits flourished, as did most varieties of vegetables. Wild walnuts and cherries grew abundantly. Blackberries and raspberries grew wild in plentiful quantities all around the mountains.

Reavis specialized in fresh vegetables, including some of the biggest and best cabbages ever grown. Reavis cabbages were famous. Heads that averaged more than ten pounds in weight were solid and firm, and as tender as young lettuce. He raised parsnips, five inches in diameter, that were extremely tender, and in fact all of his vegetables possessed the most superior qualities.

There are some very interesting Indian ruins not far from the Reavis ranch and a cave in which many relics have been found. They are situated on Rogers Creek and but few white people have ever visited them and none in a scientific way. The whole neighborhood is full of interesting features, and the place, a splendid summer resort, although comparatively few were ever privileged to take advantage of this very delightful place.

Reavis was a typical frontiersman; active, restless, hardy and hospitable. He was nearly six feet in height, very straight, and strongly built; his massive head covered with a long hirsute matting of auburn hue, innocent alike of shears or comb for perhaps years. His deep-set gray eyes looked out from under shaggy brows, leaving no feature visible except his nose, which was straight and large denoting character. He wore overalls, a flannel shirt and a seedy coat, and this costume, it is said, he had never been known to vary during the time he had been in the country. He was affable and intelligent, a thorough scholar and great reader. He possessed an excellent library of standard books, and from each trip to a settlement he carried back a bagful of newspapers and it is said that his acquaintance with the affairs of the outer world was thorough and surprising. The story of his life and adventures surely would have made an interesting volume of historical value.

Reavis had many peculiar eccentricities, such as never cutting or combing his hair; at least it gave the appearance of never having been given any care. He was really more of a recluse than a hermit, and although he attracted the attention of strangers because of his odd appearance, his burro train and dogs, those acquainted with him paid no more attention to him than they did any other mountain rancher. Once while he was visiting in Phoenix a tourist took a snapshot of him with a kodak. The picture was finished, enlarged and made a part of the Arizona exhibit at the Columbian Exposition where it was said to have been recognized by a woman from California as her long lost brother, and that there was an attempt at correspondence and a very romantic story that the old man had left a daughter in San Francisco whom he had educated and was secretly supporting. The only thing though that really resulted from the exhibition of the picture was a threat sent down the mountain side by the hermit that if he ever met the amateur artist he would send a bullet through his brain. His picture, however, had been taken some years previous to that and an enlargement of it hung in a Phoenix saloon. It represented a man whose face might have looked upon a century. The hair was long and matted and crowned by a slouched and ragged hat. A Winchester lay across his lap, the fingers of the right hand grasping the stock of the gun.

On the occasion of one of Reavis' visits to Phoenix he was entertained by a couple of gentlemen who had been at his home in the mountains. The entertainment evolved into a circuit of saloons. In one of them he was introduced to a concert-hall singer. He was a model of courtesy, a reminiscence of a former life somewhere. But when he was asked to drink a glass of champagne with the painted singer he refused laughingly, politely but firmly. He would drink with the boys, but he had never learned, wherever he had been, to drink with a woman in a saloon.

—A composite of Arizona newspaper items, 1896

The Four-Footed

Lord of the Plains

BY MARI SANDOZ

¶ *The quadrupeds, wild and half-wild, indigenous or not, that roved the plains and mountains of the West rivaled the bipeds in importance and in interest. Many books have been written, and many are still to be written, about the wolf and the coyote, about the grizzly bear and the antelope, about the Longhorn and the mustang and the buffalo. Most majestic and imposing of all was the buffalo, the American bison, numbering in the many tens of millions until the great herds melted before the long-shooting guns of the white hunters. An estimated ratio of five hundred buffalo to every Indian in the pre-paleface days suggests how important they were as source of sustenance to the tribesmen. The following selection shows the great beast in relation to its herd-fellows.*

FROM ABOUT November twentieth to late December the buffaloes were at their finest; sleek and fat, the pelage thick and glossy-dark; the calves, all except the latest ones, smooth and brown. It was at this time of the year that the sight of the great herds moved visitors from the far world, sportsmen like Prince Maximilian and Sir Gore, and naturalists like Hornaday, to call the American bison the most magnificent of all ruminants. True, the south Indian bison or gaur and the aurochs, the European bison, both surpassed him in height if not in actual bulk. The bull of the American bison usually weighed around two thousand pounds and up, the cows about twelve hundred. With much longer and more luxuriant hair on the head, neck and forequarters, the buffalo was vastly

From *The Buffalo Hunters*. Copyright 1954 by Mari Sandoz.

more imposing even singly. In the vast, dark herds of the plains, he was fabulous and unbelievable.

Towards spring, however, the buffaloes faded swiftly, their bleaching hair giving them a rusty, seedy appearance. They began to shed early, sometimes by the last week of February in the Republican herd, and took over half a year to do it, dead, matted hair clinging to them in ragged and dirty tufts. To rid themselves of this loosening hair and the vermin in it, they scratched on everything—rocks, banks, trees, telegraph poles and buildings. The only unprotected habitation that the frontiersman could maintain for long was the dugout set into a bank or side hill too steep for footing. They upset any wagon left on the prairie and rubbed down the flag poles at the army posts. To prevent over-eager defenders of the colors from cluttering up the area with stinking carcasses, orders were still issued at posts like Ft. McPherson, Nebraska, against shooting buffaloes on the parade ground.

On the hump and shoulders the new hair pushed the old off as it came in, dark and often well-matured as early as May, the heads a glossy black. The rest of the body, however, was often still nude as a badly scalded hog into mid-June. Raw, scabby and tender, the buffalo was driven wild by the flies and by the buffalo gnats that were like whirling clouds of fine clinging dust around his nose and eyes and in the sores of his bare skin. Often flight was the only remedy and a thundering run out into the wind of the tablelands left the gnats behind. But the sun burned the buffalo too, and so he retreated to the first mudhole and rolled in it like a great pig, coating his tender hide all over. The mud gathered in thick lumps on the long hair of his forequarters and his head and beard, making an appallingly hideous creature of him. Yet the Indians pursued the mud-caked buffalo as hotly as ever, although they had no illusions about the meat of spring. But hunger sharpens the tooth and the winter parfleches welcome the leanest jerky. Then too, the Indians always preferred freshly killed meat for the cooking fires, and pointed to the unloveliness of the habitual carrion eater, the buzzard, compared to the grace and beauty of animals that fed on flesh or blood that was still warm with animal heat—the eagle, the mink, the ermine and the mountain lion.

By summer the herds were full of romping calves, mostly born from April through June. They followed their mothers many months, perhaps over a year. They were reddish-yellow until August, then the hair fell in patches and by October they were brown, fat and adventuresome.

During the calving season the cows gathered off to themselves, leaving the bulls scattered, or drawn into small herds that were dangerous for the unwary hunter. Often without a cow to take the lead, to draw them away from danger, they stood their ground in sullen stubbornness, and did not try to save themselves at all. Even in the regular herds the bulls were less wary, easier to approach, and meat hunters could creep past them to get at the more desirable but wilier cows. At any pursuit or even the smell of man, the buffalo, unconscious of his strength, fled, and would only fight at bay. Now and then in a hot chase he might turn, swift as light, and overthrow horse and rider, and so was dangerous within the close range of the fuke, as the old hunters called the sawed-off double-barrel shotgun loaded with ball, or with the bow and arrow or spear that the Indian generally had to use. One of the warrior sons of Dull Knife, the Cheyenne chief, was gored to death by an arrow-shot buffalo in a surround. Yet the hunting could be dangerous even with guns, as Bill Cody discovered the time a wounded bull gored his horse and chased him afoot. It got him the name of Buffalo Bill from the laughing soldiers who rescued him.

The flamboyant Cody, with an eye for the publicity, adopted the story as one more exploit, and elaborated it into a duel to the death between the infuriated monarch of the plains and Buffalo Bill Cody armed only with a knife. It had an element of probability. Experienced skinners and butchers sometimes had narrow escapes from buffaloes apparently dead. Up north toward the Yellowstone a hunter was killed by a bull whose tongue he had actually cut out in the belief that the buffalo was dead.

A cow with a new-born calf could be more dangerous than any bull. Usually she left the herd and returned a few hours later with a lanky, new-dropped yellow calf that would follow at her side until driven away by his successor. For the first week or so the cow was "on the prod" as the hunters called it, but they often caught calves a few weeks old, after the mothers had been shot or driven off. Given a finger to suck a while the calf followed a man as closely as it had the mother, doggedly, silently, with only a pig-like grunt for hunger or thirst. At five months the wild calf could outrun a relay of three fresh horses and not be overtaken until worn out by a chase of twelve, fifteen miles, perhaps to die quietly in the pen or on a rope that night. A buffalo hunter named Charley Jones discarded the rifle for the rope and built up a little herd of buffaloes for the ranch he established at Garden City, Kansas.

The running season, as the westerners called it, was from July well into September, when the calves were two to four months old. At its beginning the ease-loving, even slothful nature of the buffaloes disappeared. Instead of the small scattered herds of calving time, they now gathered in great excitement. The bulls chased cows half of the time and fought each other the rest. The encounters, bull against bull, were long, threatening and dusty. Heads lowered almost to the ground, their narrow flanks heaving, their beards jerking, they roared until the earth shook, their bloodshot little eyeballs rolling as they pawed up dirt and threw it high over their backs. With thousands of bulls in the herd the roaring was discernible at one to three miles, even five if the wind was right and a change of weather in the air.

The actual fight, however, was usually short and harmless. The great heads finally met in a dull thud, insulated, deadened by the thick mats of hair. There was a frantic struggle, a pushing this way and that, the sharp hoofs straining for footing, the power of the great shoulders apparently sure to crush the skulls like the browned puffballs of the prairie. Suddenly one or the other, with a sudden twist, slipped his head sideways to turn a sharp curved horn into flesh. But the hair and hide lay thick over the shoulders and the massive neck. Perhaps the heads met again and again, usually until one or the other of the bulls turned and fled into the milling herd, to take up another stand, with more roaring and pawing of earth. Once in a while a hoof slipped, the adversary's horn cut in under a rib or into a flank, blood ran and the fury grew, until one lay gored and trampled or dragged himself away, every young spike bull, and even an occasional cow now taking a safe hook of a horn at this sudden outcast.

After the breeding season the buffaloes settled down again, separating into small bunches of from twenty to a hundred. Quietly they spread out until the herd covered many square miles, moving as the wind drew them. With their small weak eyes practically lost in the matting of curly hair, they depended almost entirely upon their noses to warn them of danger and so fed into the wind. In this way they sometimes wandered from good range into badlands, or out upon arid waste expanses. When thirsty the whole group set out for the water hole on common impulse. The leader, usually a four-year-cow, started down the nearest draw, the rest as if by signal immediately fell in line with perhaps no more feeding beyond grabbing a mouthful of grass on the move. The trail of a herd in search of water was usually as fine a piece of engineering as any railway surveyor could produce and was governed by the same principles. The buffaloes followed the level of the valley, swerved around high points, crossed and recrossed stream beds in order to avoid a grade. The Indian followed these trails for food and ease of travois travel, and later the white man's roads and railroads. Although the buffaloes used the trails season after season, they were not over twelve inches wide, just enough to let the small hoofs pass with ease. When a trail became deeper than perhaps six inches, whether by wear or washout, it was no longer comfortable and another was started alongside until on slopes there might be fifty trails running close as corduroy.

There was often great crowding and fighting at the water holes and perhaps trampling and death in mires and bogs. Stinking Creek, draining a wide dry region of the upper Republican, was named for the rotting buffaloes caught in its bogs. But once watered the herd settled down to rest with almost every nose pointing into the wind, the young calves playful among their ruminating elders, their tails raised high as scorpions over their backs as they ran, jumped and butted; they rolled in the dust. After a while the herd rose to feed again, gradually strolling off perhaps at right angles to the course from which it came as the wind shifted with the latening day.

Grown buffaloes liked to roll in dry dust, looking, from far off, a little like a flock of black hens dusting themselves. This was not just during the shedding time but in the fall and winter too, the bulls more than the cows. Stretching out full length a bull rubbed his head hard on the ground, using a small curved horn like a sled runner. Then he rolled over his great hump as easily as a horse and scratched his other side, raising a haze of dust all around him. Old bulls usually had over half an inch of the thickness worn off the outside curve of the horns. In wet spots one would get down on a knee, plunge a horn into the wet earth, then the whole head, thrusting the mud up on both side as he plowed his body into the hole and rolled. Soon another drove him out and then another came, until the little water hole was a deep wallow, empty of the last bit of mud that might cling to wool.

The migratory habits of the buffalo were regular so far as the wind permitted, and usually on a rather grand scale. Sometimes the great herds made their southward move before winter in easy stages, slowly; other times in a headlong rush over long distances, perhaps in a thundering, earth-shaking lope. They might come like a great dark army, four to ten animals abreast, the ragged column reaching clear back into the horizon; or perhaps in a dense mass, the leaders in danger of being trampled into quicksand, bogs or mire, or driven out on treacherous ice. Often thousands were lost in the frozen Missouri, to float up later and lodge against islands and sand-bars, the stink driving Indian villages and later white-man camps away. There is a legend of a great herd whose leader, a sacred white buffalo cow, was shot. Without direction the herd drifted out upon the fall ice of Lake DeSmet in Wyoming and crashed through, every one lost. The water turned gray so no man would drink it, and for many, many years afterward only white birds settled on the water there—gulls, white geese, and the great white swans that made their nesting homes around DeSmet clear up into the time of Crazy Horse, the 1870's.

The tremendous electric storms of the High Plains destroyed buffaloes too; sometimes one bolt of lightning killed a dozen or two close together. Sometimes while they were gathering into the great running herds, they were overtaken by the tornadoes that swept the southern plains. The buffaloes were very sensitive to the slightest weather disturbance and before a twister they became extremely restless, milling, grunting, pawing the earth, running a little this way and that, tails up high. Then suddenly, perhaps, all broke into a gallop simultaneously, as though some vast unborn wind swept them across the prairie. The instinct that made them rely on their keenest sense, their noses, keeping them into the wind, usually carried the buffaloes away from the gathering storm centers, but the Sioux tell of seeing a long funnel cloud dip down into a stampeding herd somewhere near the bend of the Arkansas River. Then the clouds broke and the rain and roaring wind shut out everything as the Indians, a little war party with two women along, flattened themselves into a washout, holding their horses down with their arms over the necks. But they were soon driven out by the boiling flood that tore through the washout and then were almost drowned out on the open prairie, so dense was the rain.

The next morning the Indians rode over to see where the herd had been. There was no sign of it now as they approached, not a buffalo left in sight, but a broad strip of the prairie was torn and washed bare. The great spreading cottonwood on the creek bottom where so many yellow orioles had nested was gone, nothing left but a stump thick as two whisky barrels, the rest twisted off, torn and scattered up the breaks, bits of it washed in with the piles of trash in the gullies. Finally the Indians saw the buffaloes, many hundreds of them, in a great long rick, as though lifted and sown along for a quarter of a mile, several deep, sometimes four, five on top of each other, broken and twisted, some stripped of their hair, some with the eyes hanging down their faces, drawn out of their skulls. Mixed in with the buffaloes were big loose clumps of hair, weeds, grass, and splintered wood, with a few other animals, antelope and coyotes too, perhaps. The Indians saw the iron of some wagon wheels, twisted and bent, but they saw no horses or men, although some could have been in the big piles or under the sand and mud washed up against the buffaloes by the rain. On a rise off to the side two big prairie wolves skulked like coyotes, looking, their tails between their legs as in fear of some terrifying thing.

"Nobody touched the buffaloes or anything among them, not until the white men came with the wagons for the bones," an old Sioux who was there recalled years later.

Even in blizzards buffaloes faced the wind instead of turning tail and drifting helplessly as cattle did, the longhorns that were trailed up from Texas. With the smell of a storm in the air the buffaloes usually sought a canyon or ravine and settled down to chew their cuds and wait it out, scarcely moving except to trample the rising snow drifts, and perhaps not even that. Sometimes small herds were almost buried and occasionally actually smothered, lost until a thaw came and the buzzards began to circle over them. After a storm the herds scattered out upon the flats and creek bottoms or along wind-bared slopes, wherever grass showed above the snow. A buffalo could last for days, even weeks. An old Kiowa chief complained at the peace council the summer of 1867 that it seemed very foolish to kill off the buffaloes who looked out for themselves during the winter to make room for the white man's cows that must be sheltered and fed.

The real winter enemy of the buffaloes was crusted snow. Their small sharp hoofs broke through the drifts that held up both the wolf and man. A lone Indian on snowshoes could run up boldly to spear the greatest bull floundering in the drifts, and wolves could tear him down. Old bulls were often in bad shape after a hard winter and yet their percentage kept increasing. By 1867 there were approximately nine or ten bulls to every cow. Even the white man preferred the cow for meat and the Indian always selected the fat young ones to eat and for robes, whether for himself or for market. Cow skins were easier for the women to tan, lighter and more pliable and not so unwieldy for bed robes and lodge skins. Old bulls were killed for shields. The thick skin of the neck and hump was stretched green over a pit of coals to shrink and harden in the slow heat, harden enough to turn an arrow or a spear, perhaps even a rifle bullet if at some distance or at a glancing angle.

The path of the migrating herds was not as fixed, not as direct as, for instance, the deer and the elk climbing to higher altitudes with the softness of springtime. The gentling days turned the buffalo from his southward movement in the first mild spell of late winter. Gradually he began to work north-ward and often westward, higher up on the slope of the plains too, as the heated air moved in from the west, until the summer nights began to chill and the portentous winds to blow into the coming storms that usually drew him south. But sometimes the nose of the buffalo betrayed him. One of the Sioux who fled to Canada with Sitting Bull told the author the story of a great herd lost because unseasonably soft northern winds had drawn them far into the frozen lands of upper Canada one fall, into the face of the arctic winter. The entire herd starved and froze there, leaving their bones to bleach through the short summers until the whole region was white as with the snows in which the buffaloes had died.

How many were lost? "Ahh-h, it was long ago, and the dead ones were very many," the old Indian replied. "Enough to feed all the women and children a long, long time. Perhaps this many—" touching his two finger-spread hands at the thumbs, moving them from the right shoulder left and downward for the sign of a hundred. Then, instead of counting the number of hundred on the backs of the fingers he made the sign again, one hundred hundred, and then once more. One hundred times one hundred hundred—a million.

But certainly there were not that many?

The old man scraped the bowl of his stone pipe "Very, very many," he said softly, as to himself.

Although several species of the American bison seem to have disappeared during prehistoric times, the modern buffalo was very vigorous, with few ailments. However a murrain, a *rinderpest* that spread westward from the settlements and the trails in the middle 1820's, left many of the great gathering places of the animals dark and stinking. A broad region in southeast Nebraska reaching up to the salt flats where Lincoln now stands was apparently cleaned of all hoofed animals so completely that in 1825 a war party of Sioux returning afoot from a foray against the Missouri tribes almost starved crossing it. Finally they found a dying old bull, his mouth and tongue so horribly swollen and rotting that he could scarcely breathe. But the Indians were so weak and hungry they killed him. Only one man, who was too revolted by the sight to eat of the meat, survived, and in the wintercounts of the Sioux, 1825 is still called the year When the Six Died from Eating the Whistling Buffalo. In 1858 a disease called the bloody murrain killed many cloven-hoofed animals—work oxen, antelope, deer and buffaloes—along the western trails. The stretch of the Overland Trail between Ft. Laramie and Bridger was one long offense to the nostrils. This scourge accounted in a measure, some thought, for the rapid disappearance of the buffalo from the Laramie Plains of Wyoming and along the Platte, although the summer of 1860 so many buffaloes were slaughtered along the trails past Grand Island, Nebraska, that the stench was fearful, and by 1862 the river bottoms to the forks of the Platte were white as fall snow in their bleaching bones.

Yet the real enemy of the buffalo was the incredible extension of the striking arm that the white man carried with him —his powder-stenched shooting stick that reached far beyond any hand-thrown rock, or the spear and the arrow. Before his arrival the buffalo's greatest enemies were the extremes of nature, quicksand, and the lightning-set fires that might be carried by the wind upon the advancing herds. When they finally turned from the fear of smoke, they were perhaps too close and soon overtaken in exhaustion, cornered against some canyon wall or driven over a bluff or cliff, to leave their bones bleaching in broken piles below. In those days the fires ran on until blocked by stream, lake or barren ground, until quenched by rain or the wind swept the flames back to feed upon their own ashes. Sometimes the Indians used fire to hold an escaping herd, ringing the terrified buffaloes for the kill. It was dangerous work in the shifting winds of the plains, and used less since the arrival of the horse, by nature even more afraid of fire than the buffaloes, although he could be trained to it. Since then the Indians fired the early spring prairie to hurry the grass for their winter-weakened ponies, and often the buffaloes were caught in these.

Perhaps the most formidable fire of the buffalo ranges was the one set by General Mitchell in 1865. In January after the Sand Creek massacre of the Cheyennes the fall before, the Indians avenged themselves on a swath a hundred miles wide from Kansas to the Powder River country, burning road-ranches and trail stations, and driving the scattered troops into their posts. Soon afterward a smoke appeared on the morning horizon, growing white and opalescent against the pale winter sky. At first a few green hunters took it for the frost cloud of a buffalo herd, but it kept climbing and stood all around the north and west like the rising wall of a blizzard. It didn't move in with the characteristic speed or send out flying tatters of fog to be followed by a thin sifting of gray flakes and the sharp, wind-driven snow that no living creature except the buffalo could face. Instead the clouds boiled up into the clear January sky like thunderheads. In reply to some uneasy telegraphing, the more remote army posts were told that the fires were started on orders from Mitchell, set at close intervals all along the line of the Platte and the South Fork, from Kearney in middle Nebraska to the foothills of the Rockies near Denver—better than four hundred and thirty miles. The fires had been started in the quiet of early morning so they could spread into a solid front before the wind grew and drove them down upon the Indians and the fleeing animals too. The experienced hunters knew what this was, cursed the perpetrators, and tried to stack their hides that were still spread out to dry on the prairie, hoping that only the outside ones would be destroyed.

All kinds of animals, from rabbit to buffalo, fled before that solid wall of fire. The buffaloes, their eyes too weak and hair-blinded to see the rolling smoke, usually did not catch the whiff of it until quite near. Then, with their ropy tails suddenly up, they turned and stampeded, sweeping in dark thundering waves over the plains, here and there one going down from age, a hoof in a prairie-dog hole, or from the burden of a heavy calf, the strong stumbling over them. All those who could, got up to run again, on and on, driven as no hunter could ever drive them, piling up in the canyons, and soon on the level prairie too.

Three days the fire swept southward, the heat exploding the dry seed tops of bluestem and bunchgrass, running up the rises with the speed and roar of an express train. In short-grass country the fire was stopped by the ice of such streams as the Smoky Hill or the Solomon and smoldered there in the bedding places of the buffaloes and in brush and marshes.

Elsewhere it leapt the streams with the wind and ran on, some fireheads going clear to the Arkansas, to spread slowly along the banks, coming together. Yet even here some accommodating wind-blown tumbleweeds carried their sparks and embers across the wide stretch of ice and, reseeded in the well-grassed bottoms beyond, the fire grew again, running itself out deep in the wastelands of the Texas Panhandle.

Millions of creatures were destroyed, all the game dead or driven from an area half again as large as all of New England. But not one Indian was killed. Some had to backfire to save themselves, their camps and their herds, and then ate of the burned game as they hurried their snorting, hungry ponies over the blackened region that lifted itself in great sooty clouds on the wind. The skin hunters, mostly close to the trails in those days, apparently all escaped except three tenderfeet who were found dead in a draw not half a mile from water, their new buffalo guns beside them, only the steel left, burnt, the fine temper of the metal gone. Along the east many settlers were cleaned out, their lives perhaps saved by their dugouts while the cows and pigs and chickens roasted, and sometimes their horses too.

Although the great fire of 1865 was intended against the raiding Indians, it was set along the south bank of the Platte when the raiders were already well across the river and headed north. Only the peaceful bands were troubled at all, bands led by men like Whistler, the Sioux, who later saved Wild Bill Hickok's life. But they all had to go to the Powder River country for meat, where their young warriors heard the exciting plans of the wilder Indians, plans to drive the white man back toward the Missouri and out of the buffalo country forever. Of course a few whites who had trading houses would be allowed to remain because even the hostiles liked their coffee now, with the white man's sweet lumps in the bottom of the cup. They liked his powder too and the lead that brought down the buffalo who was growing so wild.

The Indians of south Kansas went into Texas, deep into the country of the Kiowas and Comanches whose warriors rivaled the wildest Sioux. But now it was 1868 and there were more white men everywhere, and more guns booming around the herds.

The commerce in prairie hides had been growing a long time. It was said that many of the British troops in the Crimea marched on buffalo soles and rode saddles of buffalo leather that came from the Red River breeds of Canada, most of it hauled from the Montana plains in their squeaking carts. Many Indian robes went southward. A partner in the American Fur Company estimated that as early as 1850 at least one hundred thousand robes came in to St. Louis every year; by 1857 an annual average of seventy-five thousand robes was gathered by the upper Missouri river posts alone. The Indians killed probably around three and a half million buffaloes a year during the 1850–1860 period for their needs and the robes they traded. This included, in addition to the Plains tribes whose entire subsistence was from the buffalo, the seasonal hunts of reservation Indians along the eastern fringe of the buffalo country, and the mountain tribes who came down for meat, robes and lodgeskins.

The High Plains had an early center of Indian trade at the present Horse Creek near the eastern Wyoming line. Here, long before Columbus, ornaments and strange products from as far as Mexico could be traded for white fox skins, say, or an occasional bit of carved walrus ivory, and seashells exchanged for quilled pouches or red pipestone. Here the Sioux got their first wonderful big-dogs that a man could ride—their first horses, for some fine quilled robes. The horse of the white man was followed by iron for arrow and spear points and finally by guns and markets and a thriving business in robes. When the government tried to stop this trade to keep guns and ammunition from the Indians, to starve them to the agencies, the villages became wealthy in robes and very poor in arms and in coffee, sugar and good flannel cloth. All those destroyed in the years from 1864 through the Plains wars were packed with extra robes and beadwork—fortunes gone up in stinking smoke.

Yet to make enough meat to feed the larger villages of the Republican with the bow called for careful management now. When the ceremonials to bring the buffalo close had been made in old Whistler's Sioux camp, scouts were sent out until some returned with news of a good herd near. Then the lodges were struck and everybody moved together, those managing the hunt riding ahead to keep the over-eager from slipping away and spoiling the surround, while some scouts watched to warn the white hide hunters away with a few flying shots, if necessary.

On the way some of the best hunters with the fastest horses were selected to kill meat for the old and the poor, led by Whistler's nephew, a very serious young warrior. The village camped back from the hunting ground, on a small tributary of the Republican, with good water and wood. In the meantime just over the hill from the buffaloes the hunters stripped to breechcloth and moccasins, bows and quivers ready. They separated into two parties and rode out both ways from behind the feeding herd, moving quietly and keeping down wind as long as possible. When all were ready, in a great arc around the herd, the head men from each side whipped around in front of the buffaloes, whooping. The grazing animals stopped, and, tails up, began to run, but there was man smell everywhere now, many men charging around the herd as the sun goes, with their whooping and the flying horses, the driving arrows.

A few buffaloes that tried to break free went down, others began to circle a little, then more, beginning to mill as in a great flood as the dedicated hunters pushed in past the bulls to the fat cows, some of the others close behind. Arrows sank in behind the running shoulders, perhaps to the feathers or deeper, clear through if they struck no rib, the hunters shouting their "Yihoo!" of triumph as each animal went down. The running buffaloes and horses were like the roar of a great hail over the hard earth, with here and there a horse having to leap a down buffalo, or go down too, the rider dodging for the open prairie. The old bulls were allowed to get away, one now, then another, but the cows and the young stock were kept running in the tightening circle. Once a curved horn dipped down and a horse was lifted up, his belly split to sudden red, the tumbling entrails gray and alive as he fell back, the rider down and dodging too, the cry of alarm that went up lost in the wild thunder of the hunt. He got away but another man had to be picked up and carried away, a great hoof gash in his side, the blood flowing where the flesh hung down like a red rag, the medicine man running up.

Now the circle of the surround was closer, and slower too, the horses tiring, even the buffaloes. Here and there one seemed to be escaping almost under the bows, perhaps pursued and brought down before the rest could try to follow. One with a dozen arrows got clear out but he fell to the crack of a watching gun, the first shot fired. There were half a dozen more bullets and then the last buffalo was struggling to his feet and falling, until struck down by a Sioux war club. Around four hundred buffaloes were scattered over a quarter-mile plot, some close as an arrow's length apart, a thick haze of dust over them all. The hunters slipped from their horses now and let them go, to be caught by the waiting boys, while each one sought out his arrows. The women, who had drawn nearer and nearer, were already running in, making the trilling cries of a good hunt, the sun glinting on their long butcher knives as they came, the men who did not hunt running too, to help.

The knives flashed in the late sun and the skins rolled back, with the stench of fresh blood and gun-shot buffaloes. Then the fine pale tallow and red meat lay clean on the skins, the visceral part too, the heads, the great bones for the marrow. Small boys ran excited among the butchers, shouting, bragging, grasping at chunks of raw liver held out here and there by some good woman, while smaller children, some on their mother's backs, chewed solemnly at strips of sinew and gut.

It was sunset when the long line of pack horses came into the new camp under the hovering layers of blue camp smoke. They were heavy with meat between the folded skins, the marrow bones tied on top like thick, pink-touched bleached wood for the roasting fires. The men unloaded the meat on spreads of clean marsh grass near the drying racks the old people built during the afternoon. Hump ribs and other choice parts were put to roast for the feast, special bits carried with formal step to the council lodge and laid down as the men sang their thanks to the meat gatherers. Even the hunter who got hurt was able to sit up and would soon be riding in another surround.

As night settled the roasting fires all over the camp sputtered and flared under the meat, and the fine smell called in all but the horse herders and the scouts far out, to watch, for

Whistler's camp was not to be surprised by enemies, red or white.

After the feast the weary ones leaned back to the piled bed robes, full and happy, perhaps nursing a warm pipe a little while, or dozing. But the drums called all the rest to dance and sing, with a special song for those who managed the hunt very well. It was no longer common to get so many buffaloes almost entirely with arrows, and in the short time that the sun moved from the head to the shoulder. Now one from those with no hunters in the lodge came forward to sing a song of gratitude that their drying racks had so much fine fat meat, for although it was fitting that the needy ones always receive a little more than the others, it was also fitting that thanks be given.

There was one more thing to be done, and for this the finest skin was selected, a soft, curly one that had a blueness on the sides, a blueness shiny as on a raven's throat. This one Robe Woman tanned very soft and worked in her best bead designs, and then it was taken to a rise where the sun came to sit very early in the morning and the winds of all the great directions blew. There it was left as a thank-offering to their brother the buffalo because so many of his kind had died that the Indian might live. By then the parfleches of Whistler's village were fat from several more good hunts and the lodges warm with many new robes, the beds soft.

The Fight of the Bulls

BY MARI SANDOZ

¶ Spanish cattle arrived in the New World a few short years after Columbus made his first landfall. By 1540, Coronado easily gathered five hundred head to take north with him from Mexico on his great expedition—the first cattle seen in what is now the United States. Thousands of their descendants were found running wild by the Anglos who came to settle in Texas in the early nineteenth century; the settlers hunted them as they did other game. These "mustang" cattle, so called to distinguish them from the Anglos' domesticated stock, later became known as "Texas cattle," and finally as Longhorns. Supplanted by gentler and more heavily fleshed animals, the Longhorn has gone; but many an old-timer thinks with nostalgic regret of the great and noble breed. Here, Mari Sandoz has written of the Longhorn, truly and powerfully, the words strong with respect.

IT WAS FITTING, considering the long deification of the cow, that the first seed cattle to reach Texas should have been brought in by missionaries, by men of God. Through the wild herds that their stock fathered, they left a permanent mark upon the region, an imprint that was to spread as the cattle climbed the ladder of east-flowing streams on their march northward, eventually to become numerous enough to feed the meat hungry of the country, and many back across the sea, to change the lives and beliefs of many men, and much of the nation. Already, in 1800, Texas was characterized by her wild cattle, by her great and fabulous herds.

From *The Cattlemen*. Copyright © 1958 by Mari Sandoz.

With the Spanish knife seldom set against the young male
and never, obviously, in the wild herds, there was much natural selection, with the young scrub driven out everywhere,
his blood given no perpetuity. But that left large numbers of
bulls to fight for supremacy, or for banishment from the
herds, perhaps even death. As with most other wild ruminants, the males usually kept apart except in the breeding
season. Some, particularly the ponderous old sires, kept entirely to themselves all winter, feeding alone, chewing their
placid cud on some sun-warmed slope alone. Others gathered
in small, loose bunches scattered over the bottoms, none turning a head toward the cows, who usually kept their distance,
most of them heavy with the coming spring calves.

But finally the grass started, grew up tall enough for good
cropping with the forward jerk of the bovine head, to make
up for the missing upper teeth in front. The faded winter hair
was rubbed off on rock and oak and mesquite, baring a sleek
and glossy new coat. The little bunches of cows had calves
bucking and playing around them, the yearlings, bulls and
heifers, were restless.

Even before this the bulls in their little herds began to
lift their noses to the wind, stretching their dewlapped throats
far out, working their nostrils this way and that, testing the
whiff of some far spring blooming, or the stink of carrion
from winter storms, from early lightning, or perhaps death
in a bog. But now there was something else, too.

Afternoons cattle gathered around the shrinking water of
the small creeks, many withdrawing to their sandy bed, perhaps leaving only a few moist threads on the surface and scattered water holes. High above an eagle might be circling
slowly, and off against a yellowish little bank a dog coyote
could be waiting, too smart to get his soft pads near the
clumps of gray-green prickly pear cactus farther down the
slope, or to risk the sharp and spreading horns of the cows
scattered over the bottoms after watering. He waited. If nothing better came up, perhaps a late cow might leave the water
holes for a little while and then he could smell out the dusty
placenta afterward. At the best there might be a good bull-
fight, with a possible cripple or a gored one left behind. The
coyote settled to his haunches, his red tongue lolling lazily

in the warm afternoon, and finally he stretched out to sleep, but alert.

Several times there was a low roaring on the wind, so far off it was barely to be felt instead of heard, perhaps a big blue-roan bull somewhere pawing dust upon himself in wrath, or a black one, six, seven years old, his shining coat touched with patches of red-gold along the belly as he showered the earth over himself, his neck powerful with the great bulge behind the head, the big dewlaps flapping from throat to knees as he tossed his thick and pointed horns. Lately he had begun to hang around the water holes instead of hastily sucking up his fill of water and then marching back to his pasturage, away from the herd of cows and young stuff that loitered sociably around the slopes until the sun began to settle.

Suddenly the black bull started toward the rise and the watering beyond. He stalked in pompous anger, on the prod, making impatient grunts and rumblings to himself, his heavy horns, with the forward tilt of the fighter, swayed with the rhythm of his angry walk. In mounting fury, like the approach of a desert cloudburst, his rumblings grew louder, settled to a steady, rolling sort of "Uh-h-uhh-uhh-hh," with pauses between the grunting roars, and pausing in his entire march as well, as though challenged. Then he lifted his head and a deep, subterranean thunder vibrated in his chest, rising to a high, defiant bellow, "Mu-uhh, mu-uhh—" neck outstretched, mouth open, trumpeting to all the wild country.

So he marched down the slope to the water holes, past the resting but watchful cows, the curious young stock. The bull drank deeply but slowly, even though he had not been to water for two, perhaps three days. Then he turned and walked in dignity to a cut bank and suddenly butted his shoulder against it, his powerfully muscled forequarters bulging, his flanks seeming even lither as he curled up the earth and sod before his thrust. Several other bulls drifted in with the little herds, drinking, scattering out over the worn bottoms or standing in the drying creek bed, to switch tails at the flies awhile and chew the cud. Most of the cattle settled down on the worn benchland dotted with cow chips, the cows groaning a little, comfortably, as they let their fore-quarters down. The yearlings were restless, or sleeping flat in the sun, the young calves shying in exaggerated terror at any convenient weed or thorn or ground squirrel or grackle—running, bucking, kicking their heels, or suddenly uneasy or hungry and blatting for their mothers.

The big black bull paid little attention to any of this or to the other bulls. They knew their rank and territory long ago. They glanced at the black's excitement, calm as the old cows. Bulls didn't cut out herds of she-stuff as the mustang stallion who watered here with his mares, fighting away all other males so long as his youth would last. Bulls, promiscuous, were free of jealousy other than the one of territorial rank. The others here were free to follow any cows that favored them, so long as they acknowledged who was boss here, and kept away from his choice of the moment, stayed out of his way generally.

Today the black bull wasn't satisfied by a simple challenge thrown on the wind. He kept getting more truculent, fighting the sod, starting over again with a kind of private bellowing deep in his chest, to himself, and pawing dirt from an old bull scrape in the soft earth. He hooked a horn into the ground, deeper and deeper. Then he thrust in the other horn and went down on one knee, still bellowing, head down, eyes bulging, and goring the earth to the bowels. Finally he rose, shook himself, and rubbed a shoulder against the edge of the bull hole as his powerful lungs sprayed the flying earth from before him.

A fat young heifer came down the cowpath near the bull's hole. He lifted his head to smell her, but only for a nose-curling instant, letting her go on past, her arrogant walk tamed by the rejection. But another bull, a tawny brindle with white and smoke upon him, got up and walked slowly to meet her at the first water hole and stood beside her, testing the smell of her. With water dripping from her jaw, she turned a backward look to the bull roaring up on the knoll and then she started down through the brush, the brindle right after her, but without too much hurry while in sight of the bellowing lord on the rise.

Over in the bull scrape the black was covered with yellow-ish earth, his horns tipped with wet clay as he thrust them into the ground as into a great and powerful enemy. He worked up a fine fighting fury, sending his threats and his challenges to the sky and to the echoing bluffs on the far side of the little creek in quick, rib-jerking bursts of bellowing that rose high and hoarsely shrill to carry far over the prairie. Suddenly he stopped, his head turned. From back over the rise came a faint and distant rumble and a bellow, twice, three times.

The resting cattle stirred. Overhead the eagle still soared, a bit of black curved hair far, far up. The coyote rose, sniffing eagerly forward without taking a step. Only the other bulls seemed unconcerned. One did lift his head, barely pausing in the rhythm of his chewing. He swallowed, and then his jaw began moving again.

The faint *uh-hing* came nearer, a deep and throaty rumble, but without the marching measure of the black's to the water holes. The trumpeting bellow came nearer and nearer until suddenly a bull broke the rise, running down the slope, switching his hindquarters this way and that as he tried to follow the zigzag of the cowpath until he broke from it in his momentum. He was a furious and magnificent specimen, a little heavier than the black, a dusty pecan dun with the golden line down his back, his sides and belly light-splotched. His horns were thick and yellowish, well-sharpened for their bloody work by long whetting on the ground but spreading, fitted to the side thrust, not forward-tipped for the head-on lunge to throat or belly.

At a hundred yards the dun stopped, pawed the earth, giving a higher, wilder bellow for every one of the black's. He charged upon a scrubby thorn, broke it, tossed it over his back. His sharp eyes spied out the coyote and he charged him, but the sly animal just side-stepped around the tall cactus clump. Plainly this was only a feint, too, for the bull had already turned, head lifted, tail arched, looking toward the black as upon an interloper, as one who had just come into the territory long owned by the dun. Purposefully now he marched toward the bull hole, eyes bulging, lower lip curled away from the foolish little teeth. The black climbed out, running heavily to meet the challenger. Some distance apart they stopped, roaring challenges, feinting thrusts this way and that, trying to out-maneuver each other under the noisy fury and the rising dust, their heavy little charges shaking loose the earth still clinging to their powerful shoulders.

Slowly they circled each other, dusty heads down, eyes rolling, seeking an opening. Once they both stopped, facing, heads down, tongues out, rumbling, and now the other cattle were suddenly up, some running in to see, but turning aside well out of the way, moving impatiently, making low, sympathetic mooings. More cattle strung in over the rise. A couple of driven-out scrubs edged up, but were ignored. The fat heifer and her bull came slowly out of the clump of brush, side by side, very close, but drawn to the impending fight.

Now the rumbling stopped. One bull lunged and then the other, taking a side swipe with a dusty horn, but met only by side-stepping, parrying, the answering thrust. Then they both lunged together, the crack of skull on skull a thunderous report. With foreheads locked, the bulls pushed mightily this way and that, the black yielding a bit before the weight of the dun, his hind hoofs struggling for solid footing, tearing up the earth as he was thrust back, their shoulder muscles standing out hard as dusty metal, the massive necks pushed up in humps almost like the buffaloes of the high regions. Then the black's hoofs caught and the dun went back, back, until suddenly he twisted his head to free a horn, drive it into a black shoulder. He was blocked with the crack of horn on horn, and then with a quick motion caught the blackish brisket, tore it to hang down, the dust clotted red.

Now the black worked with blood fury, trying one side twist after another, working to unbalance this opponent, drive an up-turned horn into a shoulder, a rib, the belly. So they thrust and parried, and swerved this way and that, with their heads tight as though sealed, hoofs digging. Curious calves were drawn up to see, and scuttled back as the fight suddenly swerved their way, scared by the brawl, and the panting, the sharp and desperate scrabble of the hoofs.

Now and then the bulls backed apart and then rushed together again, apart and together, the sharp reports echoing over the creek, the dust rising like smoke, the ground torn. Foam flew, their tongues hung out, their breath rasping, tearing. Once the black's horn raked the dun shoulder, cutting to the blood, but he had to pivot against the heavy drive to his belly, and was caught in the brisket again. Now there was a strong smell of blood on the dusty air and a bellow rose from the wild cows, heads down, angry tongues out, eyes bulging, the younger cattle pushing up closer. The coyote thrust his nose around the cactus, sniffing impatiently.

By now it was plain that the fight was more than a test of strength. Neither bull dared to turn and flee. Instead, they fought it out head to head, swerving, twisting, thrusting, glancing, butting together, their throats almost silent with the straining, all but the panting, tearing breath in the dust. The sun lowered, a flock of wild turkeys came flying over toward their roosting trees along the far bluffs. The cattle stirred uneasily, hungry, looking off toward their range, yet still held. Both the bulls were reaching exhaustion, their heads still coming together, but without the sharp crack of bone, the twisting struggle slowing, hesitant.

Here and there an old cow struck out over the rise, and stopped when there was a sudden confusion of hoofs and grunting in the fight of the bulls, and a low rending bawl of pain. Then, in a swift scrabble and turn, one of the bulls, the dun, was running with a bulging of gut bursting from his torn belly, the panting black hard on his rump, trying to hook him between the legs, but too worn out. Once the dun stumbled but pawed himself up with desperate hoofs, and ran again, the black, with ragged skin flapping, still after him when they disappeared over the evening rise.

As the sun rose next morning an eagle was circling lower, followed by several buzzards in more awkward spiraling, dropping fast beyond the rise somewhere. The coyote was gone and on the whole slope of the little creek there was only the dusty black bull, lying flat, ragged, torn, with hide loose at the shoulder and the brisket, one thick, powerful horn brown-coated in dried blood and gut.

After a while three vaqueros came up along the drying creek. When they saw the bull just rising to escape to the brush, they spread out, riatas down. The black was cramped and lame but he tried to run a little before a loop settled over his horns.

"It is a good way to do, this watching for the fights in the spring," one of the dark-faced men said.

"It is the best way to get good bulls—the winners of the fights, before they can run fast again," another said a little sourly. But they did not look sour. They sat their horses admiring the black.

Wild Horses

¶ *Like the cow, the horse was alien to the American continent, introduced by the white-man invader, and like the cow it soon was running wild, adapting to the conditions of the new land. But while cattle did not find a place in the economy of the native tribes, the horse quickly became an important part of the Indian's life, increasing his mobility and likewise his ability to resist the white man's incursions. Scores of thousands of the mustangs kept their wild freedom, though, and until fairly recently were an important part of our natural heritage. Now, having been hunted relentlessly —even from the air—their ranks are decimated and the future for them is a bleak one.*

ARIZONA'S WILD HORSES are disappearing from the box canyons and open grasslands, where once they roamed unrestricted and multiplied by the thousands. Like the Indians they have been forced on to the high mesas and into the roughest country, and even here they are meeting a terrifying end. They are chased and hunted like predatory animals,

From *Arizona, A State Guide.* Copyright 1940 by The Arizona State College at Flagstaff; 1956 by Hastings House, Publishers.

trapped or shot to become chicken feed, fertilizer, dog food, or even steak. Stockmen say that wild horses eat too much grass, drink too much water.

History records that after the prehistoric American horse had become extinct there were no horses in America until 1519 when Hernando Cortes came on his first voyage of conquest, bringing with him eleven stallions and five mares of Arabian stock. Frightened by the strange animals, the Aztec of Mexico made no attempt to capture the few that escaped when Cortes's soldiery fled from attack. These beautiful horses were never seen again by white men.

In 1540 other horses escaped from Hernando de Soto's camp on the west bank of the Mississippi. At some spot westward from the Gulf plains and northward from Mexico the descendants of these two bands, in all likelihood, met, probably in the region that is now Mexico or Arizona. When the Spanish padres trekked across Arizona some rode horses brought from the homeland to New Spain. It is probable that many of these animals broke their hobbles and joined their wild cousins in the open.

When Zebulon Pike and his company traveled through Colorado and New Mexico and as far north as Nebraska in the early eighteenth century, they found thousands of wild horses and many half-wild ponies used as mounts by the Indians. All these animals, undoubtedly, were descendants of the score or so of horses that escaped from the Spanish expeditions. The pioneers in New England and the Northwest had to cope with red men who slipped through the forests afoot, but two generations later the first settlers of the west battled with Indians who were expert horsemen. The Indian bands swept over the hills on their fleet little ponies and wiped out emigrant wagon trains—thus, incidentally, setting free more horses of varied breeds to roam at will.

It was not until the Mormons moved into their empire in Utah that the white men fully realized how extensive were the herds that thundered across the valleys. The Mormons in northern Arizona saw Indian mounts that were small and unkempt, often not weighing more than 800 pounds. But these ponies had great endurance and could carry 180-pound braves for many hours in country that exhausted the heavier horses of the white men.

Big cow outfits moved into the virgin grasslands of Arizona and increased their *remudas* from the wild horse herds. From the Indians they learned that the best way to capture the horses was to run them down. Cowboys worked in relays to keep the wild animals moving day in and day out over many miles of territory, changing mounts frequently so that their own animals would not be killed by the pace the rugged mustangs set. The cowboys worked through long shifts and finally found it possible to haze entire herds into corrals, where the best horses were cut out from the exhausted band. Because the range riders, with their love for horses, were reluctant to kill the inferior animals, these were turned loose to run the range again.

In dry country it was much simpler to build a fence around faraway water holes and await the arrival of the animals. Because the odor of man is a danger signal for horses, at times the trappers had to stay away from the corral for several days until the wind carried off their scent. The horses entered the trap through a gate that could not be opened from the inside.

The wild stallions and their mares lived and fought with the wolves and panthers, but man on foot terrified them. Sometimes the horses would turn and run recklessly against the corral or pasture fence, often smashing the fence and escaping to the range once more. Entire herds have been known to stampede, breaking barbwire fences by sheer weight of numbers, leaving behind a few dead and torn mustangs, the first to hit the barrier. One western writer tells of a wild horse, corraled on the rim of the Grand Canyon, that chose to plunge to death over the precipice rather than await capture by a man coming toward him afoot.

In terror, the wild horse seems to lose possession of his senses and plunges ahead regardless of obstacles. But once he is caught and handled, he soon loses his fear of human beings. One of the quickest ways to gentle a wild horse is to feed him.

In the summer of 1927 a wild horse movie was taken in Arizona. Local punchers were paid a dollar a head for each horse they brought in. More than a thousand wild horses were gathered in a big corral and for a week were fed and watered.

One scene called for a stampede of the entire herd, but the wild horses refused to be stampeded. By some chance two Shetland ponies had been penned with the bunch, and when the corral gates were opened the Shetlands came out in the lead! The director was the wildest thing on the lot.

The stallion must fight for life, mates, and herd leadership. He is also the guardian, directing the band to water by running behind his mares, nipping the flanks of any who would turn from the desired course. It is the stallion who keeps watch until his band has watered out. Only then will the leader drink. At any sign of danger he breaks the mares into flight, and takes the lead in headlong flight for some refuge he knows in mountain or valley.

The day always comes when the leader's place is challenged by some stallion of a smaller band that wants more mares, or by a young stud that does not yet possess mates. Then there is no flight but a battle which the mares watch with interest. They are willing to belong to the stallion that survives the kicking, biting, and striking bloody encounters that sometimes end in death. Because leadership passes by might from stallion to stallion, the rulers are not usually the glossy-coated and beautiful animals sometimes seen posing on bluffs, but more often are scraggy and battle-scarred old veterans of countless battles. At times hunters find a youngster in command of a band, and often—though this is disputed by some men who profess to know wild horses—a wise old mare actually directs the movement of the herd and is its watchman, relinquishing only the breeding rights to a stallion. The females, as well as the males, can and do fight chiefly to protect the colts from wolves and panthers.

Sometimes the wild horses welcome the gelded cow horses that stray into their herd from a near-by ranch. But more often the stud drives the visitors away. It is not uncommon to see a gelding following at the outskirts of a wild herd and giving affection and motherly care to a spindle-legged colt.

The thousands of wild horses that roamed the valleys have ruined much of the forage for stock and saddle horses and, it is also charged, have ruined waterholes and polluted water by playing in the streams. Cattlemen and speculators have carried on a relentless warfare against them. Driven together in huge roundups, the best horses are broken and shipped away as saddle mounts. Many went to the British Government for use of soldiers in Africa during the Boer War. The unsatisfactory, the smallest, and the old horses are killed for dog and chicken feed—hence the term "chicken horses," used in many localities.

Undersized and often underfed, these light-bodied wild horses still possess remarkable endurance and can travel many miles in a day. But their number has grown pitiably small, and they have been driven into mountains where grass is sparse and springs are few. So starved have they been in recent years that many horse hunters swear by all that is holy that wild horses have changed their food habits, that today they will ignore oats and alfalfa hay for the dry range grass and browse that is their steady diet. The hunted wild beasts can live on scanty rations, going for days at a time without a mouthful; still more remarkable, lack of water for one to three days seems no great hardship. After longer periods without water they sometimes become frantic. They have been seen, after a long run to a water hole, pawing viciously into dried ground, digging and churning the earth to get water.

Driven hard across land where feed is scarce, inbred with inferior animals, and with the best blood of the range cut out, the bands of wild horses have become weakened and subject to disease. Many are found, clean-picked skeletons, in lonely spots far from water and forage. In the hot months blowfly eggs laid in scratches on their hides torture them and often result in death. In summer hunters drive them from the high mountains to the barren lands below. When blizzards blow in winter the horses are forced to remain on the high mesas, away from the valleys where cowboys would run them down. It is estimated that fifty thousand wild horses still live in the north and northeastern sections of Arizona, hunted and frightened. They are totally without the glamour the movies have given them for there are no currycombs in the wild country to remove dried blood, burrs, and thorns.

Only the Indians are vitally interested in the preservation of wild horses. They want to be able to capture the best for mounts and to sell others for a few dollars, with which to buy a bright velvet jacket or a silver-mounted bridle. Then, too, the Navajo have no objection to horse stew. A few nature lovers also seek to prevent the extermination of the horses but with little success. Hunters, disease, hardship, and the demands of cattlemen and sheep-raisers are powerful forces allied against the once thundering herds.

Long Shadows

The Story of Print Olive

BY MARI SANDOZ

¶ *The frontier gave short shrift to the tenderhearted and the faint-spirited. Many who succeeded in its hard environment did so at the price of a certain loss of humanity—as a more settled society reckoned humanity, at least. The successful, those who survived the frontier's long winter of adversity, bore calluses of the psyche. They were, as a rule, unloved, but if they were accorded little genuine affection they generally were respected. Often they were feared, and with reason; among such was Prentiss ("Print") Olive, a Texas cattleman who brooked no resistance to the execution of his ambitious designs. He pursued his arrogant course for years, riding roughshod over others. That he eventually met a violent end himself was perhaps inevitable. The identity of the man who finally administered leaden-pelleted quietus to Print Olive is uncertain: perhaps he was rangeland's Everyman, at last rising in wrath against the tyrant of the prairies.*

Soon after the Mexican War James Olive had moved his family from Louisiana to Williamson County, Texas, and started in cattle. He and his wife were quiet, religious, churchgoing, but there was trouble between the father and the eldest son, young I. P., called Print, for Prentice. In Texas this grew like the thorns, with the son's taste for bad companions, hard liquor, cards, and gun play and the mother still shielding him as she had from birth, keeping his actions hidden from the father when she could, standing before him with her broad skirts outspread between him and the son when his misconduct was discovered. Finally Print was drawn into the war, wounded, and, recovered, made a mule skinner and captured at Vicksburg. Paroled in an exchange of prisoners, he was appointed to garrison duty at Galveston. Here, in idleness, he found drinking and gambling even more attractive and more available, as well as several shooting scrapes that involved no one that an Olive could possibly have termed a damnyankee.

When the war ended, Print went into stock raising near home. Pleased at what looked like a sober settling down at last, the father and two of the other sons bought more stock. Print and the other three had their farms separate but they ran a ranch farther west on a large tract of state land together, each with his own brand. Under Print's hard riding, hard cussing, they built reservoirs to catch any water that fell, dug wells, and later put up windmills. Their cattle grew into thousands. For a while they neighbored with the ranchers around them, particularly with the Snyders, J. W. and Dudley, also of Williamson County. It had been Dudley who trailed beef to the Confederacy, swimming his herds behind the two oxen who drew his trail wagon but led the steers across the swollen rivers. Dudley Snyder was known as a good man to tie to, and Print Olive missed few tricks.

In 1866 Print had bossed the general roundup of the region, really only a great cow hunt for stock branded before the war, the unmarked, the mavericks, to be divided among the ranches represented. At night the men gambled in the light of brush fires with the unbranded stock, a top critter worth $5 in chips, down to a yearling valued at fifty cents. The Moore boy who was along watching for his father's strays kept the fires going for two bits a night. Print Olive furnished the grub: coffee, corn meal, salt, whisky, and all the beef a man could eat—so long as it wasn't Olive beef. But that was customary.

By the 1870's many were complaining about the Olives, not aloud, but among themselves. Their stock was shrinking while the Olive herds, particularly Print's, more than doubled every year. There were some complaints at the courthouse but nothing came of them except that a couple of the belly-achers seemed to quit the country. At least, as Print said, nobody saw them around any more. Then there were rumors of trouble with a new settler, a young man called Deets Phreme, who went into cattle. One spring day Print Olive, his brother Ira, and some hired help starting on a cattle drive ran into Phreme and a couple of his hands. It seemed that the Olives accused him of killing their cattle and pistol-whipped him until his face and head were cut and swollen, knocked him down, and told him if they caught him on the range again he would be shot.

Old-timers warned him to go, get out, but Phreme was determined to stay. He had a legal right here. He was still as stubborn when he heard the Olive version of the encounter, saying they had found some of their brands in the Phreme herd and while the men cut out their stock, Print and the settler had words. Later Phreme and his hired man had shot at young Bob Olive, Print's brother, tried to bushwhack the youth.

Plainly they were setting the young settler up for a target, the old-timers said.

A few days later Print Olive managed to meet Phreme out on the prairie. "Did you shoot at my brother Bob?" he demanded.

"No, I didn't," the settler replied, "but I sure as hell would like to take a pop at you!"

The two men fired almost the same instant and fell together in the stinking powder smoke, both badly wounded. Phreme died soon afterward and Print Olive was several years really recovering. This time he was tried for murder and acquitted. "Easier to move men than cattle," he was reported to have said after the celebration.

Now the rumors about the Olives were more open, some perhaps spread by them to scare the settlers from the range they claimed, and harder to hold with so many pushing into the San Gabriel and Brushy Creek region. This man or that one vanished, and while few in Texas reported their comings and goings, some were settlers or little ranchers who left families without so much as a pone or a spoonful of hominy grits.

Maverickers, as well as out-and-out rustlers, and anybody that Print Olive decided fit these terms, were given fair warning to keep off the Olive range, claimed by the only right possible on public lands—the guns to hold them. Cattle prices were coming up again and large rustling outfits followed the rise like the eagle's shadow follows him on the ground below. Some of the ranchers had been hiring tough, gun-fingered cowboys, men who didn't care whose cattle they burnt with the ranch brand or whose milk cow they whooped off into the passing herd. In return the little outfits and the settlers stole back as much as they dared, and a little extra for their trouble.

Here and there suspected rustlers drew together in gangs for self-protection by lies, perjury, intimidation, and murder. Not that these methods were unfamiliar in a country largely unorganized, and where many a man even in high position was traveling under a name that never belonged to his father.

An old man called Pea Eye because his eyes were squushed together, although apparently large enough to see one of these gangs stealing cattle, appeared in court as a witness against them. Not long afterward his faithful ox team drew him into his home yard, down in the bottom of the wagon dead, full of buckshot. It seems nothing was done about that, except that one man was found hanging to a pecan tree and another vanished. Some of this was not far from the Olives, grown into a powerful clan of farmers, ranchers, and even peace officers, as peace officers went on the frontier.

The pointed complaint that stock was still vanishing in the Olive region Print Olive switched as handily as a spinning bronc switches ends. "We mean to kill any man found skinning our cattle or running off our horses." He said this half-tipsy in a bar but even those on fair terms with the Olives stood away a little, silent, remembering some of the things told of this fierce-eyed, gaunt-gutted man.

In a little while everybody knew that Print Olive meant what he said. The *Austin Statesman* reported the death of Turk Turner and James H. Crow over near McDade, adding:

Two beeves had been killed and skinned and in the absence of the parties who did it, the carcasses were discovered and watch kept to see who would return to carry away the beef and hides. Finally the above parties returned with a wagon and after having loaded up and started away they were fired upon by unknown parties and both killed.

It seemed the bodies were found by Crow's young son sent to look for his father after school. The dead men were several hundred yards apart, the team tied to a tree. Later it came out that there was more than the *Statesman* printed. Turner and Crow had been wrapped tightly in the fresh hides of the cattle they killed, while still alive, and left on the prairie to suffer the slow and horrible Spanish "Death of the Skins" as the burning sun drew the green hides tight and hard as iron about the men. The brands had been turned up conspicuously for everyone to see—brands of the Olives.

There was alarm in the region, the women afraid, their eyes filmed with the horror of what had happened to Turner and Crow when their own men rode away, for the skins drew as tightly about the innocent as the guilty. Turk had been regarded as a desperado but Old Man Crow, though he had a son in the pen, had been considered honest. Besides, there was a courthouse and law here against rustlers.

Although Crow's son accused the Olives of the murder, nothing came of it. They were still on close terms with two of the region's most prominent citizens, Dudley and J. W. Snyder. The Snyders had a newly-purchased herd over on the Olive range. Young Moore, who as a boy had kept the fires burning for the roundup gambling back in 1866, was hired to keep an eye on the stock and was boarding with the Olives.

Early in August the brothers, Print, Jay Thomas, and Ira, with four cowhands, including two Negroes, were branding a new herd. Although they were working the stock at the ranch, at night the men stretched out on the prairie beyond the corrals to sleep, their guns ready, apparently expecting a raid on the cattle. Around one o'clock, when the moon was well hazed, they were awakened by shots, men setting fire to the ranch buildings and shooting at anyone seen moving out on the dusky prairie. All the Olive outfit except young Moore were well armed. They fired from behind banks and bushes in the rising flames from the ranch house. There seemed to be fifteen, perhaps twenty in the attacking mob, some scattered in a wide circle around the ranch, others closer up, apparently with shotguns. In that first stiff fire in the light of the burning ranch Thomas was hit with several blasts of buckshot. Dying, he thrust his rifle into young Moore's hand and motioned to

him to unbuckle the cartridge belt. Print was struck in the
hip and crawled painfully for better cover, growling his curses
against the men who killed his brother. One of the Negroes
was dead, too, the other badly wounded. Inside the corral the
cattle were milling hard from the shots fired into them and in
terror of the flames rising high from the burning logs of the
ranch house, sparks, and rolling smoke over them. As they
surged against the poles of the corral, the attackers jerked
the gates back and the big steers stampeded for the breaks,
almost running over the defenders scattered behind the
shadowy clumps and banks.

The fire of the buildings died rapidly and the lowering
moon was lost in the smoke that filled the valley. In the darkness the fight became a watchful preparation for dawn, but
with the first graying that might show a known face, the attackers slipped away. The ranch hands got Print stretched
out to ease his wound a little and covered the half-naked body
of Thomas. Then they discovered from the wounded Negro,
who had been the first to awaken, that the place had been
robbed of seven or eight hundred dollars Print kept on hand
as down payment on cattle delivered.

But plainly this was not just a robbery; it was a plan for
extermination. Many blamed the Turner and Crow killings.
Crow's son, who had served time, promised vengeance. It was
known that he headed a lot of toughs and desperados, probably the mob that attacked the Olive ranch. But immediately
another gang loudly claimed the honor in saloons and the
country post offices. Not even Print seemed certain who the
attackers had been, with a dozen enemy outfits long itching
for a showdown. In addition the Olives still had the trial for
the murder of Turner and Crow before them. When court
convened, the Olive forces camped at one side of Georgetown, the county seat, with an estimated forty armed men
ready to drag the jury out to the trees down along the San
Gabriel if the verdict went against them. On the other side
of town it seems another camp had gathered, sixty men
against the Olives, determined to uphold the law of Texas,
here so close to Austin, to stop this bloodshed practically on
the capitol steps.

All through the trial the town was divided into these two

armed forces, the main street a barren and dusty sort of dare line between the waiting belligerents. But in the end the Olives were turned loose and without bloodshed.

By now more dead men had been turning up. Two were found hanging by their picket ropes near the Williamson County line, with plenty of money still on them, so it wasn't robbery. Later in the summer another dead man was found in the timber, stripped naked except for a hickory shirt and a blanket over him. "Almost like he was ambushed in bed, like Thomas Olive was," some said.

The law-abiding people of the region were furious as a bull at the smell of blood. Here, within a twenty-five-mile distance, ten or twelve men had been killed during the past few months, and more farther out. Newspapers agreed in their protests, pointing out that more men had been killed in Texas the last year than she lost during all the lamented war. The editor of the *Austin Statesman* suggested a remedy, "—instead of hanging, have horse thieves and robbers surgically rendered incapable of crime and of the procreation of knavery."

As Print recovered enough to get around in his buggy, the bold attack and the death of one of their brothers stirred the Olives to a revenging fury, particularly young Bob, and the eldest, I. P., Print, his small eyes always burning in one rage or another. The women of the region pitied his wife, even those who envied her the wealth of her husband's ways. She had been an orphan reared by her grandfather, and was now the mother of a growing family, including a son who roused his father's anger and contempt as Print himself had infuriated his religious father. It was said that both Print's wife and his parents begged for a quieter life, for peace for the children. But families counted very little in these days of cow feuds, and Print and young Bob were laying for the killers of Thomas. Then one day two Negroes stopped in at the home ranch and asked Mrs. Olive for a drink of water. Although Negroes outside of the army were not allowed to carry guns, Print saw they had pistols strapped to their saddles. He ran to the house for his rifle, for once not beside him. With it across his arm he got between the Negroes at the well and their horses. When they started to leave, he pulled down on them, ordered them to halt, to explain their business.

Oh, they were just out hunting stolen horses and needed a little water this hot day, one of them answered amiably.

"Then why was you asking my wife where her husband's at?" Print roared. "Don't make a move!"

Scared, one of the men jumped for the horses and was shot dead on the spot. The other surrendered and was driven off the place with a bull whip, so it was rumored, perhaps to explain the deep red and swelling cuts on his dark face and the bloody shirt slashed from his crusted back. Within a month Print Olive was tried for the murder of the Negro and acquitted.

"Just another of them biggety Lincoln Niggers gettin' an Olive ticket to hell," a sympathetic southerner said, and counted the dead Negroes credited to Print and to his brother Bob on his fingers, moving to the second hand and grinning. But no one counted the white men openly.

Even those friendly to the Olives were getting uneasy about Print. He was drinking more, brawling more, too, perhaps with the Union vets who had returned to Williamson County but often with long-time associates as well, until one or the other of the more peaceful brothers or a trusted ranch hand had to coax him out of the bar. Not even his brothers were spared Print's violent tongue now. And there were so many ways to get even with a rancher, ways that didn't involve actually facing his gun. He had cattle to be stolen, scattered, or destroyed, range ready for the lucifer or even flint and steel. He needed some who passed as friends in the emergencies common in the wilds, not only in prairie fires, stampedes, or attacks but in accidents and sickness. Even in ordinary times he needed someone to offer a pleasant word not forced by the fear of a low-slung gun, particularly a man with children, with a growing boy. There were rumors that even Print Olive's wife dared a little gentle urging for a move to new, less-crowded range.

Following more trouble, including the fatal shooting of a cowboy by young Bob Olive, the Olive brothers pulled out,

lock, stock, and barrel, for the northern ranges. They didn't
stop until they reached the Republican River country.

With the Indians so recently pushed out of much of Wyoming and Dakota and most of the Yellowstone basin, and the
cattlemen just beginning to move in, many wondered why
Print Olive squatted in the rapidly settling Republican country. Still, he had clung to the San Gabriel and Williamson
County region with settlements from before the days of the
Texas Republic, when he could have started out in open
country as King did, or moved, as Goodnight and a hundred
others. Perhaps he needed the fighting, as the gunmen of
Griffin and Abilene, of Newton and Tascosa and Dodge City
needed gunplay.

Before many weeks on the Republican River Print Olive
was informed he had moved in on grass saved for winter range
by cattlemen who claimed the region for years. He discovered
that he was hemmed in by ranchers and homesteaders, and
that there was no grass for any Johnny-Come-Lately except
through an army of guns, and it was plain there were too
many guns here already, Texans, too, and British money,
never shy about putting unruly natives down. Besides, many
of the ranchers and the settlers were old buffalo hunters, men
who put their trust in long-distance rifles, long-distance
marksmanship. From their faces he knew they had heard his
reputation and were not afraid.

"Yeh, I hear you killed nine niggers down in Texas," one
of the old hunters now running cattle told Print in a bar.
With his mouth tilted up he said it and then took deliberate
aim on the spittoon, hit it squarely, and walked away.

But there was more to make I. P. Olive uneasy. The whole
region was organized into counties, with officials and law, law
that could be bought, certainly already bought, and would be
mighty expensive for Rebel money or any outsider's money to
unbuy. Before long Print led a wedge of his riders up to the
Platte and across it into the long-grass country of the sandhills, where the fall bunchgrass ran orange in the wind of sunset. But the Texas cowman realized that this handsome sweep
of grass was perhaps longer on looks than on feed value, or
the other grasses around would show less grazing. Yet there

must be plenty of good range farther on, in the rolling chop-hills, sandy as some of the region that Richard King had drawn into his cattle empire down in the gulf country. As they rode in deeper the cow chips became scarcer, and not a cow in sight, only an occasional antelope to turn and run with a toss of white rump hair, but to circle around back to look.

The region was without a rock or tree or even a shrub beyond a few little buckbrush patches or perhaps a dwarf willow shorter than the stirrup, in some low spot. The only thorns to make the Texans feel at home were those on the low clumps of red-hipped prairie roses in the grass, the spears of the soapweed clumps on the sandier knobs, and an occasional patch of bull-tongue cactus—patches like greenish hearthrugs scattered around, the sections small and dainty to the eye accustomed to prickly pear that grew taller than a man on horseback, with the gray-blue sections over a foot long, the barbed spines the size of darning needles.

Finally, riding over a low ridge, Print Olive and his men looked down on a sandy little valley, as empty as all the others except that a stream clear as spring water ran through it, filled almost level with the grassy banks that showed little variation from drouth or flood. The men bellied down to drink, the water very sweet to the alkalied tongues of the Olives and their cowboys. Wiping his bristled mouth with the red bandanna about his neck, Print took out the little map he carried and saw no humor in the name, the Dismal River.

The Olives sold a fine lot of late-fall grass-fat beeves, certainly finished out better than any they ever marketed from Texas. This was meat country and the Olives were the outfit to produce it, so Print bought around 150 two-year-old Shorthorn bulls and the next week he was stringing 15,000 Texas cattle northward in one close-trailed herd after another, across the sand-choked Platte and into the foothills beyond. Many of the Republican ranchers had been out to see him go, stopping their horses on the far ridges, as down in Texas, the men here not to be contented until the last hoof tracks of the Olive cows were blown over. Along the Platte men watched, too, the sun glinting on the rifles across their saddles. They knew it was Olive stock coming through and were prepared to see that the range-hungry Texans did not linger overlong.

Finally the last of the drags were in the protected hills of the Dismal country. Print had a few shacks thrown together for his riders. He was satisfied with the wintering, but by spring he was looking around for something nearer the railroad, nearer the comforts of town for his family, his hands, and himself, too, for I. P. Olive liked to spend the evenings in one bar after another, feeling big as he stalked through the swinging doors and saw the faces at his coming, the Yankee faces showing they knew him. True, there was no vacant range near the railroad and he would have to clear the settlers off their homesteads and push some small ranchers from the land they had been holding ten, twelve years. But they had no rights beyond the gun, not even the settlers, no matter what the law said.

Print settled some of his best men into a log house on a rented school section on the South Loup River and took a house at Plum Creek on the Union Pacific along the Platte. Almost immediately old Plum Creek, a stagecoach station not so long ago, became Olive Town, taken over by his outfit. Some Texans were surprised that Print would move his headquarters to the railroad, where there was law and courts, the latter certainly with the local cattlemen against the outsider.

"Hell, no law's ever stopped Print. Nor no courts, neither. Maybe he likes to know the men he's going to buy up got the power to deliver."

By now Print Olive, through his biggety ways, was called Nebraska's richest cattleman, the top cattle king, although some restricted the region of his supremacy to the Plum Creek and lower Loup country.

Soon after they moved in, Olive's men discovered what a fire could be in the largely long-grass region, with no large streams and no barren wastes to stop it. At the first cry of "Prairie fire!" and a pointing to the pearly, iridescent little cloud rising against the sky, teams were hooked up, breaking plows thrown into the wagons, water barrels loaded and sacks piled in to soak for pounding out the smaller flames, particularly in backfiring. The wind was gentle at first but it swelled

in the heated air. The men fought as well as they could, with
the help and direction of men from the surrounding ranches
and some settlers, too, and fought until they fell scorched and
worn out under the fierce drive of Print Olive. He was curs-
ingly certain the fire was set by an enemy. The plowed fire-
guards saved the ranch buildings, but the flames swept on, the
Longhorns fleeing like the occasional deer and antelope, the
coyote and the rabbit. Many were caught in the deep grass of
the bottoms and burned to death or had to be killed later.
Settlers lost their homes, their little accumulation of corn
and fodder. Finally the fire hit the South Loup and spread
along the banks, making little sullen headway, edge-on into
the wind, and so it died.

The transplantation of the new cattle king and his methods
to Nebraska from south-central Texas, where he was almost
literally driven out, caused much stir. Everything he did was
big, highhanded, overbearing, bulldozing. At the ranch
Print's word was law to the white men as it was to his "gun
Niggers" as he called them, men who had known slavery and
could bend their necks. There was soon trouble among the
men now, however, all gun-armed—white, Negro, Mexican,
Texas white, and the northern whites that Ira put on. Print
had them fight it out—egging them against each other in his
half-drunkenness, whether bare knuckled or with knives,
even guns a time or two. Afterward there were the fiddlers
for a little good time, regular hoedowns, generally. Often
there was Sunday bronc riding, calf roping, and steer tailing
around the corrals. Men from the neighboring ranches were
encouraged to come, including foremen and range riders.
Phil DuFran from up on the Missouri River in Dakota, foreman for the neighboring Durfee and Gasman ranch, was
usually there. He was as black haired as the Olive brothers, a
Frenchy and a little Indian, too, some said, but a genial fellow who could make Fred Fisher, Olive's foreman, laugh and
sometimes even the dark-mooded Print himself. When the
Pawnee Indians came through the region they had called
home not long ago, there was trading and horseracing and
betting at the Olive ranch, until Print, with a sudden wave of

his gun, shouted the alarmed Indians into hurrying their families out of his way.

When the ranch hands went to town, they emptied their guns into the store windows and shot out the large red lamp globe of the hotel, spreading a stench of coal oil over the place, and then paid for the damages with their supper bill. Olive gave them all a surprise raise in pay because the cattle increased so surprisingly, growing and fattening beyond anything he had ever seen. But then he had never seen grown cows in any region that nurtured and fattened the great buffalo herds, and very recently here.

Before long the little ranchers who ran cattle on the government land were commanded to keep their stock out of it, and homeseekers warned not to come in. This range was now Olive property. The settlers already there, and there were many, got orders to kill no cattle, brand no mavericks and no calves, and to keep their cattle off the grass, including that on their own claims. This was Olive law, issued from a ranch on a leased school section, set up over the surrounding public domain and the land legally the property of the settlers. Those who had heard rumors from Texas were certain Print Olive was preparing to shoot down everybody he wanted out of the way on the pretense that they stole Olive cattle. A man didn't have to come from Texas to know there were ways of planting a settler's brand on the calf of a rancher's cow to furnish the excuse for a shooting—or a lynching.

Several of the settlers, some with families, well-built homes, and crops planted took the hint and left their homesteads. By now the brawling, gun-jerking young Bob Olive had come down from Wyoming and even the other ranchers left the outfit alone as much as possible, put on extra line riders, ordered more guns for the hands, and waited. It was a particularly hard wait for the settlers, and hardest of all for those with wives and children. Someone would have to be the dead owl the Olives were planning to use as a scare for the others.

The expected blowup came very fast and no one could ever know the whole of it, so complex were the factors involved in this fight for grass for the cow—certainly not Print Olive or his brother Bob, with their gunmen, white, black, and brown.

Conspicuous among the settlers who would not scare out were Mitchell and Ketchum over near Clear Creek. They had filed on adjoining homesteads and built a long, double soddy across the homestead line, with Ketchum's end of the house on his claim, Mitchell's over on his. Mitchell was a slight, middle-aged man, old for homesteading in a raw country, although the Loup region was not as new as some, with a railroad in reach for ten years. He had his wife with him and two stepdaughters, the elder, Tamar Snow, a pretty sixteen-year-old who was to marry young Ami Ketchum. Like his brother Lawrence Ketchum, a government scout, Ami was a crack shot. He had brought his forge and anvil and started to set wagon tires, shoe horses for the icy ground of winter, sharpen plowshares and sicklebars, and braze an occasional gun with a broken breech tail. They were sociable people, going to the country dances and house raisings, even if two, three days away by wagon. They sat up with the sick and helped bury the dead.

Unfortunately the homesteads of Mitchell and Ketchum, although several townships away from the Olives, were a rallying center for the settlers around there, on range Print intended to take over. Soon it was said around that Ketchum was overeager to get enough money ahead to marry and that when a rancher's herd ate up his shirttail patch of corn, some of the cows left their calves in his corral. At least that was the story the Olive hands were spreading. Their friends, including Phil DuFran, foreman of the neighboring Durfee, were glad to follow the lead of this Texan if he could clear the range they had about given up. Print Olive got his brother Bob appointed stock inspector, in spite of the $400 reward for his return to face the murder charge in Texas. He was to watch Ketchum. Maybe plant an Olive calf in the settler's corral or some fresh Olive hides around his place somewhere, old-timers from Texas and Wyoming warned. One even rode over to tell Ketchum about the "Death of the Skins" killing down in Texas, in which two men were smothered, rolled in drying hides with the Olive brands.

Ami Ketchum laughed, but others warned him, too. "You better think about hittin' it out of here," an old cowhand told him at a dance. The fiddler, who was a preacher on Sundays, agreed, and offered to loan Ami the money to go back to Iowa. Once more Ami laughed and swung pretty Tamar in a dough-see-dough.

Yet all that first fall there had been trouble in the region, stirred up, some said, by the Olives. It was inevitable, this trouble in an old range country already half taken up by settlers when an Olive outfit pushed in with their big herds, after the local ranchers were already hard pressed. Some bodies showed up on the new Olive range when the snow cleared toward spring, missing hunters, all full of bullets. Nothing was disturbed in their camp, no money or watches taken.

"That's how it went down in Texas," the southern cowhands said.

By now everybody knew that both Mitchell and Ketchum had been warned to get out of the country. Then in April word got around that the Olives had a man named Roberts arrested for stealing cattle and took him up before a justice of the peace. Roberts had dared to hire an attorney, Aaron Wall, county judge in the next county, for his defense. The Olives kept Wall out of the justice court with their guns, although he opposed the half-drunken brothers and their outfit all afternoon. Finally, by a trick, Wall got them to let the prisoner come out to consult with him a minute, and got him away, for an open trial elsewhere.

Furious, the Olives went over to Wall's court to arrest him for interfering with justice, Bob leading the cowboys. Once more, with drawn guns, they bulldozed him, but did not quite dare shoot a county judge at the bench before witnesses. Finally Wall got a deputy to grab Bob Olive and fined the outfit for contempt of court. They didn't all pay but agreed to leave town, swearing they would get even.

Things crippled along this way for a while, nobody knowing where the guns would be drawn next. Then Print Olive and Fisher, the foreman, found cattle with the Olive brand at the homestead of Christensen. There were several neighbors at the place. They agreed that Christ had bought the cattle with a brand release. He went to the house to look for the paper, with Print's boots stomping after him. Roaring and impatient, Print struck the settler across the cheek with his

.45 and broke his jaw. Standing over the fallen man, Print gave him five minutes to prepare for death. But Christensen begged so through his pain and terror, promising to fetch the release to Olive as soon as he found it, that Print agreed, particularly with the armed settlers still outside. One of the men was George Brill, stepson of the Judge Wall who had defied the Olives. Besides, Brill had ridden the range with Bob Olive up in Wyoming and knew about the reward out for him. Christensen was too frightened to hunt up a doctor and the neglected jaw grew so stiff he could never open his mouth more than about an inch. In a short time he was gone, quit the country.

Afterward Print claimed that Brill and the other man at Christ's shot at him and Fisher from the brush when they left the place. "I should have killed the goddamn Swede when I had him down—"

The release on the Olive brand showed that Manley Caple sold the cattle to Christensen. Manley, son of an early rancher in the region, had been gambling heavily and was suspected of rustling to keep in chance money. The Olives had him arrested. In his confession he seemed to implicate Ami Ketchum, although apparently it was no more than an implication or the Olives would have acted at once. But in the end they got a warrant for Ketchum and had Bob Olive deputized to serve it, although everyone, including the sheriff, knew about the Olive threats to kill Ketchum, make buzzard meat of him if he didn't get out.

Then one night the Olive hands had some news to tell around the bars at Plum Creek, news about a raid planned on some rustlers over on Clear Creek. The news reached Mitchell and Ketchum, some said by the gentlemanly Texas cowboy become horse thief and traveling under the name of Doc Middleton. Others said it was Buckskin Bill, who claimed young Bill Olive shot at him twice for dancing with the kid's girl.

"Startin' early—that kid of Print's is scarcely bearding out," he said.

Although the stories of the next few days differed very much, all agreed that a stranger to Mitchell and Ketchum came to see who was home by pretending he wanted his horse

shod. Probably trying to separate the two men, get Ketchum
over to the blacksmith shop, perhaps away from his rifle. But
the settlers were hooking up to the wagon to return a borrowed bull, and Ami asked the man to come back next day.
By the time Mrs. Mitchell and the girls had climbed into the
wagon the Olives and their cowboys, mostly Negro and Mexican, charged out upon them, riding low on their horses, giving a Rebel yell and shooting.

Mrs. Mitchell pushed the girls down into the wagon bed
as the bullets whistled past. Bob Olive led the outfit, shouting
something about "Throw up your hands, Ketchum! Throw
up your hands!"

But Ketchum had already pulled his gun and fired. Mitchell grabbed the Winchester from the wagon and shot, too,
while bullets splintered the wagon box around him, the
younger of the girls inside crying in the hay. At first the settlers didn't shoot to kill, only brought down some horses and
grazed a man or two. Ketchum had jumped out into the open
to draw the fire from those in the wagon box and got a bullet
in the arm. Now Mitchell took aim and at the double report
of the rifle and Ami's pistol Bob Olive jerked himself straight
in the saddle and started to slide from the running horse but
was caught and held by cowboys on each side and carried
away as the rest turned, too, spurring for cover. Ami Ketchum
got in one last shot from the rifle that Tamar helped him
hold.

"Goddamn 'em!" he swore in fury. "I could kill the whole
damn outfit, attacking when there's women and children
around—"

Off in the brush Print decided to take his brother to a
neighboring settler's dugout, less than a mile off. He ordered
the man to get his team and wagon ready and laid Bob on a
bedding of hay. With the settler driving, Print riding alongside whipping the team along, the cowboys following, they
got Bob to the eastbound train. But he died, died, it seemed,
on his twenty-fourth birthday.

The body was shipped home to Williamson County, to his
respectable parents and sisters, and laid beside his brother
Thomas, riddled with buckshot. By rights, some said,
Ketchum should have the $400 reward offered for Bob Olive's

return to Texas, but perhaps that was for his return to stand trial for murder.

From the moment that Bob Olive wavered in the saddle, Mitchell and Ketchum knew they would be mobbed by the whole Olive outfit, with perhaps DuFran and others bringing their cowboys, too—clear the range by stringing up the one man nobody had dared to touch, Ami Ketchum. At least Mrs. Mitchell and the girls must be taken away before anything more happened, with Ketchum's arm swollen and useless, Mitchell a scared old man. They turned the neighbor's bull loose to go home, piled blankets into the wagon, and started across the country, whipping the team hard, the wheel tracks so pitifully plain over the late fall prairie. They didn't dare go to a doctor, for with so few in the country it would be easy to have them all watched. Instead, they hurried to Judge Wall, even though they realized that the Olives would strike there immediately, settle two grudges at one time. The judge advised them to get as far away as possible, to friends who would hide them, preferably friends the Olives knew nothing about. But all such friends were around Ami's old home in Iowa.

In the meantime a mob of cowboys gathered under the leadership of the Olive gunmen, burned the roof off the deserted sod house on Clear Creek, all that would burn. From there Print Olive sent his gunmen to scour the country, some pursuing the wagon tracks, others cutting across from settler to settler. The railroad towns he had put under guard by telegraph long ago. Within a few hours notices appeared in every saloon, post office, and crossroads fence post: Print Olive was offering a $700 reward for the apprehension of Mitchell and Ketchum, murderers of his brother Robert Olive.

Nobody dared to help the fleeing settlers now, not even give them a handout of dry biscuits, let alone shelter. To save the woman and the girls, the men let them go on ahead to some acquaintance and struck out alone afoot. But Mitchell was soon worn and limping, Ketchum burning with fever and pain, his arm swollen double in size. They made one more desperate and guilty appeal to Judge Wall, knowing they were endangering his life. Sadly, and in helpless fury, he admitted he could neither protect them nor advise them now. Wherever they were caught they would be returned to the sheriff who threw in with the Olives.

"Only the governor, with the militia, could save you and we can't get them in time. I sent a telegram. Got no reply yet."

The two settlers had known it was hopeless, and slowly they started away into the night. Olive's posse appeared at Wall's home. The judge managed to escape them but only because there was an old tunnel out of the house, big enough for a crawling man, dug back in the days of Indian scares.

In a short time the two settlers were run down on the prairie, put on horses, their feet tied under the bellies, and taken to Kearney for trial. There Print Olive refused to pay the reward until the men were delivered to him in his own region, Custer County. Over the pleading of the two settlers and men sympathetic to them they were smuggled out of jail without the knowledge of their lawyers and turned over to Sheriff Gillan of Keith County, west of there, but the only man of the captors who was willing to claim the reward. He took the two prisoners, handcuffed together, to Plum Creek by train. There, at Olive Town, Print, his foreman, and his cowboys were waiting. The settlers were thrown into a light spring wagon and with Phil DuFran driving, Sheriff Gillan in the seat beside him, they headed north, the mob following, in and out of sight. The moon came up, red on the prairie, just past full, and was lost in streaks of cloud. The cold of the December night chilled the manacled men but they were silent with only now and then a low word between them. They reached the burnt-over region, dark in the fitful moonlight.

About three miles from the Olive ranch and well within Custer County the mob rode up and Print handed the sheriff the $700 and took over the wagon. While Gillan and DuFran stayed behind watching, the Olives turned into Devil's Gap, a wild little canyon. There, in the light of the December moon, the wagon with the prisoners was stopped under a tree. Lariats were thrown over a limb and two of the cowboys put nooses around the necks of the settlers, still handcuffed together. Ketchum pleaded that they let Mitchell go. Old and sick, he was the only support of a woman and two children.

To shut him up, Ketchum was drawn up first, jerked up by a dally of the rope around a saddlehorn and a spur set to the horse. Mitchell's arm was yanked up by the chain of the handcuffs and held there, as Ami Ketchum kicked his life out. Then Olive put a bullet into Mitchell as pay for the one that killed Bob, and gave the signal to the cowboy with the dally.

Afterward a can of coal oil was brought from the spring wagon and doused up over the men. Print struck a lucifer and the two hanging men shot into flaming torches, the clothing and hair blazing, the brush under them burning, too, flaring up, the sooty smoke carrying the stench of the burning cloth and hair and flesh, too, out of the Gap and over the prairie to where sleeping cattle raised their heads a moment.

After a while Mitchell's rope parted and he fell into the burning brush and accumulated leaves amid a gushing of smoke, one arm still uplifted to Ketchum by the handcuffed wrist.

Nodding to his men, Print Olive turned his horse toward the ranch, the rest following, leaving two of the hands behind to keep the fire from spreading to the range.

It was the next day before anyone dared to follow the wheel tracks to find what everyone knew would be there. But no one was prepared for the burning. Now shock spread over the state, even to the hiding place of Mrs. Mitchell and her daughters, including the twice-bereaved Tamar Snow. It reached over much of the cattle region and over the nation. "Alleged Rustlers Burned Like Witches and Heretics!" one of the headlines cried. "Nebraska Settlers Victims of Heinous Crime Out of Inquisition!" another added. But mostly the headlines screamed out the same two words, over and over: "MAN BURNERS! MAN BURNERS!"

Those cowmen who had approved Print Olive's burning of the settlers as a good example got a little uneasy as more stories spread. Even after the burning of Mitchell and Ketchum was reported to the authorities, the men were left out in Devil's Gap several days, until Mitchell, on the ground, was gnawed by the coyotes, so strong was the fear of the Olives. Finally Print, sensing the feeling against him, seems to have given a poor dim-witted man $20 to go out and bury the bodies. He dug a shallow grave in the frozen ground but the bodies couldn't be fitted into it, even after chopping off an arm and a leg. So he threw them on top and scraped leaves and dirt over them. Finally several men, led by a Union veteran, went out from Loup City, dug up the settlers, and after photographing the bodies, took them to Kearney for decent burial.

This was the story that sifted through the whole cattle country, and still no arrests were made. Print Olive still stalked from bar to bar in his town of Plum Creek, threw back his buffalo saddle coat, hitched his worn holster around a little, and reached for the bottle the bartender set out. To any remark he might overhear he roared that there weren't enough men in the whole goddamn state of Nebraska to take him.

"Looks like he's right," one of the men who had hung back from drinking Print's liquor finally admitted. So he had to move to the bar, too, but let the whisky slop to the sawdust. Not even the Ketchum brothers had been seen since they came for Ami's body. They had been bragged up as crack shots but somehow their aim seemed to wobble before an Olive.

There were stories that Print was making plans for expansion, for a Platte River kingdom. This was the region for him, he shouted out one night against several men who stood away from his liquor. Texas might drive him out but a man with guts could make himself king of all the yellowbelly Yankees. The Plum Creekers, the settlers, and the ranchers of all the region kept quiet and as the days and weeks passed, they began to pull to I. P. Olive's side, or quit the country.

Then a rumor got out that Mrs. Olive wanted to leave, didn't want her young son Bill brought up in such violence. "Violence, hell!" one of the settlers from the Loup snorted when he heard this. "That kid's already pulled his gun on a dozen men around here. Only the reputation of the outfit's kept him alive."

It seemed, too, that Mrs. Olive couldn't bear the newspapers with their denunciations of her husband, the demands that the governor act against the murderers, the looks she got in the stores and on the street. No matter how carefully her carriage was watched, every time she came out there were the chalk words scribbled on the side: MAN BURNERS.

Then there was a rumor that she and the younger children were packed to leave the next Sunday, maybe Print going, too, and taking his lawless gang along. Perhaps Phil DuFran, who had brought the settlers to Print, would join them, better join them, some said. And Sheriff Gillan from over in Keith County who had collected the $700 for delivering Mitchell and Ketchum, too.

Although neither the governor nor any county official acted, the frontier's energetic Judge Gaslin had been working quietly. He found that every possible witness had been warned that the talking tongue would be cut out at the root. Warrants issued for the arrest of the Olive gang were refused by two sheriffs who said they were not ready to die. But there were a few men ready to go through hell to see Print Olive locked up. They were deputized and with a few more willing to risk their lives, Judge Gaslin headed for Plum Creek.

The men scattered casually into town, stopping for a little business here and there. After the mail train came through, Print Olive went to the post office, the waiting crowd parting to let him through. Someone introduced two strangers to him.

"The Ketchum boys, Print. You know, brothers of Ami—"

Olive growled something, his hand hooked over his holster, and waited for the men to flee from his angry face. But they didn't. With one on each side of him they put him under arrest and before the astonished eyes of the crowd snapped handcuffs on him. In the meantime out on the street somebody picked up Fred Fisher, Olive's foreman, and a few more of the gang.

By then a crowd, a mob, was pushing up around the men. "Get a rope!" somebody yelled back toward his horse and a dozen coiled lariats were handed in over the shoulders of the pushing mob, the owners calling out, "Here! Here! String 'em up!"

But one of the arresting deputies elbowed in to face the leaders. He spoke quietly, so quietly that the mob had to silence itself to hear. He said he had taken an oath to protect the prisoners and he would do it with his dead body. He handed Print a pistol. "Shoot the first man who lays a hand on you," he ordered.

To the angry roar of the crowd, the yells of "Sell-out! Sell-out!" the deputy held up his hand for silence. "This man killed my brother, Ami Ketchum. If the law fails to punish him, then it's time enough for us and I'll do it my own way."

By dawn the two Ketchums and Sam Snow, stepson of the dead Mitchell and brother of Tamar, and their posse had twelve of the Olive gang, including Phil DuFran and Sheriff Gillan. The last man they took was the keeper of the hotel and saloon where the Olives hung out. Then they were taken away, chained in pairs, and all without a shot fired by the man who a few hours earlier had seen himself king of the whole Platte country.

"Sure caved in easy," some Nebraskans said.

There were, however, some Texans around who had seen Print Olive in the hands of the law for murder before, but none had ever seen him serve a day for any killing.

Still Olive and eight others were indicted for the murder of Mitchell, taken up first as the older, the family man. It was done despite the rumors that Print had a standing offer of $1,000 out for any and all men drawn on the jury who voted against indictment. There were threats against the attorney general's life, too, and Judge Gaslin's. Nobody expected the judge to take this seriously, not the judge who had learned to lay two loaded six-shooters out before him when he opened court, to see that there would be no gun play. He was doing this back when Print Olive still shot Mexicans and Negroes down in Texas.

Olive, Fisher, and two more of the gang were taken to the pen at Lincoln for safety. Brown, who was one of Olive's trusted hands, and the affable Phil DuFran had turned state's evidence. Sheriff Gillan certainly "criminally connected with the affair," as the newspapers put it, was unwilling to take up quarters with his fellow prisoners, suddenly mighty holy, it seemed.

The trial came up in the April term at Hastings, considered a little safer because farther from the crime and the Olive gang. But there were threats of a great mob of Print's cowboys coming to raid the court, burn the town to ashes. Many were afraid, for a man burner is a man burner. The sheriff petitioned the governor for protection. A company of troops pitched their tents opposite the courthouse and stayed.

There was suddenly a great deal of money loose in the country, particularly among those who might be witnesses, money from the Olives and from ranch acquaintances and connections. Some said that included the fine old Texas cowmen, the Snyders, somehow connected with the Olives left in the south.

Print's parents came up from Texas and at first none could believe that this I.P. of the violence, the whisky, the foul mouth, the ruthless brutal killer and defiler of men could be the son of such a gentle and religious old couple. Then they heard the mother speak of the goodness of "my boy, Prentice," always "my boy," as though he were still at her breast, as though she were still hiding his childish little naughtinesses from his father. "My boy, my poor baby," she murmured into her lace handkerchief, with no eyes for his brother Ira or even Marion, the youngest.

Two of Print's hands weakened and told of a plot to shoot Judge Gaslin and Attorney Dilworth during the trial, and added that I.P. said he had no fear of such proceedings. He had attended a dozen such weddings.

"Meaning killings?"

"Yes."

Olive and Fisher were found guilty and went to the pen, with high praise for Judge Gaslin from all but three newspapers of the whole state. Steps were taken immediately for a new trial. The case hadn't been tried in the jurisdiction of the crime—the new Custer County, which by an oversight of the legislature, was attached to no judicial district and so had no district court. A thick file of documents, including some shockingly revealing depositions, was presented to the state supreme court for a change of venue. The change was granted and one of the attorneys who got the decision was said to have received the 10,000 head of three-year-old Olive steers sold for him on the block at Hastings. "No telling what the others involved got," was the bitter comment, one way or another, over much of the state.

In the meantime the local lawyers of Olive and Fisher had

been driving and riding over the entire region giving many people a choice of a roll of bills or the threat of a tongue cut out. When the rehearing came up in Custer County, in the only court that existed there, the county court, no complaint was found on the docket and no complaining witnesses came forward. The already celebrating cowboys roared and fired bullets into the ceiling of the courtroom, it was said, and Judge Boblits rose and announced, "Prisoners, get the hell out of here. It is time for another drink—on I. P. Olive and Fred Fisher."

Some said it was also time for Judge Boblits to add a good-sized herd of fine range cattle to his ranch, but then it was a good buying season. Anyway, on December 17, 1880, the court ordered "that the prisoners be discharged until further proceedings can be had." The case of Print Olive and Fred Fisher was never closed.

But I. P. Olive, said to be the wealthiest individual cattle-man in Nebraska two years before, was now reported stripped of at least $250,000 in gold and property, with perhaps as much more added by others. "State supreme courts come a little high sometimes," Judge Gaslin was reported to have said. Perhaps they should have used the ropes offered them the evening they got the Olive outfit arrested.

Print, his family, and most of his ranch hands except the hated state's evidencers left for Kansas. Attorney Dilworth, marked for death by an Olive bullet, later became state attorney general but by then only Ira Olive was left in Nebraska, Ira who managed himself judiciously now, so much a good neighbor that when he needed any help it came as to any other, as though he had been orphaned, without sibling, without brother.

Down in Kansas Print Olive had joined with other cattle-men, pushed himself, some said, into a cattle pool in the region north of Dodge City and tried to recoup his herds and money any way he could. Perhaps he was right; perhaps the day of the lone hand in the cattle business was past.

On August 18, 1886, a dispatch from Trail City was picked up by newspapers all over the cow country but read most closely in San Gabriel, Texas, and up in Nebraska, where the settlers passed the papers around until they were worn and tattered, perhaps reading where a work-blunted finger pointed: MAN BURNER KILLED BY COWBOY, saying, "Well, they got 'im; finally got 'im!"

Or perhaps: "So Old Print Olive finally got what he was askin' for for years."

All who could read had to savor the print for themselves, and those who could not, or had no glasses, had to hear it over and over. I. P. Olive, cattleman from Nebraska, now located near Trail City, Colorado, had been killed by a cowboy named Joe Sparrow.

"Sparrow—it say Sparrow?" an old Texas cowpuncher asked through clamped lips, his jaw tipped up to hold his tobacco juice.

"Yes, that's what it says."

Nobody up in Nebraska seemed to know such a man although some up along the trail this summer thought they might have seen Sparrow down there, a Hard Case, so it was said. Anyway, the news of the shooting started all the talk of the Olive killings again, both in Texas and Nebraska, and brought out the story of Print's son killing a man in the Smoky Hill country not long ago. Now this fellow Joe Sparrow came out of some place away to hell 'n' gone and picked off the head of the outfit, the old bull himself, Print Olive. A man ought to know more about a cowboy like that.

Soon there were many rumors, some saying that the fight was over a livery bill Sparrow owed Print, others that it was an old grudge from way back in Texas or that Sparrow was just traveling under that name, a man who had been living for nothing except to avenge Mitchell and Ketchum and that he had a son with the same hatred, planning to vent it on Print's son Bill. Some claimed that Bill had already been shot over a game of billiards and that the father, the Joe Sparrow, disguised as a cowboy had killed Print at a roundup of the Olive cattle.

But all these stories had to be changed later because it turned out that young Bill Olive was alive and hanging around the saloons drunk and fighting, much like his father for so many years. He had been mixed up in a killing but it was Bill who did the shooting—shot the man who killed his father. That didn't seem probable, either, not with a J. J. Sparrow standing preliminary examination for the murder of I. P. Olive, with a dozen or so eyewitnesses called in and at least a hundred more who saw the murder.

In the end it seemed that Bill Olive had killed a man up in the Smoky Hill country just to show he could do it and stood trial, one more case Print Olive had to win. He got the son acquitted but it cost a lot of money—not as much as his own release up in Nebraska but enough. Somehow putting Mitchell and Ketchum out of the way had stirred up the animals more than all the troubles in Texas, as Print complained at the time, so it was handy that the defense of his son came cheaper for he no longer had the kind of money he spent up in Nebraska.

Apparently nobody, not even around Trail City, knew much of the story behind the killing, although a Garden City, Kansas, paper reported that Sparrow had worked for Olive at one time and had some trouble, apparently over a herd of cattle. Later other stories made the rounds. Perhaps it was true that Sparrow had come in from Dodge on Sunday and happened to run into Print Olive next morning, had a few words with him, Olive pulling his gun. The cowboy grabbed it. Furious, and sour drunk, Print promised to kill Sparrow before sundown, Joe arguing all the time he wanted no trouble. The sheriff took Print away and got him to bed.

Some suggested to Sparrow that he better get out of Trail City but the man said he wasn't running. Besides, he didn't plan to have any trouble with anybody. But in the afternoon Print came through Haynes' saloon, found Sparrow, and everyone could see there was a storm coming up, that Olive had to carry out his threat but intended to make out a case for himself this time. Everybody, including the bartender, looked for shelter, preferably where they could see, most of them agreeing later that Sparrow was still trying to avoid trouble. But when Olive reached for his gun, Sparrow fired and missed—deliberately, some thought, and still talked quietly to the drunken man. Now Print fired, seeming to graze Sparrow, and this time the old rancher got a bullet through the left breast. He went down, striking his head on the doorcasing, falling on his gun hand. He seemed suddenly cold-sober but whimpering as he eased his gun out from under him. "Oh, Joe, don't shoot!" he begged, shifting himself for a swift draw.

Now Sparrow knew he had to shoot fast. This time he put a bullet through the left temple of the man who had killed so many. Then he gave himself up.

Before long some were remembering that Ami Ketchum's brother had held the mob off when they wanted to lynch Print Olive, and his words: "If the law fails to punish him . . . I'll do it my way." Perhaps Sparrow was the brother.

But that couldn't be. Surely somebody would have recognized the brother, or so it seemed. But was Tamar Snow's brother so well known? He had his stepfather to avenge, and the betrothed of his pretty young sister.

The Olive family came for Print's body and took it by train to Dodge City. The Texas relatives came up and stood sorrowfully by while the Independent Order of Odd Fellows carried out a very formal and impressive funeral for I. P. Olive, the big cattleman from Texas.

Two of Populism's Favorites

BY DALE KRAMER

¶ *Far, far different types, but still showing the lineaments of frontier individualism, were the leaders of the Populist movement that roiled the waters of Western politics in the late nineteenth century. Reacting with characteristic violence, on the verbal and electoral levels, against the Eastern*

From *The Wild Jackasses.* Copyright 1956 by Dale Kramer.

financial interests that were busily taking toll of agrarian enterprise, the Populists wrathfully, but also often joyously, stirred up the farmers, garnered votes, won elections, and alarmed the ranks of the respectables throughout the nation. Here Dale Kramer presents two leaders of the farm revolt— that capering, eccentric quasi-genius, Ignatius Donnelly; and blue-eyed, melodious-voiced Mary Ellen Lease, who exhorted Kansas farmers to "raise less corn and more hell."

THE SAGE OF NININGER

AT PHILADELPHIA in the spring of 1856 an elegant, ebullient young man of twenty-four mounted the gangplank of a steamboat. He was in even better spirits than usual. His plump, rosy face rippled with merriment and his mellifluous voice and infectious laughter were well-nigh ceaseless. And why should not Ignatius Donnelly be happy? For this young Irishman it was a grand day indeed. Was he not setting off to build an empire in the wilderness? And was there not at his side "the noblest and purest flower of womanhood," his wife Kate? Barely five feet tall, she was a beauty, with her upswept brown hair and great blue eyes. The groom himself was of no more than Napoleon's stature.

Young Ignatius waved good-by to Philadelphia without regret. He had nothing against his native city. It had treated him well and a district of it had even wanted to send him to the legislature. In his eyes, the only trouble with Philadelphia was its age. In his heart he knew that his destiny lay in carving and molding new empires.

He had already visited Chicago, its population now rising a hundred thousand, and had listened to stories of the vast fortunes that had been made in speculation during the last twenty years. But even Chicago was too old for this young man. He expected to found a new Chicago farther west. More exactly, he *had* founded it—on paper. The plat of his empire city rested in a pocket of his fawn-colored coat.

The son of a well-to-do Philadelphia doctor, Ignatius had studied law and been admitted to the bar at twenty-one. He had got off to a flying start in his profession, and it was not long before the Democrats wanted to nominate him for the legislature. But for Ignatius the party was much too ancient. The old established way of doing anything was always apt to make him nervous. Named though he was for Ignatius Loyola, founder of the Jesuit order, he had already left the Mother Church for a mild deism of his own manufacture.

The new pioneer wave was rolling across the Upper Mississippi into the Minnesota Territory. In the half-dozen years since 1850 a deal of money had been coined by speculators at St. Paul. Ignatius had gone out the year before to scout the prospects, including the village of St. Anthony, just across the Mississippi from St. Paul. He was not impressed by it, nor by the nearby squatters' nest called Minneapolis.

He had chosen a virgin bluff about twenty miles down the river for the center of his empire. The thriving village of Hastings, only three miles distant, would of course be engulfed as the new metropolis spread.

Probably no mightier dreamer than Ignatius Donnelly ever chose to settle the frontier. To him the new city was already a thing of timber and stone, pulsing with rich commerce. In truth it was something more than a dream, for besides his plat and an eloquent pamphlet he had financial and political backing. A fellow Pennsylvanian, Alexander Ramsey, until recently the governor of Minnesota Territory, had given his blessing. Another Pennsylvanian now residing in Minnesota, John Nininger, was Ignatius' chief financial angel. Nininger was indeed so heavily involved that when the time had come to name the future metropolis, his name was given precedence over Donnelly's. The neat plat on the clean white paper of the promotion pamphlet was titled Nininger City.

It was true that Donnelly Avenue appeared destined to be the main thoroughfare. To begin with, Ignatius had laid out a mere 20 streets, commencing at Front Street overlooking the Mississippi, and 14 avenues bisecting them. The location of Donnelly Avenue corresponded roughly to that of Fifth Avenue in New York City.

One of the first things Ignatius did after arriving in the Minnesota Territory was to found a newspaper, which he called *The Emigrant Aid Journal*. In it he assured all and sundry that when a railroad was built into Minnesota, certainly it would cross the river at Nininger City, linking the

soon-to-be-thriving community with the East. Meanwhile a
ferryboat would, he said, be put into service to connect
Nininger City with the rich St. Croix Valley of Wisconsin.

Although the promise of a railroad lacked any concrete
basis, Ignatius was not aware of raising false hopes. His mind
was not capable of accepting the possibility that the railroad
builders, whoever they might be, could fail to see the wonderful advantages of his city. Already the railroad puffed and
thundered in his mind. In his ears were the sounds of a ferryboat churning the waters of the great river.

The emigrants devoured Donnelly's newspaper and flocked
in, some five hundred of them. They purchased land and
erected houses with the money they had saved or borrowed.
Nininger City boomed. Ignatius put up a mansion befitting
an empire builder. And yet he was restless. It was his custom
to pace up and down his wide veranda overlooking the Mississippi.

"Here I am," he would say to himself, "only twenty-five
years old, and I have already acquired a large fortune." And
then he would inquire of himself, "What shall I do to occupy
myself the rest of my life?"

As if in answer, the financial centers of the East exploded
in the terrible panic of 1857. As it spread into the West the
papier-maché empire of Ignatius Donnelly crumpled about
his ears. The dwellings in the shadow of the mansion were
pulled down for their lumber.

It was a mortifying comedown for the grand young man.
He had to console himself with becoming lieutenant-governor
of the new state of Minnesota, admitted to the Union in 1858.

In the new state's first election Donnelly was the running
mate of Alexander Ramsey, who valued his gift of tongue.
They campaigned under the banner of the Republican Party,
which, being new, had fired Donnelly's imagination.

Ignatius, being still under thirty, was fairly content as
lieutenant-governor. But he preferred acting as governor,
which he did occasionally in Ramsey's absence. The two were
re-elected for a second two-year term.

When the Civil War broke out, Ignatius promptly offered
himself as the commander of a regiment in the field. "Where
the wrath of the nation falls," he cried, "it must fall as of old

fell the wrath of God, in fire and ashes. We must make rebellion synonymous with desolation; and the track of our armies must be as a shining track of ruin."

Governor Ramsey, however, did not appoint him, giving out for public consumption the reason that men of military experience were required for high posts. The young would-be conqueror, who had a bust of Napoleon in his library, was pretty sure that Ramsey feared that the addition of a hero's halo might make him too dangerous a potential rival.

The rising young leader of the people had to be satisfied with going to Congress, in which he served from 1863 to 1869. At thirty-two he was the youngest member of the House of Representatives.

The record of Donnelly's three terms in Congress was ambiguous, although this was hardly surprising in view of his mixture of humanitarianism and craving for personal grandeur. He agitated successfully for a Bureau of Education. In that day of virgin forests he gazed into the future and demanded the sowing of new woods. He opposed the excesses of the reconstruction period after the close of the war.

Yet the great railroad magnates found no stauncher advocate than Donnelly in their quest for land grants and other favors. All the Western legislators were able, of course, to justify support of the railroads, asserting that these latter were bringing transportation to their constituents. But Donnelly was among those who accepted personal subsidies. From financial buccaneer Jay Cooke, his fellow Philadelphian and good friend, he got $10,000 worth of stock in the Northern Pacific Railroad. Ignatius was pursuing his old dreams of empire, for he hardly needed railroad support to win elections.

The ordinary people dearly loved to hear Ignatius Donnelly make a speech. Connoisseurs of stump speaking ranked him as the most entertaining orator to be heard anywhere in the land. None were quicker with the ad-lib thrust. In one campaign a spectator threw a cabbage at him. "A Democrat has sent up his card in the form of his head," Ignatius commented, and resumed.

The best stock in his oratorical trade was the funny story. He relied heavily on "Paddy and his friend" jokes, there being a large proportion of Irish among the early Minnesota settlers, and he was a master in the telling. On one occasion a political enemy who had memorized his best jokes told them all in the opening portion of a debate. When Ignatius' turn came he repeated every one to trebled laughter and applause.

Some blamed Ignatius' love of a joke for his defeat in 1868. In replying to abuse on the House floor he charged his opponent and all members of his family with wearing the letters "M.C." (for Member of Congress) engraved on their posteriors.

Back home this language was considered risqué, and the incident rebounded against Donnelly. But more powerful opposing factors were at work. The machine dominated by Alexander Ramsey believed that Ignatius had designs on a Senate seat for himself—the very seat which Ramsey filled. In a confused election in 1868, a Democrat won Donnelly's place in the House.

At the ripe age of thirty-eight, therefore, Ignatius announced his retirement to the quiet of his extensive library, except for the overseeing of the wheatlands where his metropolis was to have bloomed. True, he sallied out now and again to deliver lectures on wit or literature for which he was able to command a good fee. In the latter days of his Congressional career he had sometimes been called the Little Giant. Now people took to referring to him as the Sage of Nininger.

Whatever high place Ignatius held or however wide the range of his ambitions, he never played the grandee among his immediate associates. He loved as much to hear a story as to tell one. It was said that a better neighbor never existed. His wife, Kate, was equally sociable and besides was a famous nurse to anyone requiring aid. Ignatius was proud of her wonderful singing voice, which he said ranged from low F to high D, and he liked nothing better than to sit in the front row while she entertained.

In his library the Sage of Nininger plunged into studies of dead civilizations and he read endlessly in ancient mythologies. Nevertheless he followed current publications as well, and now and again he put an ear close to the political ground. He was not at all satisfied with the way General Ulysses S.

Grant, the new President, was running—or not running—the country. The rough-hewn soldier appeared to have turned to putty in the hands of the financial barons. And now that Ignatius was without his empire, dependent on his crops for a living, he was not in sympathy with money lords. He had been a high-tariff man, but his views were shifting. There was no doubt that Ignatius was prepared to dart again upon the stage.

GOLDEN-VOICED GODDESS

Mary Ellen Lease was Populism incarnate. It has been said that the emotional heat of the flames sweeping the Kansas prairies in the early 1890s can never be fully realized by one who lacked the opportunity to hear the remarkable Mary.

Parades were a mile longer when Mary Ellen was scheduled to give the oration. Hayricks were more gaily decorated, the floats were decked higher with evergreens to symbolize the "living issues." Bands played louder. Drill clubs stepped livelier, the skirt dancers leapt higher. Balloon ascensions were not required to attract crowds, for the handbills carrying Mary Ellen's name were enough to fill the excursion trains to bulging and to line the roads with wagons headed meetingwards.

And oh, the singing when Mary was there! Mary always said it was time to stand up and be counted, and she gave the glee clubs a smile as they sang:

> I'd rather be a pollywog, a lizard, or a snail
> Than wear a double face and sit
> A-roosting on a rail.
> I'd rather join the weaker side, and take the consequence,
> Than be a "dummy stuffed with straw"
> A-straddle of the fence.

Somehow a time and a place and a personality had fused to create the greatest woman orator of her age. "I have never heard a lovelier voice," William Allen White said long afterward. "It was a golden voice—a deep, rich contralto, a singing voice that had hypnotic qualities."

Others believed that Mary Ellen's overawing quality was her stage presence. She did not scorn the theatrical. Her beautiful clothes—often fine imported silks and satins—were black, or heavily accented with black, both in winter and summer. Black set off her pale skin. At her waist she generally wore a small bunch of roses. For jewelry she wore no more than an emerald heirloom pin.

Mary Ellen's blue eyes, viewed close up, were undeniably lovely, if sometimes curiously dreamy. Otherwise Mary was no beauty. Her legs were long, her hips overwide, and her upper body slanted to narrow shoulders. Although her features were good enough, they somehow lacked the ephemeral substance of feminine beauty.

Mary Ellen had not always worn silks and satins. In one period of her life she had washed the clothes of others for fifty cents a day. That had been while she was a housewife raising children.

A certain vindictiveness toward the world held Mary Ellen in its grip. She had been denied the privilege of being brought up by both parents, for her father, a Pennsylvanian, had died in Andersonville prison during the war. After graduating from an upstate New York academy she had emigrated, a poor and not very attractive girl, to Kansas, where she taught in a parochial school. She married a young drug clerk, Charles Lease. They homesteaded and went broke.

Mary Ellen bore four children. She cared for them dutifully and took in washing besides, for her husband made a small wage after he had returned to his old line of drug clerking. As Mary washed, she often consulted law notes pinned over her tub. At thirty-seven she passed the bar, hung out her shingle in Wichita, and struck upward.

It was as an Irish orator that Mary Ellen polished her gifts. For two years or so she lectured all over Kansas, raising money for an Irish anti-eviction league. Many listeners thought that she had been born in Ireland, and not surprisingly, for she occasionally said so. This may have been simply oratorical license, since indubitably she was of Irish extraction. Or, carried away, she may have been unaware of what she said. Mary Ellen had the strange gift of automatic, or unconscious, oratory.

Mary Ellen believed that she possessed a "hidden power." She was an instrument in the hands of, as she put it, "a Great

Force." Her speeches—especially her Populist exhortations—were "felt" rather than prepared. Sometimes she read the newspapers to learn what she had said.

Mary Ellen was quite aware of her hypnotic powers. She tried to avoid mention of armed revolt lest her eloquence lead to bloodshed. It is well known that subjects of hypnosis must be willing to be entranced. The Populists were always ready to fall under the spell of their goddess, Mary Ellen.

King of Wheels

BY ELLIS LUCIA

¶ *Proprietor of the Holladay Overland Mail & Express Company and of sundry other large-scale transportation enterprises, Ben Holladay was a frontier tycoon, in some ways perhaps qualifying as one of those so-called "robber barons" who dominated sectors of our national economy in the nineteenth century. Bluff, hearty, shrewd, daring, and imaginative, Big Ben worked and built, manipulated and acquired, expanded and, finally, overexpanded because the man had a drive and a restless vitality that wouldn't let him stand still. He could be generous and warmly human on occasion, but his guiding principle of action was to forge ruthlessly ahead, expecting all who were not for him to get out of his way or be crushed. At the end of his life, he was a lonely and rather bewildered figure, but Ben Holladay had played a real and significant part in the opening and developing of the Far West.*

ON DOCTOR'S ORDERS the big man with the black beard was
spending a few restless days in bed. It was out of character
for him, and rough on the hired help. He was stiff and sore
and ornery, but even though he'd had a close call fighting off
those Indians in Utah he was nowhere near ready to cash in
his chips. Too much needed doing.

He stared restlessly out the window of his mansion on Holladay Hill, down upon the bustling life of San Francisco in
1865. His eyes ranged out over the broad bay, where the masts
of sailing ships made a dense forest in the harbor. Suddenly
a messenger burst through the door and, brushing aside attendants and nurses, thrust a telegram into the patient's thick
hand. The bearded man came upright, his white teeth biting
down hard on the fat cigar between his heavy lips.

The news was bad. Congress might not renew his transcontinental mail contract, the lifeblood of his far-flung Overland Stage Company. His enemies were making political hay
during his absence. He scowled and pulled at his beard. Lob-
byists and congressmen—spurred by Wells Fargo and Butter-
field, he had no doubt—charged that his stages were slow,
inefficient, undependable. He was running a buckboard stage-
line. His equipment was falling apart. The mail wasn't getting through. It made no difference that Red Cloud's war-
iors had the West bottled up.

A series of smoking expletives sent red-faced nurses scur-
rying from the room. The nightshift-clad giant jumped out
of the bed.

"Where's my clothes? Wire the stations! Have my best
teams and drivers ready! Have a strong coach at the ferry
landing in Oakland at dawn. I'm going East, faster than anyone has ever done it by stage! You understand?"

His knees were still shaky, but by the gods, it was good to
be in action again!

From California to Kansas the Overland's most skillful
drivers, its strongest coaches and its fastest teams were poised
for the historic run. Before dawn a specially consigned ferry
creaked into its Oakland mooring. Not waiting until the gang-
way was down, Ben Holladay leaped ashore, an imposing figure in finely woven wool pants and a flannel shirt open at the

neck. His boots were highly polished and he sported a wide-brimmed black hat. Under his heavy overcoat, a Colt was strapped to his side in a worn holster held by a jewel-studded leather belt. A weighty watch chain of gold nuggets dangled from his pocket.

Holladay gave the stagecoach and six fine grays the once-over. His sharp eyes spotted a loose cinch which he quickly tightened. Bags of eastbound mail were placed inside the red and yellow coach for ballast. A spare wheel and axle were lashed to the top. Rifle in hand, he swung to the box beside the driver.

"I'll see you in a few weeks," Ben Holladay promised his watching aides. "Let 'er rip!"

"Hi-ya! Hi-ya!" The driver lashed out with his long whip, slapped the heavy ribbons against the broad backs of the team. They lunged forward and the stage picked up speed. The greatest transcontinental stagecoach crossing in history was under way.

The jouncing coach reeled through the rolling yellow foothills to the east, across the broad Sacramento Valley to Folsom and Placerville, pausing only long enough to change the hard-breathing teams. Then they were on again, high-running through the narrow gorges and hairpin curves of the Sierra Nevada. Cursing drivers whipped tons of pounding horseflesh along at an insane clip.

"Faster, dammit!" Ben Holladay clung fiercely to the seat, his eyes fastened on the narrow road ahead. This was a race against time to save the empire Ben had parlayed from a country store and a fist fight.

Night and day the high-balling Concord thundered eastward, rocking on its thoroughbraces. Coaches fell apart from the terrific pounding of the rough roads. There was no time to rest or eat a luxurious meal of the kind Ben Holladay most enjoyed. A chunk of bread and a fistful of meat kept him going. They bolted through Mormon Station and over the arid wastelands of Nevada toward Salt Lake. Holladay was constantly on the box, eating out the drivers, snatching the ribbons himself. Only now and then did he curl up inside for an hour's nap.

The lurching coach rumbled onward. The trip was beginning to attract national attention. Beyond Salt Lake they rocked through Echo Canyon and into Fort Bridger. Then they were in hostile Indian country. Ben saw some of his stations in black ruins, the attendants dead, the stock gone. They kept going with the same teams, which dropped in their traces at the next relay. Several times they had to shoot fine animals and rehitch the string.

They sped across the Great Divide, swaying and groaning on springs of leather. They threw a wheel, leaping for their lives as the coach spilled over. They got it righted, fitting the spare while Ben bellowed exhortation. They were beyond Green River now, with the broad plains and the big sky stretching forever ahead of them. Off to the north, an electrical storm flared and muttered. The wind came up, and rain beat into the earth. Salt Wells . . . Sulphur Springs . . . Medicine Bow . . . Big Laramie. . . . They fought through a prairie dust storm and kept going. They were swinging southeast now to Virginia Dale, where the notorious Jack Slade had served Holladay as division superintendent. Then on into the main street of Denver.

Ben Holladay didn't pause to do any business in Denver, western headquarters for the Overland. The news from Washington remained dark. The route stretched across Colorado to Julesburg and over the plains of Nebraska and Kansas. Sioux gave chase, and Holladay scrambled onto the roof, his rifle blazing. His insistence on good horseflesh now paid off. The war party's ponies were buried in the dust of the prairie's dry washes, outclassed by the Overland's finest.

At last a foaming black set of six roared into the streets of Atchison, Kansas. Ben Holladay jumped onto the roof, spreading his thick legs as the coach plunged toward the Overland headquarters. Whooping, he fired his rifle into the air as they pulled to a clattering halt before the Overland's offices where an anxious crowd had gathered.

He leaped to the ground while the dead-beat driver slumped in the seat. Ben, who appeared none the worse for wear, jerked out his great gold watch on its five-pound gold chain of Comstock quartz.

"Twelve days and two hours." He scowled. "Shouda been better!"

Veteran stagemen gaped at him. The Overland chief had just peeled five days from the normal cross-country schedule, by far the fastest run ever made. Still their boss wasn't satisfied! Behind him lay the wreckage of broken horseflesh, battered coaches, and nerve-frayed drivers who sought the nearest saloon. The trip cost him $25,000, but Ben Holladay didn't care. It brought him where he wanted to be, got him what he wanted to have, and all at the hell-for-leather, slam-bang pace he liked. Moreover, it was a sound investment.

The news was banner page-one copy in this country and in Europe. Ben Holladay became an international hero overnight. Excited people called him The King of Hurry. Mayors presented him keys to their cities. Pretty girls kissed him. A cigar and a race horse were named for him. New Yorkers paraded him through the streets, and he tossed gold coins to the crowd. He loved every minute of it.

What was most important, the dramatic demonstration turned the trick in Washington, as Holladay had known it would. The opposition was drowned in a sea of adulation over Ben's spectacular ride. Congress quit dillydallying. Hadn't Holladay demonstrated the Overland was still the fastest, the finest, of all stage lines, worthy of Uncle Sam's mail? The contract was approved.

Ben Holladay was America's King of Wheels. His far-flung transportation system—stagecoaches, freight wagons, river boats, steamships, mail carriers, and later a Pacific Northwest railroad—bound half a world together.

Noisy and boisterous though he was, his energy and drive made him a man to be reckoned with. In business he was as tough as the situation warranted. He argued, fought, smashed and trampled on anyone who stood in his path. He had to have his way. Anything was fair, he believed, in war, love, business and politics. One of his bitterest rivals, Joseph Gaston of Oregon, once described him in print as "energetic, untiring, unconscionable, unscrupulous, and wholly destitute of honesty, morality, or common decency." It was the way a good many of his foes felt about him. Holladay knew this, and he drank their health in good Scotch whisky.

Nevertheless, Big Ben moved mountains in an age when

mountains needed moving. He got things done when pounding fists were more effective than a ready tongue. Feared and
assailed by his enemies, Holladay was beloved by the people
on the plains. Affectionately, they called him "Ben" and sang
a song about him. He was one of the boys. This was the life
he loved best. He would champion the underdog, donate land
for a church, and grubstake a down-and-out prospector. He
possessed great family loyalty. His doors were always open to
his children and their problems, but he spoiled his first family with too much money, too many lavish pleasures, and too
little parental discipline. Yet he worried about them, often at
odd times when he was under the greatest pressure and in the
midst of one of his Gargantuan business battles. He almost
abandoned the greatest project of his career, with millions at
stake, to be at the side of a son who was seriously ill. And
when his country called on him Ben Holladay placed all his
wealth and power at its disposal without a second's hesitation.

Ben Holladay was a man of many parts. In the East he lived
in the sumptuous grandeur of an Old World emperor. West
of Atchison, Kansas, he was trader, explorer, scout, Indian
fighter, and lord of nearly everything that rolled. He was
equally at home drinking dog soup with an Indian chief or
enjoying champagne at a fancy Washington reception. He
faced death many times, and always his dynamic physical
strength saved him. He was one of the most publicized and
controversial figures of his day.

Joaquin Miller described him as a "splendid specimen of
American energy and Western manhood . . . one of the
finest types the West can boast of." *Harper's Weekly* proclaimed him "the greatest organizer of transportation that the
West ever produced." Henry Ward Beecher called him "a
magnificent barbarian."

Old Hell-on-Wheels could outtalk, outfight, outride, out-
drink and outcuss anyone he came up against. He feared no
man. Rangy and tall as a doorway, Ben stood six-feet-two in
his stocking feet, which took a size twelve shoe. His bull-like
neck sank deep in a massive chest between broad, powerful
shoulders. His long legs were thick as cordwood, his arms
solid as a blacksmith's, his temper fiery as the forge. His fists
were granite-hard; his huge, oversize hands could be gentle

with a pony or fast on the trigger. Ben was Scotch, black-haired and dark-skinned. His life in the sun and wind turned him several shades darker, so that on first appearance many thought him a Mexican. He was shaggy, with a thick shock of unruly hair that refused to lie down. It matched the coal-black beard of which he was so proud.

He traveled in a blue cloud of cigar smoke most of the time. His clothes, from buckskins to costly tailor-made Paris suits, reeked of the rich tobacco odor. Always restless, always in motion, he smoked incessantly and his big teeth were yel-lowed from the nicotine which also stained his fingers. The swarthy stagecoach king was physically tough and he had a steel-trap mind. His wife often said he never really slept. The dark eyes beneath his bushy brows never missed a trick, at poker or anything else. He was a prime opportunist and a shrewd, fearless gambler, with an explosive temper that could be set off by the spark of a chance remark. He had a con-genial, warm, friendly way about him that made him easy to like. A glorious glad-hander, with an infinite zest for living to the fullest, he was at his best when a problem appeared insurmountable. He thrived on danger and excitement. Money, he believed, could achieve anything, and every man had his price. Nothing was too costly or too big for him to tackle.

Jest and Departure

BY MARI SANDOZ

¶ *Few biographies have the bite or the impact of Mari Sandoz's book about her Swiss-immigrant father, Jules Ami Sandoz, homesteader, land locator, and fruit grower in northwestern Nebraska's upper Niobrara country from 1884 to 1928. In the parlance of our own day, he was even more of an "inner-directed" person than most of the other High Plains settlers; perhaps that was why he survived and, eventually, prospered in a land that gave little and demanded much. This chapter from the best-selling, award-winning* Old Jules *gives the reader a close look at an individualist par excellence, who feared neither god, man, nor devil and who seemed to glory in bending to his will every element in his environment.*

BY THE FIRST OF JULY Mirage Flats was settling up, a covered wagon here, a dugout and the square, patient faces of oxen there. Strips of nigger-wool sod lay straight and flat as bands of metal or greened into rows of two-speared, heat-curled corn. By now no plough would penetrate the brick-hard soil. Dry-land whirlwinds picked up bits of grass and weeds, tossed them high into the air, dropped them capriciously back upon the prairie, and zigzagged on. Heat dances and illusionary lakes rippled away the noon hours on the whitish horizon. Already some of the settlers turned their bronzing faces from these signs of aridity and, with a deepening of the sun scowl between their eyes, lifted the lids of their water barrels, wondering how long before the rising yellow sand bars of the

Niobrara would choke the little channel a man now could almost jump across.

But the hardier, the more ambitious, were not content with drinking water from the tepid little stream. They turned their faces toward Valentine, to file before some claim jumper did it for them, to bring back provisions if the money lasted. Anyway to bring back well supplies, rope, windlasses, buckets.

The well Jules started early in the spring he gave up as more than a one-man job. What he needed was a strong wife. Several Sundays he rode his Jim horse up to Rush Creek, near the railroad survey. Although Matilda Lehrer never had much to say, her laugh was like beading cider at the bunghole. But to Jules her fragrant hot bread and her sure hand on the hammer and the spade meant more just now. Then somebody told her that the romantic foreigner was married.

"I don't see what difference that make," he argued. "If she want me I get a divorce."

But Matilda's mother, with cheeks hanging like a gray dish towel from the peg that was her nose, folded her hands over her stomach. Jules got on his horse and spurred out of her sight.

July was brittle with sun. Through the noon hours grouse squatted behind the ragged sunflowers along the soldier trail, mouths open, wings out, tame as chickens under a Slav's table.

The drouth sucked up the water holes south of the river and the Hunter ranch stock came in droves to the Niobrara. Any night the wild steers might drift up on Mirage and eat out the settlers. Shotguns boomed along the river. Jules filled several shells with salt and laughed as the cattleman's stock retreated.

One afternoon, when he had worked a furious half hour chopping the sod about his whips of trees and cleaning out the tough weeds, two homeseekers stopped for their last filing instructions. Glad of the respite, Jules squatted on the shady side of the wagon with them and filed his gleaming hoe.

A cowboy, headed west for the upper Hunter ranch, reined off towards the loafing settlers. His wild-eyed dun side-jumped at Jules's pile of bleaching buffalo skulls and broke away in a run. The rider jerked the horse to his haunches, bloody froth flying from the spade bit. Back before the settlers, he shifted his heavy Colt, tossed a leg around the saddle horn, and rolled a cigarette. He had been up to the tent town of Gordon, about thirty miles away. It was going strong as a sheepman's socks. Everything wide open; draw played in the dust of the street.

So?

Yeh, even had a resident sky pilot who organized a church along in May, with seventy-five people scattered around his tent, sitting on the woodpile, wagon tongues, empty whisky kegs, and the ground making a noise fit to stampede a herd of longhorns clear down on the Cimarron. But the collection was a mite disappointing, and after the praying the new congregation milled into the nearest saloon to wet their gullets and celebrate the organization of the first Methodist Church west of Valentine, much to the consternation of the rustling, straight-shooting parson.

"Rustling—shooting?" Jules inquired. "Preachers steal cattle too?"

The horseman grabbed for his cigarette and laughed.

"Naw, you got the wind wrong. The parson ain't a rustler, he's a *rustler*—works hard scratching souls together for Kingdom Come. He wouldn't chaw slow elk, starving. But he's bit off a tough chunk—saving souls up there. They's liquor enough running in the street of Gordon to lay anything excepting Nebraska dust."

It might be worth going up.

"Yeh, but better not tie your Sunday-school money in your shirt tail."

"What you mean?"

The horsebacker slapped his worn chaps. "You'll lose it when they steals your shirt, you greenhorn." Suddenly the man leaned forward, his arms crossed on the saddle horn, his light, sun-squinted eyes cold upon them. "But you grangers'll never have no money. It don't never rain in this damned country and you'll stop lead or stretch rope if you keeps shootin' cattle."

The two newcomers dropped back. Jules stood his ground, and pushed his cap away from eyes hard as the file in his hands. Deliberately he spit upon the ground at the man's stirrup.

"You don't run me off! I see the cattle business in hell first."

The ranch hand caressed the worn butt of his Colt absently. "Fighting words, hoe man," he said. "But it'll be a different tune—and you better roll up this snag of fence you got strung around here or it won't be healthy for you."

With that he pinched the fire from his cigarette butt, flipped it into the breaking, and sank his spurs. The clean-limbed half mustang dropped into a short, easy lope, stringing a trail of dust across the Flats.

Jules had no heart for more weed chopping.

After supper several neighbors came across the curled, dead grass to sit on the piles of dirt. They talked and looked at a newcomer's pamphlet on railroad land sales. "The New Canaan," one called the Panhandle.

Big Andrew, who could lay twice as much sod in a day as any other on the Flats, lifted his buffalo shoulders a little and pulled his pipestem from his red beard. "Canaan—Promised Land they call it?" He looked off over Jules's corn, dark, rattling a little in the wind of dusk. "Yah, a panhandle, to the Promised Land."

"I ain't seen much milk and honey," a truck gardener from Missouri complained.

Jules stirred from his preoccupation. "It will come," he said.

They laughed comfortably, as men who had known each other for a long time instead of weeks and days.

Off to the west lightning winked almost continuously, but no one said anything about rain. "You can see the flash three hundred miles," Jules had told them earlier in the summer.

"Three hundred miles? Who in hell you stringing now?" they scoffed.

"Stringing—fooling? I don't fool when I talk business."

So they smoked in silence now, or picked their teeth with grass. Before night settled they walked out to Jules's sod corn, dark figures plodding through the late dusk. The corn was still good, would make thirty bushels to the acre, maybe, with a little rain. Chewing the drying leaves, they talked of the coming railroad, with markets for their produce. Then there would be law, with probably a new county cut off from Sioux as Cherry had been, with county officials.

"It will be important to get good ones, in sympathy with the settlers," Jules pointed out, and told about the cowboy that afternoon.

"Hell, no cattleman'll bother us much on the Flats. Grass here's too short for nothing but sheep or horses."

Jules did not answer. They could not see that the Flats were almost settled. They knew nothing of the world's hunger for land. He left them and brought out his smoky lantern and his rifle and ran a soft-brushed ramrod through the barrel. Blinking a little in the light, the others talked—of drinking at Valentine and Gordon, about women; particularly about women, and for once Jules had no smutty story to offer. Nor did he bring out dripping tin cups of new currant wine from the keg working in the corner of the dugout. Big Andrew cupped the fire in his pipe with his palm and noticed that Jules's shirt was torn clear down the back, and that when he stooped white skin showed—white skin over delicate bones. There was something defenseless about the human back, particularly Jules's.

The settlers scattered early to-night, the newcomers taking Andrew to their wagon to ask about the locator. Funny cuss; cleaned his gun twice this afternoon.

The big fellow moved heavily on the wagon tongue. "Yah, maybe he see what we don't. He is like the tree that grow on the bluff of the river—the pine. He get the wind and the storm that do not touch us who are the cottonwood and the willow near the water. But his root is strong and he see the cloud from far off—and the sun before she shine on us."

"Talking about water—I don't see's any of you're getting much."

Jules didn't leave his corn while the Hunter cattle grazed the Niobrara Valley. Once when three steers wandered up through a gully he took half the powder out of two shotgun shells and peppered their tough hides with buckshot.

When his corn was curled and gray, and the potato and bean plants seemed harsh sticks with dry leaves, the rain came. It fell for three hours, so hard that the Flats was a sheet of water. Jules pushed out to throw up a ridge of sod about the mouth of his dugout. Even so he had to rescue his bed, his catalogues, and his guns from the floor.

The rain brought a buzz to the Flats. The settlers, young with the land, talked big as the surviving sod corn and the potatoes pushed their bursting bosoms up under the shadows of the new vines. But the first week in September brought fog, a flurry of snow, and a clear, bright morning that spread ice over the water barrels and whitened the unmatured corn. It killed the beans and the big melons that Jules and the coyotes watched so jealously.

The next morning wagons rumbled away over the Flats towards Pine Ridge for lumber. Unless another hard soaker came soon there would be no sod cutting for building.

Here and there hunched tiny stacks of hay, not enough for the cattle, nothing at all for the horses. Jules had only his team, accustomed to desultory care, and some of the settlers who did not have even the three dollars locating fee he now charged hauled dry brush from the Niobrara for him to a pile behind his dugout. This he chopped when needed, in three-foot lengths, and pushed through the fire-box door of his cookstove as it burned, disregarding the smoke.

"Well, I'll be damned! You are the laziest yet," a neighbor remarked.

"Me lazy? I got the best sod corn and beans in the country and a couple hundred trees growing. In addition I located over a hundred settlers that will stay."

"Yeh, I guess that's right enough," the man admitted, not convinced.

During the late summer Jules's letters brought three young French Swiss from Ohio. Paul Nicolet was the light one, with a small, pointed head and a delicate upper lip. Jules Tissot, nicknamed "The Black," was narrow-eyed, and yellowish skin grew far up between his bony fingers. Jules Aubert, the writer and spokesman of the three, was like his letters, judicious, cautious, articulate without brilliance—an open handwriting in blue ink on good blue-gray paper. He found work at once at a new ranch on Minnetonka, Pine Creek, as the white man called it, at fifteen dollars a month.

The three accepted Jules's dugout, still without wood floor

or door, as their headquarters. Within a week they were calling themselves "the Company." Because three by the same
name were too many, and perhaps, because of his aversion to
practical jokes, the current frontier humor, their host became
Old Jules. Soon he was Old Jules to all the Flats.

Nicolet and Tissot helped with the well. In return the
locator would take the newcomers to Valentine to file on land
he had managed to keep covered for their coming. A holiday,
a little wine, a little music, perhaps a little women—who can
say? And as they planned they ate young prairie chicken
flavored with wild garlic and roasted to the point of disinte-
gration in the army kettle. And with it they drank deep red
wine of the black currants from along the river.

Then they talked of the Old Country and of course of
women, Tissot the loudest. He was the sort who jerked a
peasant girl's head back by her thick braids and pressed his
kisses upon her.

"Conquering a woman who hates you—a-ah, that is worth
the effort!" and the red of his dark lips showed wet.

"I like mine tame."

Aubert agreed with Jules. But The Black was a devil of a
fellow.

Jules told of his pranks in the mountain village where he
had been sent to learn German among fat cheeses and buxom
blonde maidens. He laughed until he choked at the recollection, swearing he had his fill of thick calves forever. A little
nostalgically they talked of the vineyards, like green robes
embroidered in purple, spreading down the mountainside, of
the wine-pressing time, the sparkle of the juice, and the
dances. They sang a little, sentimentally in bad German, or
lustily in French about the "Little Pot under the Bed," and
the "Boatman's Daughter." Then there was the "Marseillaise." For Jules there was always the rousing "Marseillaise."

During the day he filled buckets in the well that Nicolet
and Tissot drew up from the narrow hole. Sometimes they
waved a coat over the opening to frighten the excitable Jules,
or made the full buckets dance over his head and laughed at
his fiery cursing until they had to lean weakly against each
other from laughing. But usually they were busy enough
pulling the rope or nailing curbing together to follow the dig-

ger. Needless expense, this curbing, some thought, with lumber scarce, but after a cave-in near Gordon upon the digger it was concluded that Old Jules's way was probably better.

One exceptionally warm evening they dried their soil-caked clothing in the evening sun. The Black Tissot teased a toad drowsy with fall. At last he dropped it into the well, listening for the plop as it hit far below. "You are a fool!" Jules told him angrily. But good humor returned easily to-night. To-day his spade had struck water. To-morrow they would clean out the well, the next day off to Valentine. There would be mail, a letter from Rosalie. Surely she would come before the first blizzard, before winter blocked the roads.

Somewhere a belated prairie-dog owl called a friendly "Who, who!" An arrow hawk fell noisily upon the fall's last mosquito. Lights winked faintly out upon the Flats. Jules's lantern had burned dry the night before, and when the chill rose up out of the river valley they went to bed.

Eighteen days later a wagon escorted by troopers swung to a halt before the log hospital at Fort Robinson, and Old Jules, his eyes sunken into a fever-burned mask, was carried away. By the time he regained consciousness, Dr. Walter Reed, the post surgeon, had examined this granger. The man was covered with dark bruises, but everything was overshadowed by the crushed left ankle, swollen to the size of a water bucket, black and green with infection, the leg to the loin swelled to a shininess and lividly streaked. Eighteen days— perhaps it was too late even for amputation.

But when the emaciated man was prepared for the operation he sat up, his gaunt cheeks flushed a violent red under his beard, his bloodshot eyes glittering.

"You cut my foot off, doctor, and I shoot you so dead you stink before you hit the ground."

The attendants pinned the man back, but they could not stop the tongue or the eyes. The doctor, tall, slight, not much past thirty, stood over this patient, so different from the regular run of stolid grangers that were brought to him sick and dying. He saw a strong, straight nose, wide-winged, a fine forehead, narrow hands, eyes that commanded even through the veil of fever. Long the doctor looked down into those eyes that never wavered, although the patient's clawed hands gripped the narrow edge of the table to retain consciousness. He was not begging but commanding that his leg, rotting though it was, and dying, be left to him, defying anyone to take it from him.

The thin line of the doctor's mustache twitched. "My orders are amputate. But your wish to die in one piece shall not be ignored." He gave a salute, one that was only half mockery. "And it would be just like your particular brand of damn fool to pull through."

The doctor was right. Jules did pull through, but not without a great deal of agony to himself and to this doctor who could never learn proper impersonality toward his patients. The first few nights it took two men to hold Jules when he tried to fling himself out of bed upon Nicolet and Tissot, when he cursed his father and his mother for driving him away to America. Then there were times when he talked to Rosalie, the Rosalie who might be waiting at Valentine, and once of the man with the Winchester in the saloon. These two came with the sleep of the doctor's morphine.

His leg in a sling, with tubes in the crushed ankle dripping bloody pus, the infection slowly drained away; the swelling went down. By then the doctor and the attendants, and through them the entire fort, had the story of Old Jules.

It seemed that when the final pail of mud had been dumped on the mottled brown and yellow piles of clay, the two helpers pulling Jules from the well could not resist a little joke. They jerked the rope several times, laughing until they had to wrap it about a corner plank while Jules, dizzy in the twisting bucket, looked down at the water far below him and knew that under it was rock. They pulled again, and jerked, pulled and jerked—once too often. Near the top the frayed rope broke and the well-digger plunged sixty-five feet to the bottom, his foot doubled under him.

Two weeks later soldiers headed for Fort Robinson found a man lying along the trail. It required three stout troopers to take the rifle from him and then he collapsed in a rush of French, German, and English curses. They gave him water and got two settlers, Scribner and Sturgeon, to haul him to the fort.

During the first two months at the hospital Jules went over the accident a hundred times. The two frightened helpers had pulled him out and, bowing before the blast of his anger, tried to bathe and bandage him, Tissot pale and a little defiant, Nicolet with tears in his light, boyish eyes. When Jules calmed he took a dose of morphine and considered. He was in no condition for a hard trip a hundred and fifty miles down the Niobrara with no hospital to receive him. And even now the land came first. The filings of the three must be made immediately. To Aubert, who came that evening, he gave his last twenty-five dollars for winter supplies, took another dose of morphine, and went to bed. They would pound the horses on the tails; be back in a week if possible.

But the ankle did not get better and the pain grated like a rasp through the mist of morphine and wine. Hunger and the need for water drove him out the third day. He crawled to the well, dragging the swollen foot after him like a wounded animal. Then he waited at the edge of the garden for an hour for a rabbit to come within shooting distance. Because he had no kerosene there was no light. Everyone thought he was gone to Valentine. No one stopped.

The seventh day Jules shot a chicken hawk that lit on a fence post. Carefully, with his gun steadied on a box, he shot, but it was a long time before he could get back to the dugout and set the gaunt, blue corpse of the bird on to cook. He drank the dark, wild broth and gnawed the meat that was never tender enough to eat.

The eighth day and the ninth the young Swiss did not return. Jules's morphine was gone, and the wine, with its dulling alcohol. Delirium and unconsciousness swept over him like wind-driven fog. At last he dragged the heavy, swollen leg to the soldier trail and lay down to die.

After a few weeks Dr. Reed saw that the patient would probably recover. He cut off the morphine and substituted whiskey and a pipe. When Jules set his bed afire at night, his tobacco and matches were taken away at ten o'clock, but without his pipe he let no one sleep and so he was told to burn himself up.

The doctor brought in some of the Frenchmen about the

fort, particularly Baptiste Garnier, half-breed interpreter, the man General Crook termed the best hunter in the West. This Little Bat had the terse, figurative tongue of his Siouan mother. Two years before, when Dr. Reed came to the fort, the tough element, still hanging about from the Black Hills gold rush and the agency days just past, sized up the slight build of the new post physician: the delicate forehead, the sensitive mouth under the narrow mustache. They laughed with peculiar unpleasantness. But not Little Bat. "He is like a new rifle, this doctor, light as nothing in the hand but shoots far and true." The comparison tickled Jules's fancy when he heard it. Yes, a fine, new rifle. And when Little Bat heard about the beaver feet Jules caught, he laughed. "Drown them—with sack of sand," he advised.

When the fever first left him, Jules, at the strong insistence of Dr. Reed, wrote to his father. The two young men found a great deal to discuss: science, politics, Switzerland; and always Jules's career as a doctor. To the young Swiss, cut off from all contact with the educated for three years, these hours with the post surgeon were fine and precious. But in Jules, as in every man, there lurks something ready to destroy the finest in him as the frosts of earth destroy her flowers. In spite of himself he became derisive.

"You don't learn nothing in the American universities. Damn poor doctoring you fellows do!" he jeered.

Dr. Reed bit his mustache, felt the patient's steady wrist, and went sadly away.

Instead of the customary Christmas letter, Jules wrote Rosalie a short, cold note, speaking of himself as a cripple who could be of little value to her now even as an acquaintance. He sealed it with three blobs of red wax pressed down with his grandfather's seal from the box of papers the thoughtful Sturgeon had brought along. For a moment he looked at the bit of brass, with its intaglio of the man and sprouting tree against a rising sun. Then he put it away and turned his face to the wall.

Now he wrote no more, saw no one except the breeds and the enlisted men who taught him American card games, profanity, and smut. They had no patience with pinochle, the only game he knew, learned secretly in his father's stable in

Neuchâtel, so he learned seven-up and pitch and blackjack.

Late at night, sometimes, he wondered what had happened to the three young Swiss who left him alone on the prairie. They should have been back days before the soldiers came. Probably let the horses run away; perhaps were caught in a prairie fire or killed by road agents. More probably they went back to Ohio or the Old Country. They owed him more than that, that Nicolet and Tissot.

So the days dragged their misery-soiled trail over him. During the nights his leg ached in the sling and the wind whistled about the adobe and log shacks of the fort.

In November Jules got a letter in the smooth, pleasant hand of Jules Aubert, on his blue Swiss correspondence paper, saying:—

DEAR FRIEND:

We arrived at your house the day after your departure for Fort R., and the following Sunday Mr. Scribner, who conducted you, came to tell us that one of us ought to go to see you during the course of a week and bring you an extra shirt and a pair of trousers. I planned to go at the beginning of last week but crops which we gathered and threshed by hand hindered me. . . .

We made hay for your ponies and charge ourself to lodge them and feed them during the winter in order that we may serve you by this little while we haul the lumber for our houses. Tissot is going to the post to-morrow and I send you a shirt which was in your trunk. As for the trousers, I haven't found any, but I think you won't need them for the moment.

Winter is approaching and we have to build a stable for four horses and a house for ourselves. . . .

We weren't able to bring back any merchandise from Valentine for the reason that we had twelve bushels of wheat and oats . . . and one of the horses got sick, perhaps the colic, going down. . . . In consequence I hold at your disposal the $25 which you entrusted to me for merchandise. Please tell me if I should send this to you. In that case I should like to have a receipt for the $25 I paid you for the forge in order that if anyone comes to reclaim it I will be able to let him see the receipt. Moreover I have sold 13 pounds of beans at 8 cents a pound and four bushels of potatoes at 25 cents each, making $2.04. I am sending a receipt for the bill from Mons. Sparks Brothers, for the $20 that I sent to them for you.

As soon as we shall have finished our house we shall go live there

and put all your property in your house and close the entrance in
such a way that no one can get in. . . .

We learn with pain that you have been obliged to go to a doctor
and that perhaps it will be necessary to amputate a foot. We hope
that all will go well and that you will recover rapidly and that soon
we will have the pleasure of seeing you here in good health. We
beg you to receive our affectionate salutations.

In the name of the Company,

Jules Aubert

P.S. We were able to take our claims as we understood them and
thank you for the good service you have done us.

"Wants a receipt for his money. Thinks I won't come back
and they can get all I got!"

In February he received another letter from the three. It
was full of news. Certain paragraphs he read and reread:

Everyone left the country at the beginning of the winter and we
are the only ones left for at least five miles around. Even Big
Andrew has gone, no one knows where. We are still staying in your
house, seeing that the snow had hindered us from hauling the lumber necessary to build. It has diminished a little these last days and
yesterday I made two trips to the river. Last night it began to snow
again and here we are, halted for some days.

It has been impossible to come to visit you. A man named Clark
was obliged to leave his wagon en route to Valentine in December
and it was not until recently that I was able to go hunt him up.

Nor has everything happened for the best here. Nicolet had six
wagons of hay burned by a prairie fire. The last of November while
going to see a timber claim for his brother coming from Ohio, his
black horse fell in the middle of the river and despite all our care
to dry him, he perished during the night. Mr. Bourne, who lives
five miles northwest, lost two horses and one mule and 55 head of
cattle and he doesn't know where half of them perished. . . . Nor
have you been exempt from misfortune. I found your black pony
stretched out behind the stable. In spite of all my efforts I could
not hold him on his feet. The next day we went to the stable again
but in vain. He died, so of the four horses we have only two. . . .

I sold the remainder of your store for seven dollars, which I hold
at your disposal.

I reclaimed your revolver and your rifle from Scribner. He
brought them to me immediately. He left his claim the third of
December, as did Bourne, Sturgeon and others. We have been to

the Hunters' ranch to look for work. We will cut posts for fences for the next month. Perhaps we could work there all summer, only I have not the $200 to prove up my preëmption and in consequence must live on it this summer.

Perhaps there will be some way of coming to an understanding about cultivating your place, if you make reasonable conditions. Perhaps I might also buy your pony if you are disposed to sell it.

Receive, dear Friend, our best wishes for your speedy recovery and for the New Year, which has just begun, also the sincere greetings of your altogether devoted,

JULES AUBERT

"Devoted, hell! Eat up my grub, kill my pony, now want my other one and my farm land!"

There were other letters; two of them were from Matthews, an Iowan Jules located on the Flats. The first letter was full of accounts of foot injuries. One acquaintance had had his leg amputated, a little at a time, up to his hip. But he was making a living selling shoe strings in Chicago. "Nerve up and you will come out all right. I wish I was with you to take care of you."

The second letter rambled on in a friendly manner and ended in a dun for twenty dollars due on his stove. They were all buzzards, these friends, like buzzards sitting on a fence waiting for a sick cow to die.

"*Soldat!*" Jules called, motioning to a private he knew who was walking past the frosting window. The man came in and they played seven-up, using Mat's letter for a score pad.

While Jules dealt, the private bit off a chew. "God, but it is cold out. I been on the border for almost three years now and I ain't never seen such a chilly spell. Man just came in from that knot of tents and shacks on Chadron Creek. Grub got scarce, so about a week ago a young feller takes his gun and busts out to bring in a buck. The wind commences to move the snow around. He didn't come back, and it being thirty-two below that night he ain't been seen since. The man that just come over on snowshoes took two days to make what's just a little jaunt in the summer time. They wants the troops to turn out and find the lost hunter and Uncle Sam's always willing to oblige."

"You think they find him?" Jules asked as he picked up the cards.

The man hit the spittoon with true military marksmanship. "Oh, yeh, they'll find him—when the snow goes off in the spring, by watching the buzzards."

Late that night another blizzard howled between the high buttes and down about the fort. Jules lay awake and thought of many things—of Rosalie and the children they might have, of the herd of a thousand elk reported wintering in the sandhills, south of the river.

He thought, too, of the other stories the soldiers told, ghost stories. Of an Indian with a buffalo robe, a knife hidden in his hand, stalking before the guardhouse, his head down, his one feather pointing into the sky: the ghost of Crazy Horse, the greatest Sioux war chief of them all. Little Bat told Jules the story: how Crazy Horse was tricked into the guardhouse and bayoneted through the kidney. It was said that ever since, for eight years, he walks.

"What he want?" Jules asked.

Nobody could guess. Some said he had to walk so every dark of the moon until the last Indian he led against Custer was dead. Others said he was looking for the man who killed him.

"Old woman stories," Jules scoffed, but somehow Crazy Horse reminded him of the man in the saloon at Valentine, the one with the beautiful Winchester. Lone men, both of them, self-reliant. It would be good to be so.

One of the warmer days in February a grinning private brought in a young woman. Jules turned as far as the sling would permit. The woman stared a moment, clasping the baby in her arms close to her.

"Oh!" she cried. Then Jules recognized her. It was Nina Haskins and her little Jules. She kissed the man's clean cheek. "Oh, I'm so sorry about your foot. I just had to come before I left for home."

"Your man, he's leaving the country?"

"No." She shook her head. "Jed's buried up on the north table. He—he got caught in a blizzard."

"Oh, hell!"

"So I'm going to Sidney to take the train—" She blinked rapidly and then smiled. "But don't you think you might say you are proud of your namesake?" The eight-month-old boy reached out his arms and laughed at the thin, white man, so different from the wind-burned, bearded one that spanked him into life. The next moment the woman was gone towards the door, burying her face in the child's wraps.

One afternoon Dr. Reed came to Jules's cot with a small envelope bearing a Swiss stamp.

Jules took the letter slowly. It was addressed to the doctor two months before in his father's handwriting and asked humbly for word of his injured son and special kindness for him.

"My reply is on the back," the doctor told Jules, and went away. Almost afraid to see what this man had to say of him, he read:—

I beg that you will pardon my delay in answering your favor of Dec. 27th '84. I am happy to inform you that your son, Mr. Jules Sandoz, still remains under my care in the Post Hospital of this Fort, and that, although not fully recovered, he is doing very well. His injury was a very severe one—being a compound, comminuted fracture of the left ankle-joint, with dislocation. He was admitted to Hospital on the 18th day after receipt of injury, & had truly a horrible joint. I at once placed him under ether, removed the astragalus entire & a part of the os calcis and int[l] malleolus. Drainage tube was then carried through joint & wound dressed antiseptically & placed in plaster of paris splint.

I may say that had I been permitted to fully exercise my judgement, I should have amputated at the ankle-joint, but your son would not consent. The wound is nearly healed, & I anticipate that he will yet have a useful foot.

You may rest assured that he shall have my best attention.

Jules folded the letter slowly and slipped it into the envelope, already addressed. It was taken away and still Dr. Reed did not return. Perhaps he had been called out. Most of the grangers left the country before the first snow, Jules had been told, but now and then a half-frozen traveler was brought to the post or a desperate, half-wild man came plodding through the snow. Perhaps forty miles out there was sickness, a woman insane, or a baby coming. Patiently the doctor bundled himself against the cold, mounted a sturdy post horse, and, with his aide, set out into the teeth of the blizzard, or across the white night at nearly forty below zero.

"This country will develop—in time," he told Jules once. "But not until the ground is soaked in misery and in blood."

"Yah, I guess that's so," agreed Jules, without looking up from the scraping of the bowl of his pipe. He admitted it reluctantly, for not many months ago the land had been almost without flaw in his eyes.